The E(

Advanced Applications of

Emotional Intelligence

To Modern Business

Dan Green, PhD

Author of the Best-Selling
The Art of Modern War

Forewords by

Craig A. Parisot
Chip Taliaferro
Dr. Claire McWilliams
J. Ibeh Agbanyim

Published by Psyndesis, LLC
www.Psyndesis.com

Publication Data
Green, Dan, 1981-
Title: The EQ Shinobi - Advanced Applications of Emotional Intelligence to Modern Business / Dan Green.
Includes bibliographical references and index.
Subjects: 1. Emotional Intelligence. 2. Leadership. 3. Organizational Behavior.
4. Psychology. 5. Organizational Effectiveness. 6. Change Management. 7. Executive Coaching.
Production Credits
Cover and Interior Design: Ian Gillespie
Printed in the United States of America
FIRST EDITION
ISBN 978-1545069264

The EQ Shinobi

Advanced Applications of
Emotional Intelligence
To Modern Business

To Kevin, A great
grandfather and a
decent father-in-law

April
2017

To Caleb and Drake, who continue to inspire me every day.
And for my Muse, My Precious.

The only way to predict the future is to create it

Table of Contents

Foreword by Craig A. Parisot xi

Foreword by Chip Taliaferro xiv

Foreword by Dr. Claire McWilliams xv

Foreword by J. Ibeh Agbanyim xvii

Acknowledgements xviii

Introduction 1

    Who This Book Is For 3

    What This Book Is 4

    What This Book Is Not 4

    My Goals for This Book 6

Part 1 10

    Recommended Pre-Readings 11

    A Brief History 12

Defining Emotional Intelligence 20

Assessments Are Born 22

    Quick Check In 23

Review of Level 1 25

The Bar-On Model of 26

Emotional Intelligence 26

The Development of the Bar-On Model 27

    The 15 Factors of the Bar-On Model 27

Composite 1 – Self-Perception 28

Composite 2 – Self-Expression 30

Composite 3 – Interpersonal 32

Composite 4 – Decision Making 34

Composite 5 – Stress Management 36

The Happiness Indicator 38

It's All About Balance 39

Part 1 Wrap Up 40

Part 2 41

If You Build it, They Will Not Come 42

Public Speaking and Work Shop Facilitation 44
Writing 44
PowerPoints 44
Volunteering 45
Cold-Calling and Snowball Networking 45
Emotional Intelligence and Selling 46
Grit 47
Does One Find Grit, or Does One Develop It? 50
Master the Spiritual 52

The 5 Major Perspectives in Psychology 54

Psychodynamic Approach 55
Behavioral Approach 56
Biological Approach 57
Cognitive Approach 58
Humanistic Approach 59
How Each Perspective Applies to Assessment Theory 60
Different Types of Assessments 61
Perspectives Wrap Up 65
Master the Mind 66

Multiple Intelligences - Advanced 360 Interpretation 68

Identity Vs. Reputation 68
Cognitive Dissonance 74
Incorporating Other 360s 75
Master the Impersonation 76

Subtle Signs from the Environment - The EQ-i 2.0 Group Report 78

How EI Can Empower Team Performance 78
Stages of Group Development 79
Forming 79
Storming 79
Norming 79
Performing 80
Adjourning 80
How EI Can Diagnose Team Dysfunction 81

The Differences Between Dysfunctions 81

The EQ-i 2.0 Group Report 83

Social Loafing 88

Groupthink 89

Group Polarization 90

Subtle Signs 91

Master the Environment 94

Advanced Emotional Balance 96

A Recap of Level 1 Emotional Balance 96

Advanced Emotional Balance – High and Low Use 98

Balancing Self-Perception 101

Valencia the Ambitious 104

Balancing Self-Expression 107

Craig the Provoker 110

Balancing Interpersonal 113

Roxanne the Good Samaritan 115

Balancing Decision Making 118

Jon the Jack of All Trades 122

Balancing Stress Management 124

Marc the Ice Dragon 127

Balancing Happiness and Well-Being 130

Advanced Emotional Balance Wrap-Up 131

Master the Balance 133

Part 2 Wrap Up 135

Part 3 137

Emotional Syndromes and Configurations 138

The Emotional Blindness of Alexithymia 139

EI Configurations that Might Identify Alexithymia 140

"No Story" Nancy 141

The Emotional Roller Coaster of the Schizoid 143

EI Configurations that Might Identify Schizoids 144

Lawrence the Lonely 147

The Emotional Destruction of the Machiavellian 149

EI Configurations that Might Identify Machiavellians 150

Mach 4 Miko 152

Emotional Syndromes and Configurations Wrap Up 154

Mastering the Art of Fire 155

Emotional Intelligence, Heuristics and Cognitive Bias 157

The Illusion of Asymmetric Insight....................................... 162

The False Consensus Effect 163

Focalism 164

Bandwagon Effect 166

Confirmation Bias... 168

Conservatism 170

Information.. 170

Ostrich Effect 172

Curse of Knowledge 173

Empathy Gap 174

Framing Effect 176

IKEA Effect 178

Allais Paradox 179

Actor-Observer Bias.. 182

Halo Effect 185

Bizarreness Effect 188

Humor Effect 191

Zeigarnik Effect... 195

Primacy Effect.. 197

Fading Affect Bias 198

Illusion of Transparency... 200

Mastering the Art of Stealth 202

Emotional Intelligence and Leading Change 204

The Decision Stage 205

The Resistance Stage 205

The Adoption Stage 210

Mastering Change 214

Determining Psychological Fit 216

Selection 217

David the Independent 219

Succession Planning.. 221

Sarah the Successor 224

Mastering Psychological Fit.. 228

A Sword That Can Only Cut Once 230

   The Kids Aren't All Right 230

   Recruiting Spies With EI 231

   The 70/20/10 Model 233

   EI is a Blade That Can Only Cut Once 235

   Master the Recruitment 239

The Battle Continues 241

   Areas of Future Focus 246

      The Hippocampus and Future Thinking 247

      Emotional Intelligence as a Clinical Diagnostic Tool 248

      Communicating with Animals Through Emotions 249

      Empathy and Violent Video Games 250

      Love is Blind 250

      Emotionally Intelligent People Can't Spot Liars 251

      EQ Radio 251

   Master the Future 252

Epilogue 254

References 260

Index 268

Foreword by Craig A. Parisot

To be a master of anything takes study and practice. However, it all must start with the desire to be the best possible version of yourself and the commitment to be great at what you do.

Over the past 20 years, I have built the reputation as an innovator and results-focused strategic thought leader, putting ethics and collaboration high on my list of values. During my time as a military officer and private sector executive leading large and small teams to win big and achieve stretch goals, I've been the driving force behind major efforts that transform the way organizations think about their future. These successful efforts include enterprise change initiatives, mergers and acquisitions, major new business pursuits, technology launches, government relations, and marketing and rebranding efforts. In addition to my current role as the CEO of ATA, LLC, I serve on multiple not-for-profit boards and engage in angel and growth stage investing. I also founded and lead a highly successful working group that engages data science leaders and practitioners across the federal government and private sector. Throughout it all, I have realized that there is one common skill that can predict workplace success across all industries and job roles – emotional intelligence.

During my career working with and observing Fortune 1000 executives as well as my own experience leading, building and exiting fast growth technology companies, I have developed some simple truths about people and organizations. As we seek to rise to the top of our chosen professions, we must acknowledge our fundamentally flawed nature as human beings and embrace the two most important leadership facets of emotional intelligence. First, a strong degree of self-awareness for individual focus on practice and mastery. Second, a sense of empathy expressed through the willingness to make an organizational investment in developing emotional intelligence, both as a team and as individuals.

We've heard these before: "awareness is the first step towards solving a problem" and "practice makes perfect." Hard to argue the first point but I recently read an article arguing that practice does not, in fact, make perfect. So, for the sake of discussion, let's set-aside any debate about the total validity of this axiom and stipulate its underlying value. While criticized, I even think Malcolm Gladwell even got this point when he illustrated a model for mastery known as the 10,000-hour rule. If you are unfamiliar, it states that if you perform 10,000 hours of any activity, you will master that activity. However, I don't want to lose the underlying point – we are not born masters of anything, even of ourselves. It takes an investment of time and energy to get good at anything, including developing and controlling our emotions and engaging in effective interpersonal relationships, especially as an executive leader.

As leaders, our job is to inspire, focus and mobilize those whom we lead formally or lead informally. It is also our job to ensure that every day we arrive ready to perform at the best of our ability in full acknowledgment of our flaws and shortcomings as human beings. To take control of that with which we can, we must invest and practice both in ourselves and in our teams. Every decision presents a choice and even when we make a 'bad' choice, we always – in an instant – can make the decision to do better and immediately alter course. This awareness, the ability to act and the ability to forgive is central to emotional intelligence and should be a central goal as leaders (as well as spouses, partners, parents, coaches and all of the other roles we find ourselves in).

The second is the deep sense of empathy expressed through the willingness to make an organizational investment in developing emotional intelligence, both as a team and as individuals. By doing so, leaders send a strong signal to the organization about standards and expectations around behavior and personal responsibility. If we can put ourselves and our teams in the right frame of mind to feel empowered, then imagine the problems that can be solved at the lowest levels and the innovation that can be unlocked (among other positive benefits). Without the organizational investment in coaching and the setting of high organizational standards centered on personal accountability, you are leaving too much to chance. As leaders, why leave this to chance when it is both our responsibility and within our control to do something about it?

In 1998, Rutgers psychologist Daniel Goleman wrote the following in *What Makes a Leader,* to establish the importance of emotional intelligence to business leadership: "The most effective leaders are all alike in one crucial way: they all have a high degree of what has come to be known as emotional intelligence. It's not that IQ and technical skills are irrelevant. They do matter, but...they are the entry-level requirements for executive positions. My research, along with other recent studies, clearly shows that emotional intelligence is the 'sine qua non' of leadership. Without it, a person can have the best training in the world, an incisive, analytical mind, and an endless supply of smart ideas, but he still won't make a great leader."

Goleman's words ring truer today than they did nearly two decades ago. The importance of emotional intelligence to leadership acknowledges certain truths about humanity and the changing nature of the global economy driven largely by seismic shifts in technology and social connectivity. We as leaders better have our act together or our competition will eat our lunch. Traditional models of the way we work, generate revenues and create value are failing as we enter a new economic age. Simply put, the rules of the game have changed.

This book comes at the right time and is a must read for all those seeking to be relevant in the new normal. Dr. Green has used emotional intelligence to develop leaders, empower teams, and lead large scale change all over the world. Through these intimate experiences, he has developed the advanced EI methodology that he is now taking the time to share with you in a systematic and thoughtful way.

In the new normal of the global marketplace, soft-side, human variables—focus, culture, agility, talent, collaboration, creativity, connection and experience—determine value far, far more than the classic flow of goods and services. Innovation and collaboration are not optional, they are demanded. For the modern competitive enterprise, optimizing the human side of the business equation is essential for sustainable success. The confidence that your team, and your customers, has in you to learn, adapt and innovate ahead of the competition is vital. The same is true for all leaders today regardless of sector, business size or industry—whether public or private; profit or not for profit. Competition has never been more intense, change more constant, disruption more frequent or the battle for top talent more intense. In this paradigm, winners think differently, work smarter and seek emotional intelligence mastery.

Craig A. Parisot

www.ATA-LLC.com
Great Falls, Virginia - March, 2017

Foreword by Chip Taliaferro

Obi-Wan Shinobi. That's who I feel like after reading *The EQ Shinobi* – ready to covertly take on any situation where emotional biases create friction or impede progress in business. The Jedi and the Shinobi have a great deal in common and would probably have gotten along quite well had they not lived eons and galaxies apart from one another.

In the modern world, we often don't stop to think about the generations of people before us who were extremely capable and innovative in the multitude of society's roles. Many lessons have been lost to time that have only recently been rediscovered or applied in new ways. *The EQ Shinobi* fantastically relates the superhero-like skills of the ninja in ancient feudal Japan and their surprising applicability in today's workplace. Through Dan's book, I came to the realization that I had been missing an entire way of not only understanding people's approach towards their jobs and colleague interrelationships, but my own shortcomings as a participant and contributor. Armed with my new Shinobi skills, I am excited to improve my performance and that of my clients.

I have had the pleasure of working directly with Dan for the past three years on a significant Federal Government program that will fundamentally shift how the agency communicates with citizens. Given the scope and breadth of the program, we have worked with hundreds of people and dozens of teams all across the EQ spectrum. Dan's Master Shinobi status has enabled us on many occasions to quickly assess and plan for the various personalities to ensure roadblocks are removed and individual motivations rewarded.

As a long time technology and management consultant in the telecommunications, mobile, and government spaces, I continually seek out new methodologies and approaches for delivering more value more quickly for my clients. *The EQ Shinobi* adds a new arrow to my quiver.

Chip Taliaferro

https://www.bluestream.cc
Leesburg, Virginia – March 2017

Foreword by Dr. Claire McWilliams

Not every day does one meet a ninja in a PhD program. I had the opportunity to get to know Dan in various courses we shared together, and over time we encouraged one another to keep pressing on in the grueling battle that is getting a doctoral degree. After nearly two decades teaching at the high school level, I chose to get my doctorate and aimed for a position at the university level. I knew the journey would be challenging, but when I reached a critical moment where my skills and resolve were tested, I felt isolated and uncertain about how to move forward. Enter Dan Green. His 'shinobi' warrior skills were apparent from the start. He could soak up complex material (hence my nickname for him became 'Stats Ninja'), apply his industry knowledge to theory and theory to industry in a genius way, stealthily flex to the teaching style and requirements of each professor, predict the next steps to stay well ahead of deadlines, and consistently kept himself in the right spiritual and psychological mindset throughout the experience. There were numerous times when I was ready to give up, but Dan would not hear of it. He reminded me of my values, the investment I had already made, and why the outcome was worth the struggle. He challenged me to be persistent. In my experience, Dan *lived out* the behaviors of an emotionally intelligent leader. He is *The EQ Shinobi*. There are professional psychologists and there are business professionals. At what point will their acumens fully combine to optimize outcomes in the workplace? Dr. Dan Green has a jika-tabi placed firmly in both of these worlds, and can empower readers of *The EQ Shinobi* to translate EQ *insights* into *strategies* to create tangible *outcomes* within a business enterprise. Many predominant psychological theories, while insightful, fall short in usefulness and application in business practice. Emotional Intelligence has, to some extent, found its way into the lexis of corporate America. Many managers are *aware* that a high EQ is linked to superior performance and effectiveness. They may have undergone EI testing and/or training via consultants or conferences. They may have experienced an 'aha' moment thanks to Goleman's book. The true gap exists in how to weave EI theory into the daily workings of an organizational team toward the ultimate goal of shaping emotionally intelligent leaders.

Dr. Green's work fills this void and will allow a dedicated reader to assume the role of an EQ Shinobi in training, and ultimately raise the bar for individual performance and organizational success. His clever weaving of ninjitsu principles will make the strategies outlined in this book memorable and inspire readers to bring forth their inner warriors. Dreams were realized for both Dr. Dan and myself. As our careers grow in new and interesting directions, we remain in a state of mutual encouragement. I *did* make it to the finish line of my doctoral journey (albeit long after Stats Ninja) and to that university teaching position I dreamed of, and I owe it in large part to Dan's empowerment and coaching. I know that I can use the resources Dr. Green provides in this book for my own growth and to help empower my students as they prepare for careers in management. These tools will also assist me in my own consulting work. I know that Dr. Green can, through this effort, do the same for you.

Note to reader: Heed Dr. Green's recommendations and do the recommended pre-reading first. This book is not for the novice, but those ready to move beyond discussion and become practitioners of EQ.

Dr. Claire McWilliams

www.clairemcwilliams.com
Phoenix, Arizona - March, 2017

Foreword by J. Ibeh Agbanyim

For decades, intelligence has always been a construct of study in psychology and humanities. Intelligence as a construct has multiple levels. So many scholars have taken stands on the topic of emotional intelligence, but no work has been published on advanced emotional intelligence. Dr. Dan Green's work is the first. Green is a sought-after expert in the field of industrial-organizational psychology and advanced emotional intelligence. His global body of work within Fortune 1,000 companies is a testament to that fact.

Advanced emotional intelligence is Green's area of expertise, bringing business and psychology into play. Green has significantly improved the narratives surrounding emotional intelligence. It is unyieldingly true that his work will contribute tremendously to how we do business in the workplace and relate to one another.

A couple years back, I was lecturing at a prestigious University in West Africa to a group of I-O psychology students. During the Q&A, a student asked whether what they learned in Africa can be applied in the Western world. It was a question that stuck with me. Although social and cultural intelligences are required in the adjustment process, I reassured them that humanity is inextricably tied. After that experience, I started to wonder how many students, employees, leaders are asking if what they do matters? As an I-O psychology practitioner who has travelled nationally and internationally, I found Green's work relevant and dynamic. It is work that promotes hope in the way we manage our emotions in decision-making and has placed advanced emotional intelligence at the forefront of how we conduct business in this fast-paced global economy. I recommend this work to anybody who has interest in personal development, healthy human relationships, and increasing the bottom-line in corporations.

J. Ibeh Agbanyim

www.fvgrowth.com
Mesa, Arizona - March, 2017

Acknowledgements

My path to becoming an I-O psychologist was heavily influenced by my teachers, peers, friends and family. There have been many along the way who have provided motivation and tutelage, uniquely crafting the conditions that fostered my curiosity for the psychological realm, developed my acumen for modern business, and hardened my resolve to make a difference.

Thank you to Chris and Ed Hennessy, who introduced me to the world of emotional intelligence and certified me to administer the EQ-i 2.0 assessment. Thank you to Dr. Kitti, who taught me the method of psychological research and the difference between mastering and adding to the current body of knowledge. Thank you to all of my college professors, who are too many to name, who helped develop my passion for the pursuit of understanding the unknown. Thank you to MHS for permitting specific characteristics about the EQ-i to be published in this book.

And thank you to my family, who believed in me, before I believed in myself.

Introduction

A ninja, or shinobi, was a covert agent who operated within the shadows of feudal Japan. Often employing methods of irregular warfare, the mission of the shinobi was to create change and disruption at all costs. The shinobi worked in teams to gather intelligence and craft war plans, all while remaining invisible. Though not much is known about the shinobi, it is believed that they had legendary skills and abilities that were unmatched, they operated without a master, and they influenced the outcome of empires. In the modern day, the few shinobi that are left employ a different skill set than the ancient ones, but it is a skill set that also has the ability to influence modern day empires – corporations. Moving from grappling hooks, kunai (daggers), hamaguri (knives) and mizugumo (water shoes), the modern-day shinobi employs psychological abilities to affect change. The mind-bending skills of the modern-day shinobi exist within the realm of emotional intelligence.

. . .

Emotional intelligence is a collection of emotional and social skills that influence the way individuals understand and express feelings, develop and sustain social relationships, and use emotional knowledge in an effective and meaningful way (Bar-On, 2004). Even though the concept of a social intelligence that differs from aptitude and is separate from IQ has been around for over 100 years, emotional intelligence in its current form has only been around for about 30 years. Before the late 1980s, when psychologists Peter Salovey and John Mayer began writing about emotional intelligence in the *Journal of Imagination, Cognition, and Personality*, emotional intelligence was viewed as a fad and regarded as having little sustained business or psychological value.

We are inculcated from birth to believe that greater technical skill equals greater career success. However, business leaders have long known, deep down, that success in the workplace extended beyond IQ alone, despite the ineluctable stance from historical leadership development views that IQ and workplace success were linked. Subject matter expertise or proficiency in a specific technical discipline never directly correlated to powerful leadership or successful people management, and leaders began to understand that something was missing from the equation. In the 1930s, Edward Thorndike discovered that a social intelligence was responsible for leadership success in the factory, which little did he know, would start a psychological revolution.

Over the following years, the idea of a social intelligence being linked to workplace success began to take shape, as psychologists looked for new applications of psychosocial and psychoemotional concepts in the business world. It wasn't until Daniel Goleman bridged the chasm between psychology and business consulting with his popular 1995 book *Emotional Intelligence: Why it Can Matter More than IQ,* that consultants and business leaders started to see the power of practical business application. Now, emotional intelligence as an applied science is here to stay.

There are many major assessment providers offering psychometrics that deliver emotional intelligence profiles, ranging from skill identification to ability discovery, according to the Consortium for Research on Emotional Intelligence. Still considered by most scientists to be in its infancy in terms of business application, many emotional intelligence practitioners today are simply performing 1-on-1 coaching debriefs, 360-degree feedback sessions, and off-the-shelf team performance workshops based off individual assessment results alone.

Emotional intelligence consultants expect that these limited skills alone will somehow transmogrify into a sustainable coaching or consulting practice.

The purpose of this book is to offer a view into advanced applications of emotional intelligence concepts and synthesize it with modern consulting best practices, psychological perspectives, and coaching techniques. Readers of this book will become masters of emotional intelligence business and coaching applications, and will learn how to apply emotional intelligence to empower teams, determine psychoemotional fit, develop EI-based succession and talent programs, battle cognitive bias, and discover multiple psychological reputations that empower a single leader.

Who This Book Is For

This book is for coaches, consultants, entrepreneurs, business leaders, psychologists, therapists, project and program managers, sales people, and anyone else that is interested in how emotional intelligence can dramatically increase performance, and is looking for advanced applications to do so.

This book is also for those who are not yet trained or certified in emotional intelligence, but want to see what the future could possibly hold, should one embark on this wonderful journey.

This is for those who want to become an EQ Shinobi. Much like your ancient ancestor shinobi, you will be one that creates change with irregular tactics, uses teams to gather hidden intelligence while operating covertly, and is comfortable operating without a master. By learning the advanced concepts in this book, you will be without a master, because you will become the master. Are you comfortable with that?

This is also for those who wish to extend their knowledge of the application of emotional intelligence toward driving desired business outcomes, executive coaching, leadership development, change management, and increasing team performance. A beginner's understanding of emotional intelligence is required to fully apply the content of this text, but if this is your first emotional intelligence book, by no means put it down. You are about to read the first book ever written on advanced emotional intelligence application that fuses proven psychology and modern business, into one methodology.

What This Book Is

This is an advanced interpretation guide that is based in organizational research, peer-reviewed journal articles, scholarly sources, extant literature on emotional intelligence, and personal experiences from my consulting practice. I am not a researcher; I am a practitioner. I have used emotional intelligence at the highest levels of the Federal Government, for small businesses all over the world, for professional American sports teams, and for global audiences within Fortune 1000 organizations, to accomplish 3 main goals:

- Create psychologically safe environments to foster powerful 1-1 coaching sessions
- Diagnose talent issues on dysfunctional teams and accelerate performance
- Create and sustain desired behaviors within leaders

There are other applications of the assessment, but most, if not all, usually tie back to one of these three areas. If you are certified in any emotional intelligence instrument, you most likely took a 2-day course with a master trainer, studied basic material and passed an online test. In this book, I will refer to this basic certification curriculum as **Level 1**, while the advanced material in this book will be called **Level 2**. You will often see me refer to emotional intelligence as **EI** or **EQ**.

What This Book Is Not

This is not a beginner's guide to EI. There is a massive amount of information that you can find for free on the Internet about EI. I will discuss beginner (Level 1) interpretation concepts to build upon the advanced (Level 2) concepts, but to get the most out of this book, at a minimum you should read *The EQ Edge* as a precursor. Working knowledge of the EQ-i 2.0 assessment, or better yet, possessing a certification in it, will help immensely. Many of the historical and introductory concepts that I will cover are also covered in *The EQ Edge* and most likely in your Level 1 certification course.

This book is also not intended to be an extension of the assessment technical manual or additional psychological research, but rather it is a blend of personal experience, industrial psychology, consulting and coaching skill, business acumen, and organizational behavior principles, woven into one methodology that yields advanced interpretation of the most powerful EI assessments to date.

I also assume that if you are reading this, you already accept EI as a performance enhancing science and a social intelligence that is positively correlated to workplace success. There are many that still do not buy into the notion of EI as a separate intelligence. Some view EI as anathema and will discredit you at the first mention of it. Some merely think that EI is simply a set of re-labeled personality traits or a byproduct of them. Others question the criterion validity of emotional skill assessment and some feel that there is not enough science yet to show correlation or causality to workplace performance. While the evidence and research cited in this book should be compelling enough for any skeptic, my intention is not to try and sway the nonbelievers. The skills of the ancient shinobi were only for the chosen, so I see no reason why the skills of the modern-day shinobi should be any different. This book is for those who believe in EI and all that it can do, and wish to maximize their supernatural abilities with it.

This book is also not an advertisement for the EQ-i 2.0, but I realize it may come across that way. This is a collection of my personal experiences using EI all over the world to make individuals and teams better, and the EQ-i 2.0 happens to be my assessment of choice. I was not asked by anyone to endorse anything, though if you can afford me, we can certainly discuss any endorsements on your mind. Did I mention that shinobis are mercenaries for hire?

My Goals for This Book

This book will be edgy. This book will be direct. *My main goal for this book is to make the psychology degree as important as the business degree, by showing that EI does more to influence organizational success than anything else.* In Part 1, I will present history and models that are ubiquitously contained in other books. In Part 2, I will discuss the proven methods that I have used to stand up coaching practices within Fortune 1000 organizations and I will introduce the five perspectives of psychology and why they are important. Part 2 will also extend Level 1 knowledge by discussing advanced 360 interpretation and how to use the Group report to empower teams. I will also advance the discussion on the importance of emotional balance and identifying emotional configurations within clients. Part 3 will be, as they say in Latin, *sui generis* (of its own kind). I will dive into the human mind, flawed cognition and decision making processes, highlight how EI can affect large-scale organizational change, and discuss how to craft bulletproof selection and succession programs that are based in EI.

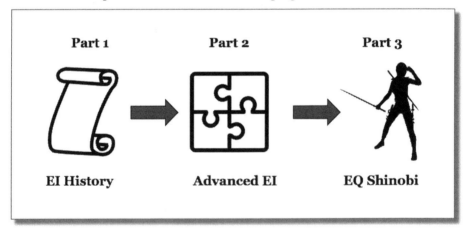

Figure 1 - The three parts

No one has ever written a book on EI that was aimed at bridging the skill sets of coaches, psychologists, and consultants, into one lethal EQ Shinobi. My goal, is that by the end of this book, you will possess the knowledge needed to make you one of the foremost experts in EI business application in the world. You will become an EQ Shinobi. What you do with that knowledge, is completely up to you. If you feel that you possess a strong background in EI and have a solid grasp of its rise as a social intelligence, feel free to skip to Part 2.

We are in the business of increasing performance, having hard conversations, and leading change within individuals and teams. The best way to accomplish this is through honest language and powerful examples. My hope is that this text will provide you with advanced working knowledge of EI in combination with organizational behavior principles. My objective is that you will walk away with high-level expert knowledge in the following areas:

- Advanced application of EI to coaching and consulting
- How EI can empower team performance
- How EI can identify team dysfunction
- Advanced interpretation of EQ360 assessments
- How to weave psychological perspectives into your coaching discipline
- Advanced understanding of emotional balance
- Discovering psychoemotional fit
- Understanding of how EI can affect change
- Understanding of how EI can empower decision making ability
- Understanding how EI can attract and retain talent
- A future view of where EI is headed

I provide anecdotal stories and scientific examples of the concepts that I introduce. Names have been changed to protect the innocent.

Warning – Generalization Just Up Ahead

My goal is to also introduce my blended psychologist-coach methodology, which fuses two paradigms that are omnipresent in this field. In my experience, many people in this field are **coaches**, meaning that they do not necessarily have an advanced psychology degree but rather subscribe to a standard of coaching such as ICF (International Coach Federation), Co-Active, etc., and *apply* coaching techniques to increase performance of teams and team leaders. Generally speaking (and I know many coaches that will jump on me for this), coaches lack the psychological understanding of many EI principles that really enables them to maximize the effectiveness of what the assessment data is saying. The coaching modus operandi is simply to have conversations.

Conversely, the other half in this field are **psychologists**, of the I/O (industrial & organizational), performance, or clinical variety, that are interested in *research*. Psychologists normally understand the science, validity, reliability, and rigor of assessments, but generally (and I know many psychologists that will jump on me for this) they lack the coaching methodology to deliver feedback in a powerful way that stimulates client growth and prosperity. The psychologist modus operandi is simply to dump data onto the client or to diagnose.

As stated earlier, I am an I/O psychologist and a practitioner, which I suppose makes me a unique blend of the two, lucky me! If you are a blend of the two as well, lucky you! But you aren't an EQ Shinobi yet, so keep on keepin' on.

By the end of this book, you will be an advanced EQ Shinobi, who will be able to create the conditions where clients can achieve sustainable behavioral change individually, within their teams, and for their organizations, using advanced EI concepts and applications that you didn't learn in your standard EI certification courses.

So, what's all this shinobi talk about? I'm glad you asked! I have aligned the teachings in this book to the ancient ninjitsu philosophies. There are many parallels between what the ancient shinobi did to influence empires and what the modern shinobi can do to influence organizations. At the end of each chapter, you will acquire the skills of the ninja, on your way to becoming an EQ Shinobi. Here is a list of the ninjitsu skills of the ancient shinobi that I have linked to modern-day EI techniques throughout this book:

Seishin Teki Kyoko – Spiritual and emotional aspects of the ninja

Inton-Jutsu – The art of escape, concealment, and invisibility

Henso-Jutsu – The art of disguise and impersonation

Ten-Mon – The art of forecasting conditions

Naginata-Jutsu – The art of spear fighting

Kayaku-Jutsu – The art of fire and explosives

Shinobi-Iri – The art of entering and stealth

Nyukyo No Jutsu – The art of timing

Nyudaki No Jutsu – The art of psychological infiltration

Cho Ho – The art of espionage

Tai Jutsu – The art of unarmed combat

If I have captivated you thus far, but you do not feel that you are ready for an advanced application guide for EI, proceed to Part 1, which will review a brief chronicle of the rise of EI, a definition of the chosen EI model for this book, and other erudition you would acquire during a beginner Level 2-day EQ-i 2.0 certification course.

Part 1

A review of the history and models of Emotional Intelligence

Recommended Pre-Readings

Below is a list of books that I have found to be extremely valuable in my consulting practice. There are hundreds, most likely thousands, of books on the subjects of psychology, EI, coaching, and consulting, and while I advocate reading as many as you can, these five are packed with applicable knowledge that will be valuable to you on your quest.

The EQ Edge: Emotional Intelligence and Your Success, By Steven Stein, PhD and Howard Book, MD. This book lays the foundations for understanding EI at a beginner level and is a must have for any serious EI practitioner.

Co-Active Coaching: Changing Business, Transforming Lives, by Henry and Karen Kimsey-House. This is a great book on the art and methodology of coaching, which is the often-preferred delivery and debrief mechanism for EI assessment results.

Million Dollar Consulting, by Alan Weiss, PhD. This book is the professional's guide to growing a consulting practice and how to sell your consulting services, which is a subject I will extend in this book.

The Millionaire Mind, by Dr. Thomas Stanley, which interviews hundreds of millionaires and asks them what is responsible for their own financial success (hint: it isn't IQ).

The Five Love Languages, by Gary Chapman. While this book is about falling in love, it is a great way to understand that everyone speaks a different language when it comes to giving and receiving love. Most coaches and consultants only deliver feedback via one method; whichever is best for themselves. This book will show you why it is best to deliver in whichever way is best for the client.

Next, a brief history of the rise of EI will catch you up to speed.

A Brief History

While this book isn't meant to be a full historical account of the rise of EI, it is important to understand that this intelligence has a deep history of evolution. Having a broad understanding of the origins of EI will help with your eventual mastery of the advanced interpretation concepts. If history doesn't interest you, skip to the next section. If this section sounds familiar, you are one of the few that needed a cure for insomnia and read my doctoral dissertation.

Charles Darwin is best known for his theories of evolution that he published in his 1859 book, *On the Origin of Species*. He developed his theories of natural selection based off work he did with marine invertebrates and other geological work, and is often described as one of the most influential figures in history. Darwin claimed that "intelligence is based on how efficient a species became at doing the things they need to survive" (Darwin, 1859). His theories and contributions to science focused on the evolutionary survival of a species, and he posited that the ability for that species to survive was largely based on its intelligence.

His work was one of the first that focused on the intelligence of a species and the implications to its survival, and provided a theoretical base to the theory that intelligence can be developed and is correlated to specific outcomes of a species (Darwin, 1859). Darwin would also become the inspiration behind Sir Francis Galton, who eventually created psychometrics.

Edward Thorndike was an American psychologist who investigated the learning process of humans and pioneered evolutionary psychology in the 1930s. He was a former president of the American Psychological Association, and dedicated his research to identifying three main areas of intellectual development in adult learning. He described abstract intelligence, which is the ability to comprehend different concepts, mechanical intelligence, which is the ability to handle objects physically, and social intelligence, which is the ability to get along with other people.

The ability to understand and manage men and women became a foundation for social intelligence, and is the origin of EI (Bar-On, 2004). He posited that success in the workplace came not from skill of a particular craft, but rather possession of a social intelligence. He wrote, "the best mechanic in the factory may fail as a foreman for lack of social intelligence" (Thorndike, 1932). This view was one of the first to apply intelligence to the workplace and specifically distinguish that expertise in a particular skill did not always lead to workplace success. Through his research on various intelligences, he provided the foundations for later EI researchers such as Daniel Goleman, who eventually brought EI into the mainstream, as well as provided a theoretical basis for executive coaching.

David Wechsler is an American psychologist who is best known for the WAIS, or Wechsler Adult Intelligence Scale, which he created in 1939. He emphasized that there were other factors and reasons behind behavior other than intellectual ability. His work was pioneering in the field of intelligence measurements and psychometrics, and the WAIS is still one of the most commonly used psychometric today. His philosophy that intelligence is the capacity of an individual to deal effectively with a surrounding environment and act in an appropriate manner, in addition to rational thinking, provides a philosophical basis for modern psychometric assessment and EI theory (Kaplan & Saccuzzo, 2010).

Abraham Maslow is best known for his hierarchy of human needs. He posited that people have social and psychological needs and that those needs must be satisfied. The process of satisfying those needs aims to decipher human motivation and behaviors. His work is some of the first to be applied to employees, since it provides people managers a framework to understanding individuals at work, what their deprived needs are, and how those deprived needs negatively influence behavior, attitudes, and thinking (Ozguner, & Ozguner, 2014). On the flip side, his theories also provided avenues for managers to positively influence behavior of individuals by addressing certain deprived needs. According to Maslow's theory, individuals have a hierarchy of needs that are arranged from lower level to higher level. Starting with physiological needs, humans have a basic need for food, shelter and clothing. Organizations can meet these needs by providing adequate compensation and working conditions. Once physiological needs are met, safety needs revolve around protection from danger and freedom from fear (Ozguner, & Ozguner, 2014). Organizations can meet these needs by providing job security and benefits programs. Social needs are addressed after safety needs are met, which involve a desire for love and acceptance from other people. Organizations provide for these needs by facilitating social engagement and a pleasurable work environment for its employees. Next, esteem needs represent the need to be respected by others. This ego portion of the hierarchy can be addressed with job titles, accomplishments, and praises (Ozguner, & Ozguner, 2014). Lastly, self-actualization is the final need that addresses the self-fulfillment potential of the individual, and organizations can meet this need by providing opportunities for personal growth. It is important to understand this hierarchy because it was one of the first psychological models to be applied to modern business that specifically targeted motivation of employees (Ozguner, & Ozguner, 2014). Maslow's work is pioneering in the field of employee engagement because he describes emotional needs, and provides a theoretical basis for modern-day organizational development as well as management of workforce behavior (Ozguner, & Ozguner, 2014).

Howard Gardner is an American psychologist and professor of Cognition and Education at the Harvard Graduate School of Education. He is best known for his theory of multiple intelligences, as introduced in his 1983 book, *Frames of Mind: The Theory of Multiple Intelligences*. He posits that intelligence isn't a singular construct, but rather a diverse ability that can splinter into eight distinct intelligences. He claims that musical-rhythmic, visual-spatial, verbal-linguistic, logical-mathematical, bodily, kinesthetic, interpersonal, intrapersonal, and naturalistic, are all distinct intelligences that humans can learn at different paces (Slavin, 2010). These eight different intelligences can be categorized into three primary areas, which are: the ability to create an effective item that is valued, a set of skills that enable a person to solve problems, and the creativity of solution solving through acquiring new knowledge. The first two are ancestors of EI. More specifically, his intelligences of Interpersonal and Intrapersonal are both direct reflections of EI, as Interpersonal has to do with the interaction of others, their sensitivity to moods, feelings, and motivations, and Intrapersonal has to do with self-reflection, emotional self-awareness, and understanding of one's own strengths and weaknesses (Slavin, 2010). His two types of intelligence form the foundation that most EI models are operated on today.

Wayne Payne and Keith Beasley are two individuals who are important to highlight because they are credited with first publishing the terms of "emotional intelligence" and "emotional quotient". Wayne Payne first used the term "emotional intelligence" in his doctoral thesis titled, *A Study of Emotion: Developing Emotional Intelligence* in 1985 (Payne, 1985). Keith Beasley published the term "emotional quotient" in an article for the British Mensa magazine in 1987 (Beasley, 1987). Until this point, the concept of multiple intelligences had been explored and generally accepted in the scientific community, and even though many of those studied intelligences had emotional components, the distinct area of EI never had its own name. These two individuals helped distinguish and identify EI as a separate intelligence.

Reuven Bar-On is a psychologist who became interested in noncognitive competencies in the mid-1980s. He sought to create a measure of social intelligence, and eventually created the Emotional Quotient Inventory Assessment, or EQ-i. According to his model, EI is a combination of interrelated emotional and social skills and competencies that determine how effectively we process emotions, express emotions, cope with challenges, and how we understand and relate to others (Bar-On, 2004). The Bar-On model of EI is divided into two parts, with the first part comprising of theory, and the second part comprising of psychometric properties. Theoretical foundations were used to develop the Bar-On model, such as Darwin's early work on the importance of emotional expression for survival of the fittest. Thorndike's 1920 theory of social intelligence, as well as Wechsler's 1940 theory of non-cognitive factors, all served as inputs into the development of the EQ-i 2.0. Bar-On's model of emotional-social intelligence provides the theoretical basis for the psychometric assessment that will be used in this book, and is considered by the *Encyclopedia of Applied Psychology* as one of the three major models of EI (Bar-On, 2004).

Peter Salovey and John Mayer attempted to develop a scientific measure of the difference between a person's ability to recognize the emotions of others, and found that there were varying degrees of ability among people to identify the feelings of themselves and others. In 1990, they published a paper titled "Emotional Intelligence". In collaboration with David Caruso, they developed an ability based emotional intelligence test, labeled the Mayer Salovey Caruso Emotional Intelligence Test, or MSCEIT (Fiori et al., 2014). While it is not the specific instrument being used for this book, it is important to examine because it highlights a differing view of EI testing. As an ability test, it examines the participant by asking the test-taker to perceive emotions by viewing faces and pictures, and measures areas of emotional management and emotional relations. It asks the participant to identify emotions and gauges the ability to accurately identify emotions in others (Fiori et al., 2014). Being an ability test instead of a self-reported assessment (such as the EQ-i 2.0), it measures the ability of an individual to recognize emotions of others in visual situations, rather than self-reporting on their own EI scores. Fiori et al. (2014) posited that items appeared too easy to challenge individuals that possessed a high level of EI. EI ability tests also measure how individuals perform at their best instead of assessing how individuals perform on a normal basis (Fiori et al., 2014).

Daniel Goleman is an American psychologist who reported on the brain and behavioral sciences for *The New York Times* in the mid-1990s. His book, *Emotional Intelligence, Why It Can Matter More than IQ*, has sold more than 5,000,000 copies and was a *New York Times* bestseller for over a year and a half. His work is considered one of the first main stream works of EI, and he further establishes the case that IQ is not the sole measure of one's abilities, and that workplace success is a matter of social intelligence, not cognitive intellect. *Emotional Intelligence, Why It Can Matter More than IQ*, was named one of *Time* Magazine's "25 Most Influential Business Management Books", and his views on leadership in conjunction with social and emotional intelligence have paved the way for further research into the field.

Goleman agreed with the work of Salovey and Mayer, and built upon their work, believing that EI may be the best predictor of success in life (Srikanth & Sonawat, 2014). He posited that unattended, ignored and repressed emotions affected enhanced learning, greater focus, optimum relationships, and effective decision-making, and sought to understand the relationship of EI to day-to-day life (Srikanth & Sonawat, 2014). Goleman helped further develop the notion that EI is a skill that can be developed within humans, and that developing this skill provided humans with a capacity to have alternative behavioral choices to anger, violence, and other undesired actions. His work is instrumental in linking EI to desired business outcomes as well, as Srikanth and Sonawat (2014) posit that Goleman's work led to further studies on how EI impacted vital organizational factors, such as organizational change (Ferres & Connell, 2014; Singh, 2003); leadership (Ashkanasy, 2002; Dearborn, 2002; Gardner & Stough, 2002; Weymes, 2003); management performance (Slaski & Cartwright, 2002); perceiving occupational stress (Nikolaou & Tsaousis, 2002; Oginska-Bulik, 2005); and life satisfaction (Palmer, Donaldson & Stough, 2002). He developed the Emotional and Social Competence Inventory, or ESCI, which assesses the emotional and social competencies that distinguish outstanding leaders from average leaders (Goleman, 1995). Daniel Goleman was not the first to study or publish on the subject of EI, but through his work he catapulted the subject into mainstream business thinking (Srikanth & Sonawat, 2014).

Goleman is often considered the key element that organized years of psychological and social research into a coherent subject that the average person could understand (Stein, 2011). The response from the general population, as well as modern business, was overwhelming. Mainstream educators, business people, the media, and academia rallied around the subject of EI, as numerous books and studies began to flood the marketplace.

Though Goleman was not the first to call it emotional intelligence, his seminal work bridged the chasm between psychology and business, between research and practitioner. Coaches and consultants began to use EI as part of their coaching framework, and used EI to facilitate powerful conversations, develop high-performing teams, and lead talent interventions all over the world.

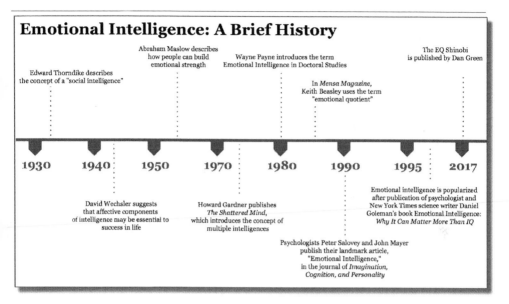

Emotional Intelligence: A Brief History

Abraham Maslow describes how people can build emotional strength

Wayne Payne introduces the term Emotional Intelligence in Doctoral Studies

The EQ Shinobi is published by Dan Green

Edward Thorndike describes the concept of a "social intelligence"

In *Mensa Magazine,* Keith Beasley uses the term "emotional quotient"

1930 1940 1950 1970 1980 1990 1995 2017

David Wechsler suggests that affective components of intelligence may be essential to success in life

Howard Gardner publishes *The Shattered Mind,* which introduces the concept of multiple intelligences

Emotional intelligence is popularized after publication of psychologist and New York Times science writer Daniel Goleman's book Emotional Intelligence: *Why It Can Matter More Than IQ*

Psychologists Peter Salovey and John Mayer publish their landmark article, "Emotional Intelligence," in the journal of *Imagination, Cognition, and Personality*

Figure 2 – Important Dates in The Rise of EI

See what I did there?

Defining Emotional Intelligence

There are a few accepted definitions for EI. Stein (2011) writes in *The EQ Edge* that: Reuven Bar-On called it 'an array of non-cognitive capabilities, competencies, and skills that influence one's ability to succeed in coping with environmental demands and pressures'. Peter Salovey and John Mayer, who created the term 'emotional intelligence', describe it as 'the ability to perceive emotions, to access and generate emotions so as to assist thought, to understand emotions and emotional meanings, and to reflectively regulate emotions in ways that promote emotional and intellectual growth.' In developing the EQ-i 2.0, emotional intelligence has been defined as 'a set of emotional and social skills that influence the way we perceive and express ourselves, develop and maintain social relationships, cope with challenges, and use emotional information in an effective and meaningful way.' (p. 156)

The core concept of EI, is that EI is a dynamic skill that can change over time, while personality and IQ are considered fixed (Bar-On, 2002).

Figure 3 – The EQ-i 2.0, Based on the Bar-On Model of Emotional Intelligence

Reproduced with permission of Multi-Health Systems (2017). All Rights Reserved. www.mhs.com

Assessments Are Born

There are many EI assessments in use today, but three have become the most predominant in research and coaching and are considered the three major models of EI, according to the *Encyclopedia of Applied Psychology*. I will provide a quick highlight and discussion of the three, but this book will then focus on advanced interpretation and application of one of them – the EQ-i 2.0.

MSCEIT is an ability-based EI assessment, as opposed to a self-report EI assessment like the EQ-i 2.0. The MSCEIT seeks to measure capacity for learning EI skills. It measures one's ability to identify and express emotions by showing pictures of faces, asking the respondent to identify the emotion. The MSCEIT also measures how the respondent understands how emotions impact thoughts, one's ability to comprehend and analyze emotions, and one's ability to regulate emotions. Fiori et al. (2014) investigated the MSCEIT and its ability to measure EI. Fiori et al. (2014) determined that the MSCEIT is best suited to differentiate between individuals on the low end of the EI spectrum, but for individuals in the medium to high range, the variation could not truly reflect EI. The researchers also questioned the availability of multiple scoring systems for the assessment, and called out that the MSCEIT could be considered too easy to respond to, with different degrees of correctness almost impossible to detect (Fiori et al., 2014).

The ESCI was developed by Daniel Goleman and Richard Boyatzis and is considered a 360-degree assessment. This type of assessment is not self-report, but rather an assessment that generates data via multi-rater input, meaning that other people take the assessment about the subject. A mixed model approach, the ESCI measures EI competencies and abilities, not EI skills, across four distinct areas of ability: self-awareness, social awareness, self-management, and relationship management.

Bar-On developed the Emotional Quotient Inventory, or EQ-i, as a self-report measure of EI that provides an EI score over five composite scales and 15 subscales. The 133-question assessment has had reliability and validity studies performed on it for over twenty years, with a consensus of findings revealing that the model is consistent, reliable, and stable (Bar-On, 2004). The overall internal consistency coefficient of the EQ-i is .97, using the North American norms (Bar-On, 2004). The assessment has demonstrated an ability to predict various aspects of human performance based on studies performed by Bar-On and various researchers. With over 80,000 Americans in its general normative sample and being a self-report assessment, it is one of the premier assessments available today.

Quick Check In

As previously mentioned, Level 1 material is the knowledge you would gain by going through beginner EQ-i 2.0 certification. Level 2 is the advanced application of Level 1. The information presented in this book is the practitioner methodology that I have developed based on my real-world application of the EQ-i 2.0 all over the world. I have found that Level 1 certification, while great to get a coach started, does very little to prepare someone to tackle some of the toughest talent challenges and most difficult leader interventions in the business world. Level 1 is great for 1-on-1 debriefs, but to lead organizational change and develop C-level executives in modern business, advanced application is needed. This is where Level 2 comes in. Below is a summary of the differences between Level 1 and Level 2:

Level 1 (what you learn during initial certification)

- Explanation of the Bar-On Model of EI
- The five Composites and 15 Subscales
- The APA Coaching and Feedback Method
- Brief EQ360 Overview
- Super Brief EQ Group Report Overview
- Overview of MHS (assessment provider), Online Account and Tokens

Level 2 (what you will learn in this weighty tome)

- Advanced application of EI to coaching and consulting
- How EI can empower team performance
- How EI can identify team dysfunction
- Advanced interpretation of EQ360 assessments
- How to weave psychological perspectives into your coaching discipline
- Advanced understanding of emotional balance
- Discovering psychoemotional fit
- How EI can battle cognitive bias
- Using EI to manage change
- How EI can be used to retain talent

. . .

Coming to prominence in the 15th century, the shinobi were specifically trained for a solitary purpose – to be stealth soldiers whose main goal was *to create change*. Change was brought about by methods such as kancho (spying), teisatsu (scouting), kishu (surprising) and konran (agitating), (Turnbull, 2003). These are the same methods that promote change within individuals and organizations today. We gather information, take account of the landscape, then innovate and disrupt.

Review of Level 1

A review of the EQ-i 2.0 EI assessment
and the knowledge gained during beginner level certification

The Bar-On Model of Emotional Intelligence

The Bar-On model is what most are familiar with that have a beginner level understanding of the EQ-i 2.0, and normally the knowledge one would possess after a 2-day certification workshop. Let's review the Bar-On model, as the advanced concepts in this book will build upon his work.

The Bar-On model of EI can be divided into two elementary parts: conceptualization (theory) and psychometrics (measurement). According to Bar-On (2013), "these two parts of the model have also been referred to as (a) "the Bar-On conceptual model of emotional-social intelligence" and (b) "the Bar-On psychometric model of emotional-social intelligence" respectively, while (c) "the Bar-On model of emotional-social intelligence" refers to both the conceptual and the psychometric components of this model combined together into one inseparable entity."

It is important to note that some publications refer to it as the EQ-i model, which is incorrect. It is the Bar-On model of emotional and social intelligence, and the EQ-i 2.0 is the assessment that measures it.

Charles Darwin's work on the importance of emotional expression for survival and adaptation influenced the creation of the Bar-On model, which claimed that socially intelligent behavior was responsible for adaptation and survival. The Bar-On model was also influenced by the ideas and findings of others listed in the history section, specifically Thorndike's view of social intelligence and its link to managerial performance, as well as Wechsler's observations on non-cognitive factors and intelligent behavior. Gardner's introduction of the concept of interpersonal multiple intelligences had an influence on the development of the intrapersonal and interpersonal mechanisms of the Bar-On model of EI (Bar-On, 2013).

The Development of the Bar-On Model

According to Bar-On (2013), the model proceeded in six stages. The following is a direct excerpt from his website:

1) identifying, in the professional literature, and logically clustering various emotional and social competencies, skills and behaviors thought to impact human performance and well-being;

2) defining the individual clusters of competencies, skills and behaviors that emerged from the literature;

3) constructing an experimental instrument based on initially generating approximately 1,000 items that were thought to tap these definitions;

4) eventually determining the inclusion of 15 primary scales and 133 items in the published version of this instrument (the *Bar-On EQ-i*) based on a combination of statistical findings and theoretical considerations;

5) norming the final version of the *EQ-i* on 3,831 adults in North America; and

6) continuing to collect data, norm and validate this instrument across cultures worldwide.

This is described in detail in the technical manual for the EQ-i 2.0, along with validity and reliability data, if that interests you.

The 15 Factors of the Bar-On Model

Emotional intelligence is a collection of emotional and social skills that influence the way individuals understand and express feelings, develop and sustain social relationships, and use emotional knowledge in an effective and meaningful way (Bar-On, 2004). The Bar-On model amalgamates the 15 factors into five composites. Let's explore the five composites and the 15 factors within, which are referred to as subscales.

Composite 1 – Self-Perception

Figure 4 - The Self-Perception Composite

The Self-Perception composite of EI seeks to measure the inner self, and includes Self-Regard, Self-Actualization, and Emotional Self-Awareness. This composite measures inner strength, feelings of confidence, our own understanding of the impact of emotions, and our pursuit of goals.

Do we accept ourselves, with the bad and the good?

Do we respect ourselves?

What do I want written on my tombstone? (morbid, I know)

Can we identify the emotions that I am feeling right now? (70% of people cannot)

This composite of EI is directly associated with self-awareness, feeling fulfilled, and being satisfied with life.

Self-Regard involves respecting oneself while knowing and accepting both personal strengths and limitations.

Self-Actualization is the inclination to consistently try to improve oneself and pursue the meaning of life.

Emotional Self-Awareness is the skill of recognizing one's own emotions and being able to understand their meanings, their causes, and the impacts they have on one's actions. Often considered the most important EI skill, as it appears in every version of social intelligence beginning with Darwin, and there is no psychometric instrument that does not possess an emotional self-awareness component.

Composite 2 – Self-Expression

Figure 5 - The Self-Expression Composite

The Self-Expression composite is the outward facing skill of the Self-Perception composite, comprising of Emotional Expression, Assertiveness, and Independence. It seeks to measure open-mindedness, how well we express certain emotions, and how well one communicates in a non-offensive manner.

Are we passive, aggressive or passive/aggressive?

Do we express emotions well both verbally and non-verbally?

Do we rely on others for our emotional health and direction?

This composite of EI is directly associated with being bold, being openly expressive, and not letting others take advantage of us.

Emotional Expression is one's ability to openly express emotions verbally and non-verbally.

Assertiveness is one's ability to communicate boldly, but non-offensively and non-destructively.

Independence is one's ability to remain free from emotional reliance of others and complete daily tasks freely.

Composite 3 – Interpersonal

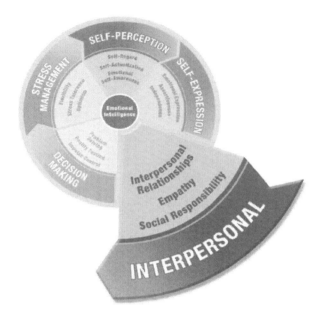

Figure 6 – The Interpersonal Composite

The Interpersonal composite includes Interpersonal Relationships, Empathy, and Social Responsibility, and measures one's skill in creating mutually satisfying relationships, understanding how others feel, and showing concern for a larger community or organization.

Are our relationships a one-way street?

Can I tell how someone feels without them telling me so?

Do I care about the greater good?

This composite of EI is directly linked to antisocial or deviant behavior, and represents essential building blocks of EI within an individual.

Interpersonal Relationships refers to one's skill in developing relationships based on trust that are reciprocally satisfying.

Empathy is the skill of recognizing how someone else feels, and the ability to articulate the description of that feeling to others, with respect.

Social Responsibility is contributing to the greater good, and is the skill of social consciousness.

Composite 4 – Decision Making

Figure 7 - The Decision-Making Composite

Reproduced with permission of Multi-Health Systems (2017). All Rights Reserved. www.mhs.com

The Decision-Making composite addresses how well we use and process emotional information, and includes Problem Solving, Reality Testing, and Impulse Control. These skills reveal what emotions do to our decision-making processes and how well we can avoid knee-jerk behaviors in stressful situations.

Do I shoot from the hip, or aim first?

Am I creative or a realist?

Do I make gut decisions or decisions based on data?

This composite of EI is directly linked to behaviors of successful Fortune 1000 leaders and managers that experience high anxiety.

Problem Solving is the skill of finding a solution when emotions are present and the ability to understand the influence of those emotions on the decision-making process.

Reality Testing is the skill of objectivity and determines how much bias comes into play during our decision-making process.

Impulse Control is one's ability to delay action or curb temptations and rash behaviors. This measures our ability to control our emotions and not let them control us.

Composite 5 – Stress Management

Figure 8 - The Stress Management Composite

Reproduced with permission of Multi-Health Systems (2017). All Rights Reserved. www.mhs.com

The Stress Management composite addresses how well we cope with emotions that come with change, unpredictability, and thinking about the future. It includes Flexibility, Stress Tolerance, and Optimism, and these skills measure resilience, perseverance, and how much hope we have.

Are we hopeful about the future?

Do we manage change, or does change manage us?

How do I handle difficult situations?

This composite of EI is directly linked to behaviors of skilled negotiators, military generals, change leaders, and overall individual health.

Flexibility is how well one adapts emotions to times of change, unpredictable events or wacky ideas.

Stress Tolerance is how well one deals with the emotions associated with difficult scenarios and tough situations.

Optimism is a gauge of hope and one's outlook on life, despite obstacles.

The Happiness Indicator

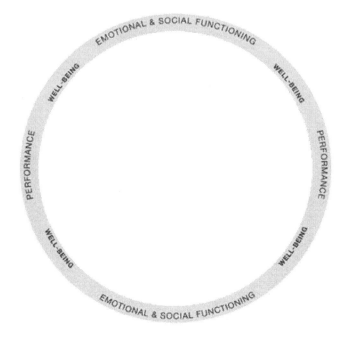

Figure 9 - The Happiness Indicator

Reproduced with permission of Multi-Health Systems (2017). All Rights Reserved. www.mhs.com

Circling the model is the happiness indicator, which addresses emotional health and well-being. It is not included within the total EI score, but it is a side-skill that identifies feelings of satisfaction and serenity in one's life.

It's All About Balance

For many years, personality assessments singlehandedly dominated the psychometric market, which delivered types and traits that comprised of a static profile. Traits and types are not skills, so there is no reason to try and raise the scores. There is no value in trying to become "more extraverted" or "more agreeable". The main goal with personality profiles is self-awareness. Like personality assessments, the goal of EI is not simply to raise every score as high as you can either. The goal is to achieve balance. Once EI assessments started to become readily available, many coaches incorrectly assumed that the goal was to raise scores at all costs since the scores represented dynamic use of a skill, but it is actually all about emotional balance. Once a profile is within balance, then raising the scores is the objective, but more on this in the Advanced Emotional Balance section.

Review the model of the EQ-i 2.0 again and you'll find that it is shaped like a circle or wheel for a reason. If you take an even closer look, you can see the colors of each composite give the illusion that the wheel is in motion, spinning clockwise. If use of any of the skills were high compared to other skills, our metaphorical wheel would have a bulge in it, making it difficult to spin properly. Similarly, if use of any of the skills were low compared to other skills, the wheel would have a divot in it, also making it difficult to spin. The goal should be balance, so that our symbolic wheel can spin and we can access all EI skills freely. More about EI balance later on.

Part 1 Wrap Up

So, that does it for Part 1. It is a review of the rise of EI and the Bar-On model of EI. Part 2 and 3 are where the advanced application begins. In Part 2, you'll learn about psychological perspectives, advanced EQ360 interpretations, identity vs reputations, Group report applications, and other high-level psychoemotional approaches. When combined with EI, they create a powerful performance boosting methodology for your coaching practice or consulting efforts. Let's dive into Part 2, which contains avant-garde methodologies that I have created and used to perform EI performance accelerations all over the world. Buckle up.

Part 2

How to stand up a coaching/consulting practice,

an introduction to psychology perspectives,

and advanced interpretation of the EQ360, Group Report, and emotional balance

If You Build it, They Will Not Come

The ninjitsu skill of Seishin Teki Kyoto referred to the spiritual education of the shinobi, and encompassed the spiritual and emotional aspects that must first be mastered, before any physical training could take place. Seishin Teki Kyoto developed the spirit within self-knowledge, understanding reality, fate, harmony, the heart, the eye, and love. This was a vital first step to developing the shinobi, as no other skills could be learned without first mastering these skills.

. . .

I have a confession to make. I used to believe that my personal accomplishments would directly translate to future success, without me having to grind and continuously work for it. More specifically, I used to believe that once I had achieved a goal, such as completing my Bachelor's degree or getting my project management certification, that work would come flying in and that I would never have to sell myself again to anyone. Almost like my degrees would create some form of passive income. Blame this on my American upbringing. I postulate that most parents just say to their kids "just graduate college and life will be good", just to get you out of the house, not because they really believe that a degree alone is all that is needed for lifelong success.

"All I need to do is build a website, and the business will come."

"All I need to do is finish college, and I'll get a high paying job."

"All I need to do is certified in the EQ-i 2.0, and all the coaching clients will come."

Sound familiar?

Well I built my website, I finished my degrees, and I got my certifications in everything under the sun, and guess what? No one came. I never realized that collecting degrees and certifications would be superfluous effort, and that in order to really be successful, I needed to realize and develop two key skills before all else.

I needed to develop **grit** and the ability to **sell**.

I mention these in the very beginning of Part 2, because if you think that you do not have the ability to sell (or could eventually learn to sell) or that you do not possess the perseverance (or the ability to eventually develop the perseverance) to grind on, then nothing else matters.

I have seen many aspiring ninjas get certified in the EQ-i 2.0, then do absolutely nothing with it. I assume most of you were dilettantes who developed a passion for EI based out of life experience, personal reading, or another non-job related method. Most coaches that I know do coaching as a side job, not dedicating enough effort to develop a full-time practice.

When you decided to study EI and get certified in it, you most likely paid out of your own pocket for the course, or you were fortunate enough to have some general training budget allocated to you from your organization and you used that to pay for the course. If your manager specifically sent you to EI training, you are one of the lucky ones!

This means that when you came back from training, your personal interest in EI had run its course. You then had to operationalize it somehow, among a sea of peers that probably couldn't care less about EI.

Did you?

In my experience, I have found that less than 5% of those who get certified, become successful enough with the instrument that they can use it as a full-time income generating tool. For the purposes of this book, I will assume you are in the other 95%.

The reason you are not as successful as you would like to be with the EQ-i 2.0, most likely lies in the depths of your selling ability and your perseverance. Now, before you go bananas at the thought of having to sell, maintain equanimity and realize that you are always selling something, each and every day. You are always selling your ideas, your pitch, yourself, everything! You now have an expertise that you must sell, convey, and communicate to the world, in a way so that others can understand your value proposition, and even better, be willing to give you money for it.

You are now a champion of EI, and it is up to you to demonstrate to nonbelievers and the yet-to-be converted, that emotional intelligence isn't esoteric and that it is tremendously powerful as a widely-applied business science. Do not worry, this isn't a book on only selling, so I will quickly highlight the top selling vehicles that I have found to be most effective in my consulting practice.

Public Speaking and Work Shop Facilitation

Nothing asserts *expert power* more than publicly speaking about a subject. Find every opportunity that you can to speak publicly about EI, its benefits, and how it can accelerate team performance. Facilitate EI seminars, webinars, coffee hours, break-outs, tiger teams, anything under the sun, where you can be the expert that all eyes are on. Create workshops that are relevant to your audience. Chances are, when a client is ready to commit to hiring an EI coach or consultant, they are most likely only going to hire one (much like a surgeon or dentist). In scenarios where clients only seek a relationship with one, it's normally the best one they can find. Be the best one they can find, because you are everywhere, speaking about EI.

Writing

Writing is a great way to share your knowledge and also display *expert power*. I personally love writing, because it forces me to think about new positions, mindsets, and viewpoints, which keeps my brain sharp and my ideas flowing. Write a book that encompasses your personal view, or write for peer-reviewed journals, trade magazines, LinkedIn, Medium, your blog, and any other platform that will have you. So many journals and magazines starve for content, that you would be surprised how easy they are to write for. Look up a few journals in your field and reach out. There are many journals that would most likely love to get your content and publish you. Get familiar with free online publishing platforms. Make sure you have a good editor though, or in my case, a thesaurus that works in real time and a top-notch spell-checker.

PowerPoints

Truth be told, I hate PowerPoint. I embody the phrase "death by PowerPoint", and I have certainly administered the lethal dose a time or two in my career. That was until I read a book called *Presentation Zen*, by Garr Reynolds. It is a fantastic book that really describes the best (and only) way to create a presentation for a speech or a workshop. Now, I consistently use PowerPoint in my sales pitches and my workshops with great success. Effective PowerPoints are a must.

Remember, finished beats perfect. There are those fastidious many that endlessly craft their presentations and waste so much time "perfecting" it, that it never gets presented. News flash, messy and unfinished idiosyncrasies are what people remember, so get out there and tell the world what you have to offer, regardless of how imperfect you feel that your pitch is.

Volunteering

Sometimes, it is difficult to get that first gig. After EQ-i 2.0 certification, you receive a couple hundred tokens that you can play around with, which are great for practice or for volunteering. Remember, that as an aspirant shinobi, you will possess skills that most people have never heard of. If people haven't heard of it before, how can you sell it? Volunteer as a teaser, but also volunteer to provide a great service. Show people a small taste of what your EI skills can do for their team and team leader, which will only help further substantiate your future high fees.

Cold-Calling and Snowball Networking

Everyone hates cold-calling, and truth be told, EI consulting services aren't exactly as hot as time-shares in South Florida. Before you start malingering, when I refer to cold-calling, I do not mean pointing to random numbers in the *White Pages* and start dialing. Instead, start reaching out to your network. Reach out to former contacts, colleagues, LinkedIn connections, social contacts, and peers. Let everyone know what you do and how you do it. For the ones that take your call, strategically decide who you will offer volunteer services to, who you will pitch, and who you will ask for advocacy.

Over 80% of my business comes from referral, meaning someone contacts me saying that they knew of work that I did for one of their colleagues (in some cases I didn't even perform any services, my name just came up in conversation when the two were discussing something unrelated). The world needs to know what you are doing, so hit the pavement and let the world know.

Next, snowball recruit. Ask each person you connect with for three more connections. When you reach out to those connections, mention how you found them. Warm hand-offs are almost always welcome. When you are done, you will have a web of connections that could span thousands. Do not worry about rejection. I know, easy for me to say, but remember this one profound principle.

"1% of your seeds will yield 50% of your flowers."

Emotional Intelligence and Selling

When things are said to be "positively correlated", it means that increase in one variable equals some amount of increase in another, depending on the strength of the relationship. In other words, the two variables are linked and move in the same direction, and working on development of one variable means that you are indirectly working on developing the other. EI and sales are positively correlated, and there is copious extant literature that highlights this relationship. The relationship of EI and sales is global and has been studied within many industries. For example, EI and sales have been positively linked in sales performance of car salesman in Kuwait (Kholoud, 2016), the financial industry in Malaysia (Wisker, 2016), global B2B sales (Borg, 2013), medical sales in the Midwest USA (Harris, 2012), retail sales in India (Munshi, 2013), and sales promotion activities in Iran (Kamal, 2014), just to name a few. By working on your ability to sell, you are developing a skill that many consider is the most important skill in the world.

By working on your own EI, you become better at selling. By working on your ability to sell, you raise your EI skills. Isn't that great how positive correlation works? Selling involves many skills, but being able to listen to others, articulate other people's needs, and negotiate positions are all sales skills that are also EI skills. If the thought of selling, presenting, speaking, cold-calling and prospecting nauseate you, then you are choosing to not develop the most powerful and applicable skill in our known universe.

Being able to sell to others, also ensures that we are not "sold" to. Proper selling involves listening, understanding, and recommending solutions based off the customer need. Being "sold" means that someone is trying to get you to purchase something that you do not need, simply for their own financial gain, and many unscrupulous salesman have developed powerful techniques to sell to others in deceptive ways. As you will discover in the cognitive bias section, being highly skilled in EI ability also comes with a dark side. Developing your own EI and sales ability will also protect you from being "sold" to from others who chose to use the dark side of EI to manipulate others.

Robert Herjavec wrote a fantastic book on the entire sales process, and his main influence for the book was Dale Carnegie's *How to Win Friends and Influence People*, published in 1936. Herjavec describes how the most important lesson, and the **first lesson** taught, is how important it is to get along with other people (a core EI skill). Here is a summary of the sales process discussed by Herjavec (2016). Good salespeople:

- They know how to negotiate
- They learn determination
- They gain confidence
- They get others to agree with them
- They practice self-discipline

Sound familiar? He highlights that the most important takeaway, from his entire book on selling, is that "eventually everyone is selling something to someone". You can learn to sell. Even if it sounds scary, you can learn to sell. You are already selling, and you will be selling something every day for the rest of your life, so you might as well learn to perfect it!

Grit

Now let's talk about grit. It is a fait accompli that perseverance is one of the most important, if not the most important, precursor to success. Perseverance is the steadfastness in doing something difficult despite a litany of failure. Someone who makes perseverance one of his or her cornerstone behaviors, is said to have grit.

"Now wait a second there," you say.

"Grit is a non-cognitive personality trait, I thought we were talking about emotional intelligence skills?" all of you I/O psychologists are proclaiming.

OK, you got me. I tried to sneak some personality in there. There is a 3-part Venn diagram of what makes you, you. It consists of IQ, personality, and EQ. If you remember from psychology 101, IQ and personality are fixed, while EQ is dynamic.

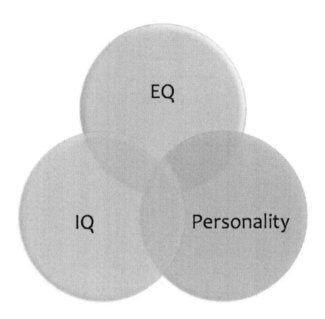

So, while personality and IQ are fixed, it doesn't mean they aren't important in the discussion. Grit ensures that you stick with it, because creating a sustainable coaching practice and convincing the masses of the benefits of organizational behavior and psychometric assessment of its leaders is not an easy task.

Salles (2016) performed a study on grit, and how it correlated to attrition rates in an equally demanding profession – surgical residency. In the study, Salles collected survey data from residents over two consecutive years that were assessed on grit and psychological well-being using validated instruments, as well as risk of attrition via survey items. According to Salles (2016) they found that:

Grit was positively correlated with general psychological well-being ($r = 0.30, p < 0.05$) and inversely correlated with depression ($r = -0.25, p < 0.05$) and risk of attrition ($r = -0.37, p < 0.01$). In regression analyses, grit was positively predictive of well-being ($B = 0.77, t = 2.96, p < 0.01$) and negatively predictive of depression ($B = -0.28$ $t = -2.74, p < 0.01$) and attrition ($B = -0.99, t = -2.53, p < 0.05$).

For the non-scientists reading this, essentially the study findings are that grit is positively associated with better psychological well-being and negatively associated with risk of attrition. So, while this doesn't necessarily directly translate to success, the surgical residents' skill in medicine would mean absolutely nothing if they didn't stay within the residency. *Grit had to be present before any other skills were learned.* Grit ensures that you stick with it, even when times get tough, and that your psychological health stays intact.

Suzuki (2015) examined associations between grit and the Big Five personality traits, self-control level, and other demographic variables, to see if grit was related to work engagement within Japanese workers. After analysis of over 1000 workers, the results showed that grittier individuals were more likely to engage with their own work versus less gritty individuals. Specifically, Suzuki (2015) found that:

Grit had a significant positive association with work engagement ($r = .26, p < .001$), and this result was consistent even after controlling for other variables in Models 2 and 3. Age ($\beta = 0.010, p < .01$ in Model 3) and education ($\beta = 0.055, p < .05$ in Model 3) were positively associated with work engagement. With regard to orientations to happiness, both engagement and meaning were positively associated with work engagement ($\beta = 0.060$ and 0.057, respectively, both $p < .001$), while pleasure was inversely associated with work engagement ($\beta = -0.051, p < .001$). Furthermore, the Big Five traits of Extraversion ($\beta = 0.015, p < .05$) and Openness to Experience ($\beta = 0.019, p < .01$) were positively associated with work engagement.

For the non-scientists reading this, essentially the study found that grit is related to work engagement despite many other demographic factors such as age, income, and gender, as well as personality factors in the Big Five. This is important because you will not be a successful coach or consultant, if you do not love your work and keep your own engagement high. Your passion for EI will need to shine through to your work, and it will be impossible to convince teams and team leaders to let you guide them through growth and transformation, if you aren't engaged and convinced yourself.

Does One Find Grit, or Does One Develop It?

I believe that one has to find grit within them, not necessarily develop it. Grit is often referred to as a personality trait, and by adhering to the mantra that personality is static, it isn't something we can develop. Rather, it is something that exists within all of us, some more than others, and we can disinter our distinctive version of grit by being aware of the mechanisms within us that encourage them.

Angela Duckworth does an amazing presentation on grit. Her book, *Grit: Passion, Perseverance, and the Science of Success*, is fascinating. I suggest picking up a copy once you finish this and all of the other recommended pre-readings, if you discover that you need to find your grit. According to Duckworth, one can discover grit through a four-part process:

- Practice – this includes learning on the fly, stepping out of your own comfort zone, and looking at failures as learning opportunities. This step is about the mindset of failure (learning opportunity instead of catastrophe) and constantly trying to push yourself a bit further.
- Purpose – this includes finding your passion (hopefully it is EI) and aligning your practice activities to this passion. Finding something you want to learn more about every day and something you will step outside of your comfort zone for is important to developing perseverance.
- Hope – failure is inevitable, and the idea of hope is understanding that it is never over unless we give up. Fall down seven times? Get up eight. It is OK to fail as long as you never give up.

- Time – to become an expert in anything, it takes time. Common lore suggests that 10,000 hours is how long it takes to become an expert, which is 20 hours a week, for 50 weeks, for 10 years. While it hopefully does not take you that long to find your grit, understanding that it does take time is important to maintaining hope and searching for purpose.

- Find others – surround yourself with other gritty individuals, so you can learn how they found their grit and also what grit looks like. Social psychologists believe that we are an average of the five people we hang around the most, so if we want to find our grit, we need to be around grit.

Master the Spiritual

The ancient shinobi refer to this skill as Seishin Teki Kyoko, which translates to spiritual refinement, and is derived from Zen Buddhism. The shinobi worked tirelessly to acquire deep knowledge about themselves and their unknown innate abilities. Exercises in mental endurance, as well as physical skills, were taught to the ninja for survival. The seven principles include self-knowledge, understanding reality, fate, harmony, the heart, the eye, and love. Unearth your sales ability and your grit, otherwise all else will fail. These are the spiritual components that lay the foundation for success to come.

– Shinobi Skill Acquired –

Seishin Teki Kyoko 精神的 教養

The 5 Major Perspectives in Psychology

Inton-Jutsu, translating directly to escape and concealment, refers to the five elements that ninjas could deploy to remain invisible. Originally referring to the five natural elements – metal, water, fire, earth, and wood – the ninja was a master of manipulating the five elements to his advantage and to remain undetected. Today, the modern shinobi can master five natural elements of the mind, to educe powerful coaching techniques in combination with EI.

. . .

Why do people do what they do? The scientific study of psychology examines how we think, feel and behave. Over the years, five major perspectives have emerged, which is important to note when discussing what is the best way to deliver psychometric feedback and maximize team performance. *Every leadership development program, coaching practice, or organizational effectiveness initiative, follows a psychological approach, so understanding them, and where assessments fall within them, is vital to success.*

Let's discuss the five major perspectives.

Psychodynamic Approach

Sigmund Freud was one of the original psychodynamic psychologists, who believed that sex drove most of our impulses. Psychologists in this school of thought believe that unconscious drives and experiences from early childhood are at the root of our behaviors and that *discovering these hidden and often repressed memories are the key to determining current day behavior.* Freud conceived that the mind was composed of three elements, the id, the ego, and the superego. The id is the part of the psyche that encompasses all primal and unconscious desires. It is responsible for our wants, desires, lurid impulses and sexual drives. It is considered to be separate from reality and solely responsible for driving pleasure and gratification. The ego is part of the psyche that addresses the demand of the real world and acts as a mediatory between the id and reality. The ego is where consciousness, awareness, and reality reside within the individual, and represents common sense and sense of self. The superego maintains our morals and ideals and works in contradiction to the id. The superego aims for perfection in all that it wants, and it is the home of spirituality and the ego-ideal (where rules and standards for good behaviors exist). The superego works to suppress the id at all times and works with the ego to act idealistically instead of realistically.

Wow, what a mess! How can anyone coach within this perspective?

Within this perspective of psychology, our primal urges are always at odds with our cognition and societal norms. A constant battle within the brain ensues and the end goal of any psychotherapy within this perspective is balance.

Anyone that coaches within this realm is either working with a vulnerable population, or is projecting vulnerability onto the client that they assume is in a deep malaise, in order to have the session fit the coaching methodology. Both are dangerous for coaches; one is a licensure scenario, the other is a malpractice scenario. Generally speaking, a vulnerable population is a group of people who are at risk for some type of danger. Clinical psychologists are trained to work with vulnerable populations (that is why they need state licensure), while I/O psychologists and coaches are not (Carducci, 2009).

I have seen far too often, coaches will use EQ-i 2.0 results and engage in psychotherapy, where the lone focus is to alleviate psychic tension in the client. The primary focus is dysfunction and all concentration is on what is wrong. This is dangerous because Level 1 certification does not equip you with the proper psychodynamic techniques to provide psychotherapy. Examine your coaching style to see if you engage in this method, and if you do, change it quickly.

Behavioral Approach

Psychologists of the behavioral approach believe that *external environmental stimuli influence your behavior* and that individuals can be led to act in a certain way if the environment promoted it. Behavioral psychologists believe that you learn through a system of reinforcements and punishment, and that free will does not exist, since our behavior is a consequence of environment and conditioning. Behaviorists believe the following:

- The environment influences behavior
- Learning is a symptom of stimuli and response
- Learning must include a behavioral change
- Animals and humans learn similarly
- Learners must associate a response with a stimulus, so they both must occur together

Within Behaviorism, classical and operant conditioning split the perspective. Ivan Pavlov did his famous experiment with dogs, where he noticed that dogs began to salivate in response to a bell ringing that was paired with feeding time. Classical conditioning involves placing a neutral sign *before* a reflex, so that the sign eventually becomes associated with the reflex. Operant conditioning uses punishment and reinforcement to create associations, assuming that certain behaviors will increase or decrease based on the introduced association with it. For more information about behaviorism, refer to your Psych101 course book.

Like Psychodynamic theory, behaviorism often operates within the dysfunctional realm because it assumes that we have little to no control over our actions. Many slipshod managers assume that motivation is simply a function of conditioning, and mistakenly use monetary factors like bonus and salary to increase employee morale and motivation. But everyone loves money, right? Not so much (at least in terms of motivation).

Economist Angus Deaton and psychologist Daniel Kahneman performed a study in 2010 at Princeton University which found that happiness caps at an annual salary of $75,000 per year. Meaning, that after that salary limit, any perfunctory increases from our magnanimous leaders no longer equated to equal increases in happiness or motivation. So, using behavioral conditioning to create desired behaviors from our teams and saying "if you do this task you will get more money", sounds great in theory, but does not work in real practice. If your coaching style aligns to the behaviorist perspective, you are either being lazy, ineffective, or both.

Biological Approach

Psychologists who take the biological approach look at how your nervous system, hormones and genetic makeup affect your behavior. Biological psychologists seek relationships between your mental states, your brain, and hormones, and how those relate to actions. For the biological approach, you are the sum of all of your parts. Your actions and thoughts are a function of your brain chemistry and physiological needs, *meaning that all of your actions are based off physical needs and internal characteristics.* While a behaviorist or a psychodynamic psychologist may assume certain behaviors are due to repressed urges or faulty conditioning, biological psychologists would associate undesired behaviors with brain damage or internal chemical dysfunction. Essentially, who you are most likely can't change without some physical change.

Most personality assessments fall within this range, specifically type-based instruments. Still adhering to the mantra that personality is fixed, many believe that personality traits are inherited from our genes and cannot be changed. Personality scores on certain assessments may fluctuate a few points here and there, but overall, personality is static (Bar-On, 2002).

If you coach within the biological perspective, you most likely subscribe to *type-based* assessments that claim to be the panacea for all corporate ills, by simply assigning four representative letters to an individual – highlighting things such as extraversion or introversion. I do believe that any coaching based in *trait-based* assessments is necessary and valid, because many leaders in organizations today are unaware of their strengths, dark-side personality derailers, and personality factors that drive motives and preferences. However, this style of coaching is normally one of promoting self-awareness only (because remember, personality is static), since there is no skill to develop. For those leaders who are already self-aware, there is little coaching opportunity left for you. I will discuss type versus trait based theory a bit later on, but there is a vast amount of research available online as well; a quick Internet search will yield many articles on the subject.

Cognitive Approach

A modern approach and born from dissatisfaction of the behavioral perspective, cognitive psychologists believe that *your behavior is determined by your thoughts and emotions*. How you act is based upon internal processes. Cognitive psychology combines behavioral outcomes with self-insight about negative or self-limiting thoughts. Essentially, your thoughts create self-fulfilling prophecies about outcomes and behavior. A quote by Henry Ford that illustrates this approach is "whether you think you can, or you think you can't, you're right."

Once brain researchers discovered the parts of the brain that were responsible for language production (Wernicke's aphasia) and comprehension of language (Broca's aphasia), cognitive psychology replaced behaviorism during WWII, as it became vital to determine how to best train soldiers to maintain attention while under duress (Anderson, 2010). Developments in computer science and artificial intelligence also paved the way for cognitive psychology to become prominent, as language was tied to working and long term memory, as well as perception within the machines, so cognitive psychologists began to research and apply those principles to human intelligence.

The benefits of coaching within this realm are quite obvious. There are now schools, degrees, practices, books, and programs designed around positive psychology – more specifically, positive-talk psychology. This perspective of psychology is powerful when combined with EQ-i 2.0 results, because the practice of positive self-talk combined with insight into use of emotional skill creates marvelous transformations within individuals and teams. It emboldens the leader to be responsible for her own success, and empowers her with the ability to claw out of any mentally negative position.

Humanistic Approach

Humanistic psychologists believe that all humans are essentially good and that *each is motivated to realize his or her full potential.* Feeling good about yourself is simply a function of fulfilling your needs and goals, or at the very least, constantly aspiring to do so. The humanistic approach works on individual empowerment, and humanistic psychologists believe in the good of mankind and emphasize the individual's inherent drive towards self-actualization and creativity. With this approach, the sole focus is on strengths.

Coaching within this perspective can also be treacherous if the coach is not careful. The view of many in the scientific community is that this approach should be used sparingly, but not solely. *Strengths-based* assessments often play exclusively within this perspective and it is dangerous because *strengths-based* assessments oftentimes avoid any weaknesses within the individual. Massive amounts of research available point to dark-side leadership derailers as being the quickest way to end a rising career (Chamarro-Premuzic, 2016). If you avoid or ignore them, no strength characteristics in the world will save your client.

For example, a *strengths-based* assessment used at a Fortune 50 company that I once consulted for, identifies an individual's top 2 strengths, then assigns a label, or type (remember what we said about type-based) and seeks to identify group performance based on the diversity of those labels, but the labels and performance associations with them are arbitrary and not widely accepted in the scientific community. In my experience, focusing solely on strengths, while ignoring environment, emotional and social skill, and personality characteristics that drive behavior, can be *detrimental and borderline perilous* when making important business and talent decisions, and strengths-based coaching can actually weaken the individual (Chamarro-Premuzic, 2016).

Here is a graphic that summarizes the above and illustrates which perspectives focus on dysfunction and which focus on performance.

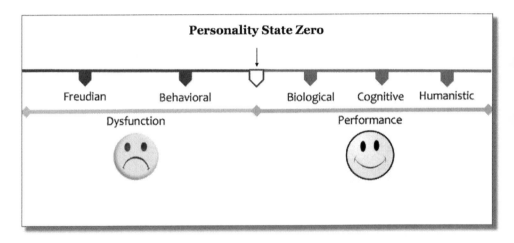

Figure 10 - The 5 Perspectives of Psychology

How Each Perspective Applies to Assessment Theory

So why is the EQ-i 2.0 one of the most powerful assessments out there? Because it has the furthest span across all of the psychological perspectives. Let's summarize what we discussed above.

The Freudian and behavioral approaches focus on diving into an individual's dysfunction, and assumes the key to increased performance and better living is a matter of **identifying these dysfunctions, labelling them, and becoming self-aware of the impact** that they have on our internal thought processes. For Freudians and behaviorists, the goal is to get back to a "Personality State of Zero." *Any assessments that fall in this range simply seek to exhume dark aspects of our personality and bring them to light.*

The biological approach also looks at **internal** *aspects* to determine behavior, but doesn't necessarily assume that an individual has dysfunction. *Any assessments that fall within this range, seek to help individuals understand internal aspects and how they drive behavior.*

The cognitive approach does not focus on dysfunction or internal characteristics, but instead focuses on **emotions and expectations.** *Any assessments that fall within this range seek to help individuals understand emotional states and how positive self-talk and thoughts can drive performance.*

The humanistic approach focuses solely on **maximizing potential and identifying strengths**, while ignoring derailers, dysfunction, and other internal aspects of behavior. *Any assessments that fall within this range seek to drive self-actualization.*

Different Types of Assessments

Let's start with the personality assessments that are *type-based. Type-based* personality assessments have fallen out of favor in recent years because they are often considered "entry level", lack scientific rigor (specifically validity and test-retest reliability), and do very little in predicting performance (Hogan, 2007). *Type-based* assessments are rarely considered for team performance activities by serious coaches and consultants.

Next, *strengths-based* assessments, focus solely on strengths while ignoring everything else. Assessing which strengths are most prominent within each individual is the lone objective. While it is important to understand the strengths that each leader possesses, *the danger with this type of assessment* is that they ignore personality and emotional intelligence factors, environmental fit, and other drivers of behavior that are vital to effective leadership development. These types of assessments make people feel good (hence solely falling in the humanistic range) but *lack any true developmental aspects* other than "strengths" as a vague concept. As of this writing, the scientific community is split on the idea of a strengths-based development approach, most leaning not-in-favor (Chamorro-Premuzic, 2016).

Differing in theory from *type-based* assessments, *trait-based* assessments (and others that measure Big-5 Personality characteristics), are a *great blend* of behavioral (environmental fit, motives, drivers) and biological (internal characteristics that drive our behavior). Assessments based off traits subscribe to the Big 5, or five-factor model, which analyzes a respondent's openness to experience, conscientiousness, extraversion, agreeableness, and neuroticism. *Trait-based* assessments are fantastic for personality based assessment needs, and currently have strong consensus within the scientific community in relation to work place success. The only limitation to *trait-based* assessments, is that personality is static over time, so any assessment of pure personality is mostly for self-awareness instead of skill development (Bar-On, 2002). I often use trait-based assessments in my coaching practice, when the specific need arises.

The EQ-i 2.0, measures emotional intelligence, which is a set of dynamic skills that influence the way we perceive and express ourselves, develop and maintain social relationships, cope with challenges, and use emotional information in an effective and meaningful way (Bar-On, 2002). The EQ-i 2.0 *covers the largest band of the psychological spectrum*, as it focuses on internal characteristics, balance of emotional skill, self-awareness, creating positive thoughts and behaviors, and maximizing self-actualization. Emotional intelligence has been proven to drive performance for over 100 years.

Leadership and organizational development fall into two broad buckets — *self-awareness and skill development*. Generally speaking, *trait-based* personality assessment seeks to increase self-awareness while emotional intelligence assessment seeks to increase use of skill. *Both drive positive outcomes.*

Now, the titillating part.

Let's discuss where each assessment falls within the five perspectives.

Disclaimer: There are hundreds of assessments out there and I chose the top few in each category (trait, type, strengths, EI) that I have direct experience administering. I was not asked by any of the assessment companies to endorse in this manner, and the graphic is only for illustrative purposes.

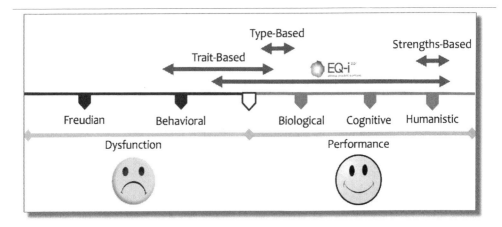

Figure 11 - The 5 Perspectives of Psychology and Where Assessments Fall Within

All assessments fall within the psychological spectrum. Your particular method of coaching is important to examine, so that you can understand what type of psychological outcomes you are encouraging. I am often asked about the difference between coaches and clinical psychologists. As I mentioned earlier, the main difference is that clinical psychologists normally work with vulnerable populations (those that fall within the dysfunctional perspectives of psychodynamic and behavioral), trying to take clients from "dysfunctional to zero". Clinical psychologists normally need state licensure for this reason, but coaches do not. Coaches, consultants, and the like, are geared toward taking individuals and teams from "zero to hero", so it is important to subscribe to coaching methodologies (like Co-Active) and assessments (like trait-based and the EQ-i 2.0) that focus solely on increasing performance.

Now that you have an understanding of psychological perspective, how does your coaching style align?

Like I mentioned before, I find it rare for someone to be both coach and psychologist. Most coaches do not think of psychological perspectives and most psychologists are drawn to the clinical nature of addressing the dysfunctional. In order to apply advanced concepts of EI to individuals and teams, a solid understanding of these perspectives, and where your coaching style falls within them, is vital.

If you feel that you simply cannot break your coaching style from the dysfunctional, I suggest you read the five books that I mentioned in Part 1. If you are still stuck, ask yourself if performance coaching and consulting is right for you. If it is, and you are still stuck, give me a ring. We can have a tête-à-tête and I'll coach you out of it.

Perspectives Wrap Up

Don't get me wrong. There is a massive need to focus on the dysfunctional. Clinical psychologists perform a great service to the world. Having mental disease in my family, I know the power and the value of a gifted clinical psychologist that pulls someone from the depths of the dysfunctional and returns them back to a state of "normal". However, in the business world, we should focus solely on performance. Performance of individual contributors, managers, technical experts, leaders, teams, and executives. EI focuses on personal development, skill acquisition, and self-awareness, and operates within the performance perspectives of the psychological spectrum.

But what about team dysfunction?

I'm glad you asked! Team dysfunction is not the same as individual dysfunction. Team dysfunction is often caused by a mismatch of personality and EI characteristics or lack of fluid conversation and effective communication. The individuals within the team are most likely not dysfunctional, but the culmination of them all together creates dysfunction. It is vital to understand the difference between individual and team dysfunction. Individual dysfunction is for clinical psychologists, while team dysfunction is for performance coaches and consultants. More on that later.

Take a hard look at your coaching style, the questions that you ask, and the psychological situations that you create. Are you acting as a compass and a mirror, guiding the individual through self-discovery? Or are you leading with questions that fit your narrative? Do you create psychologically safe environments that allow individuals to develop at their own pace? Or are you engaging in a more modern (and hopefully less extreme) version of psychic driving? Your coaching style, and the assessments that you use, fall within one of the five perspectives, and the only way to foster true spiritual transformation within teams and team leaders is to understand your own style first.

Master the Mind

Now you understand the skill of Inton-Jutsu, which are the unseen and undetected perspectives that underpin coaching and consulting processes. The ancient ninja was a master of manipulating the five elements to his advantage to remain undetected, and now you have acquired working knowledge of the five elements of psychology. You can now wield them to your advantage and safeguard against misuse of them. Enjoy your newly obtained power.

– Shinobi Skill Acquired –

Inton-Jutsu 隠遁術

Multiple Intelligences - Advanced 360 Interpretation

The ninja skill of Henso-Jutsu, roughly translating to disguise and impersonation, was essential to the shinobi of antiquity. Essential to the ninja's espionage work was her ability to create false personalities and remain hidden through her area of operation. More than merely just putting on a costume, the shinobi's disguise system involved thoroughly impersonating the false identity of the character. Personality traits and body subtleties of the identity assumed were entrenched into the shinobi's way of thinking. She literally became the new identity.

. . .

A 360-degree assessment is a process in which individuals receive confidential, anonymous feedback from the people around them (referred to as raters) such as managers, peers, direct reports, friends, family, and others. Normally, a minimum of three people per rater category should respond to the assessment, about the subject, in order for that category to be accurately represented. The subject of the 360 also takes the self-assessment portion, and the self-assessment results are compared to the results of the external respondents. What the 360 actually does, is deliver to the subject her *identity and reputations*.

Identity Vs. Reputation

Since self-awareness is a key component of development, whether we are assessing personality or EI skill, what is the best way to become self-aware? Freud and historical thinkers like Karl Marx believed that self-awareness could be achieved through a process of self-reflection and introspection, but what we now know about modern psychological thought shows this to be untrue. Humans cannot simply contemplate about our past actions and determine the reasons for them. The nature of personality makes this so, since our personality consists of an *identity and reputations*.

Your identity is the you that you know. Only you will know the you that you know because, hopefully, you are the only one inside your own head. Your reputation is how the rest of the world sees you. The other 7 billion people on this planet know your reputation. So, not to ruin your solipsism, but only one person knows your identity, and 7 billion know our reputation. You can see why many psychologists who study this topic say "the you that you know, is hardly worth knowing". Let that sink in for a minute. Over 100 years of research on identity has yielded little in the areas of measurement or taxonomy, but 20 years of research on reputation has generated reliable ways to measure it and a generally accepted classification system (Big-5 model). Extant research on identity and reputation shows that successful career progression evolves from social interaction, highlighting that social status (how others view us) is vital to a successful career, not self-view. Psychologist Robert Hogan claims that self-awareness comes from experience, not introspection, and objective knowledge of those experiences can only come from external sources that rate our life experiences and social interactions. According to Hogan, the distinction between identity and reputation is essential to correctly comprehend self-awareness. He posits that over 100 years of research suggests that there is nothing to learn from introspection, self-analysis, or rumination. Understanding how others perceive you (your reputation) is the key component for career achievement. "People hire you, fire you, promote you, trust you, confide in you, or loan you money based on how they perceive you. This means that, in an important sense, self-knowledge is other knowledge. We need to know how others perceive us, what we are doing to create those perceptions, and what we should do to make sure our reputation is aligned with our career goals and aspirations", (Hogan, 2007). Essentially, Hogan claims that observer feedback is the key to self-awareness. So, if self-awareness does not come from self-reflection, how do we become self-aware? Let's compound this a little bit.

Imagine you and I are old buddies and we are drinking in a bar (order me a bourbon and coke if this scenario ever presents itself in reality). In our two-person conversation, there are actually six completely separate "people" present. There is:

- Who I think I am
- Who you think I am

- Who I really am
- Who you think you are
- Who I think you are
- Who you really are

By all accounts, that is six completely separate people, consisting of two identities and four reputations. A 360 assessment psychometrically delivers to the subject her identity and her reputations across all the different categories (often referred to as rater groups) and is the only true way to become self-aware.

How cool is that?

Solomon (2016) took it a step further in her study that appeared in the *Journal of Personality and Social Psychology*. This study examined interpersonal accuracy, specifically how well an individual could guess their own self-view (identity accuracy), how well an individual could guess their external view (reputation insight), and if the individual was aware of the discrepancy between her own impressions of a target and how others see the target (reputation accuracy). Mapping to the Big Five Personality traits, the results were as follows, taken directly from Solomon (2016):

For perceiver-**identity** agreement, the correlations were $r = .61$ for extraversion, $r = .40$ for agreeableness, $r = .33$ for conscientiousness, $r = .49$ for neuroticism, and $r = .31$ for openness (all $ps < .05$), and for perceiver-**reputation** agreement, the correlations were $r = .61$ for extraversion, $r = .40$ for agreeableness, $r = .42$ for conscientiousness, $r = .48$ for neuroticism, and $r = .31$ for openness (all $ps < .05$). Thus, perceivers' own perceptions of targets showed moderate to strong agreement with both targets' **identities** and **reputations** for each of the Big Five. These results suggest that perceivers could successfully use assumed agreement to achieve **identity** and **reputation** *accuracy* because there is in fact agreement between their own perceptions of targets and targets' actual **identities** and **reputations**. However, these results also indicate that this agreement is not perfect—there is still substantial disagreement between perceivers' impressions of targets and targets' **identities** and **reputations**, which is what we need to test whether perceivers have insight into the discrepancies between their own impressions of targets and targets' self-perceptions (**identity** insight), as well as targets' **reputations** (**reputation** insight)...we also found that friends have accurate perceptions of how targets are seen by others (**reputation** accuracy), but, in contrast to **identity** accuracy, these inferences are entirely accounted for by assumed agreement. That is, friends generally (and correctly) assume that others see the targets the same way they see the targets, leaving no room to achieve insight into discrepancies between their perceptions of targets and others' perceptions of targets (**reputation** insight).

For all of the non-scientists reading this, essentially the results of the study found that people do have accurate self-views, and somewhat accurate views of how others see them. However, the accuracy of those views is only present if the reputation and identity are similar. But you are about to see, this is not always the case, especially in the corporate world. The only way to truly understand our identity, our multiple reputations, and our accuracy in identifying the discrepancies between them, is via a 360 assessment. Let's take a look at an EQ360 report.

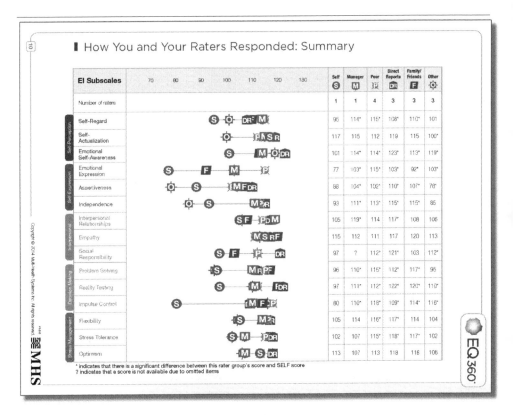

Figure 12 - A sample 360 Report

Reproduced with permission of Multi-Health Systems (2017). All Rights Reserved. www.mhs.com

This is a summary report that shows the average response of each rater category, or in psychological terms, each reputation. It is perfectly normal for the identity (self-assessment) and all of the different reputations (different rater categories) to vary wildly. Look at how far apart the "S", or self-identity, is from most other reputations. I refer to the variation as "reputation distance." Each of these reputations is a completely separate "you" that the rater category knows.

Look at each column as a completely separate entity. The columns labelled Self (identity), Manager (reputation 1), Peer (reputation 2), Direct Reports (reputation 3), Friends / Family (reputation 4), and Other (reputation 5) are all of the different people, existing within you, that the world sees.

Think about it, do your friends and family know a different "you" than your peers and direct reports? Most likely. Many coaches erroneously believe that the opportunity for growth and performance enhancement lies within trying to shorten the distance between the identity and reputations, but this isn't necessarily true. It is perfectly feasible to assume that some individuals act differently toward peers, family members, and her manager, in comparison with their self-view. This is perfectly fine, **as long as this is by design.**

There is no psychological benefit to merging multiple reputations and identity. Each one of those reputations can exist in their own reality for all of eternity, as long as they *each produce the outcome that you desire.*

Are you a great father who is silly with your kids, but is a fierce manager who drives deadlines among your engineers?

Are you a driven mother who demands tyrannical perfection on the piano from your toddlers, but has fantastic bedside manner at the hospital?

Reputations that vary wildly in distance are perfectly acceptable, as long as it is on purpose and delivering the outcomes within that reputation's reality that you desire.

When you are faced with a coaching client that has large reputation distance, here is the advanced EI application methodology:

1) the coach needs to clearly articulate the concept of identity vs reputations
2) the coach needs to articulate that trying to merge all of the reputations is not necessarily the desired action (this will be the natural inclination initially when a respondent first sees the results and the reputation distances)
3) the coach must question the subject on if this difference in reputation is by design
4) If not, the coach must dive deeper into reasons for the major difference between reputations and then coach accordingly, as this is now a self-awareness discussion
5) If yes, the coach must help the subject understand that largely distant reputations are psychologically sound, as long as cognitive strain isn't being produced, and that the distances are by design

Cognitive Dissonance

Cognitive dissonance is when an individual experiences mental stress and discomfort due to holding two or more contradictory positions at the same time. If multiple reputations have a good amount of psychological distance from each other and that is not by purposeful design by the subject, cognitive dissonance will be present. It is up to you, the advanced EI coach, to determine if the reputation locations are by design, and if the subject's brain is creating any stress maintaining those reputation distances. Stress is a major killer of performance, creativity, and innovative thinking. Focus on the stress created by the reputation distance, and apply EI concepts to that stress. If the reputation distance is by design, discuss with the subject the methods that she employs to create those reputations, and discuss how to reinforce those reputations and the positive outcomes that they provide.

The 360 assessment is a powerful tool, because it delivers self-generated feedback (identity) and multiple external feedback (reputations). There are many assessments that offer 360 feedback, but the EQ360 is powerful because it measures skill, as opposed to personality. Remember, personality is fixed, EI is not. Performing an EQ360 assessment can provide a baseline for leadership development for company executives. The coach can kick start a development program that spans months and then re-assess at the end of the program. In theory, the results will change, hopefully for the better. McAbee (2016) wrote in the *Psychological Review* that too many performance psychologists rely on only self-reports, and rarely implement multi-rater assessments to disentangle a subject's psychology, leading to error, inaccuracy, and ineffective coaching.

Incorporating Other 360s

In my experience, anyone going through a 360 assessment has most likely gone through other leadership development assessments previously. I am often asked "how is this assessment different than others that I have taken"? While trait-based 360 assessments also deliver similar identity versus reputation type feedback, it is important to elucidate the difference between static personality and variable skill to the subject. One is fixed, the other dynamic. The whole idea of performance enhancement within individuals begins with self-awareness and extends towards self-actualization. Only EI based assessments can truly deliver both, and identify key areas within an individual's identity and reputation that can use a performance boost. Start any 360-feedback session with a historical debrief of any previous 360 assessments or developmental feedback, so that you can start to determine if the reputation distance that the subject possesses is by design or on accident.

Master the Impersonation

To master Henso-Jutsu, often referred to as the methods of becoming invisible, ninjas had to master sociology. They observed people in other towns for long periods of time, learning the habits, language, and mannerisms of the locals. Much like an actor of today, the shinobi had to appear as a priest, merchant, performer, beggar, farmer, samurai, and many other different personas to accomplish their mission. Unbeknownst to most, everyone within corporations performs similar impersonations at all times. A new hire joins the organization, waits, learns, and observes, only to assume multiple roles of manager, leader, project manager, technical expert, confidant, or political assassin. The EQ360 is the only assessment that delivers a scientifically validated snapshot of the success, or failure, of the respondent's ability to maintain invisibility. Your advanced interpretation of the EQ360 will provide the client the path to achieving success through "the methods of the invisible".

– Shinobi Skill Acquired –

Henso-Jutsu 変装術

Subtle Signs from the Environment - The EQ-i 2.0 Group Report

Many believe that the external environment consists of only what one can see. Ten-Mon, directly translating to meteorology, is the ancient ninja skill of forecasting conditions based on observing subtle signs from our environment that aren't directly in front of us. One could use elemental signs, surrounding nature, and animal behavior to predict circumstances and create strategic advantage. The shinobi used everything that was not in direct sight, to plan his next move.

. . .

Within organizations, many workers use what is directly in sight to plan their next moves. What they read in their email, what the financial reports say, and what their managers direct them to do. Managers (and coaches) are not equipped with the proper tools necessary to forecast environmental conditions and recognize subtle signs. That is, until the EQ-i 2.0 Group Report arrived.

The EQ-i 2.0 Group Report is a powerful tool that essentially takes the individual results of all team members and merges them into a team-based report. This report presents an overview of group results that identifies group strengths as well as group weaknesses. Furthermore, the EQ-i 2.0 Group Report examines the organizational implications of the results and recommends strategies for action that can further develop the group's performance and potential.

How EI Can Empower Team Performance

Motivational speaker Jim Rohn once famously said "you are an average of the five people you spend the most time with." There have been a few studies on the effect of personality on group performance within animals, and most have found that in many species, such as hermit crabs, bees, fish and wolves, the right combination of personality is vital to success (Milius, 2012; Briffa, 2013). Humans are the same way, but extending past personality, we also overlay use of emotional skill. As explained earlier, EI is all about balance within an individual, and it is the same within teams. A team of 10 where every member exudes maximum Assertiveness, will most likely be a team with a lot of shouting and minimal effective communication.

Stages of Group Development

The report also gives insight into what "stage of development" the team is in, but that requires some interpretation and discovery. First introduced by Bruce Tuckman in 1965, the most commonly used model of group development is the forming-storming-norming-performing-adjourning model. Originally published as an article called *Developmental Sequence in Small Groups*, he hypothesized that groups went through two realms of development on their way to becoming an effective group: interpersonal relationships and task activity (Bonebright, 2010). Within these realms, stages of group development occurred.

Forming

In the first stage of the model, the group orients itself with the task, establishes rules, and then creates tacit and official boundaries of interpersonal and duty behaviors. Within this stage, relationships are established and standards are solidified.

Storming

In the second stage of the model, inter-conflict occurs. Group polarization, social loafing, and groupthink occur. Political positions and stances on various issues are hardened and group members can become hostile. It is not uncommon for group members to react emotionally to tasks, especially when change is involved. Bonebright (2010) wrote in the journal of *Human Resource Development International* that emotional responses and positions are responsible for much of the resistance during this stage, but they are often not discernible.

Norming

In the third stage of the model, personal idiosyncrasies of team members are accepted and general roles become established. Conflict resolution takes precedent as the goals of the group become clear and direction towards those goals takes priority.

Performing

In the fourth stage of the model, the team begins to realize its full potential as a team and problem solving ability compounds exponentially. Psychological energy begins to accelerate team performance and task completion is normally within sight.

Adjourning

Sometimes referred to as adjourning and/or transforming, this final didactic stage is simply the resolution of the team, or the team moving onto other tasks and objectives. Lessons learned are captured during this stage, and a post-mortem analysis takes inventory of the group performance that took place.

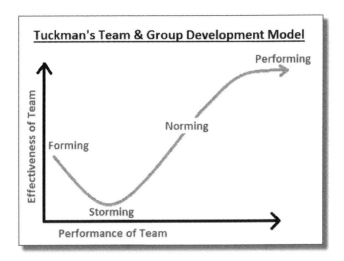

Figure 13 - Tuckman Stages of Group Development, Tuckman 1965

How EI Can Diagnose Team Dysfunction

Why is this important? For two reasons. First, according to Bonebright (2010), Tuckman's model is the most common framework used among organizational teams (there were over 250 different models and theories included in the survey), and second, most teams never make it out of the Storming stage. Emotive conflict, psychological dysfunction, and political posturing keep teams wedged in the Storming stage. Much like melodramatic team leaders, teams themselves can be capricious, mercurial and volatile, oftentimes without warning. While each team member may be psychologically sound individually, certain combinations of personality and EI skill can create a team psychosis that lacks conscious experience, qualia, or sentience. Paradoxically, each team member may feel he or she is acting in the best interest of the team, but selfish individual motives normally drive this stage as team roles, standards, and outcomes are most likely not yet formed (Bonebright, 2010). Each team member's EI profile, when combined with the other team member's EI profiles, create an overall team profile. The combination of these EI skills can create dysfunction on the team (even if each individual is not dysfunctional themselves) because it is the combination, or mismatch, of EI skills that causes team distress.

The Differences Between Dysfunctions

I discussed the five psychological perspectives earlier, and how coaching within the dysfunctional realm was dangerous for non-clinically certified psychologists and therapists. Diagnosing and tackling team dysfunction is different, however. Individual dysfunction is a result of: repressed memories, childhood trauma, biological factors, chemical imbalances, brain damage, and other many inconspicuous internal elements. Team dysfunction is a result of: mismatched personalities, poor use of combined EI skills in group settings, poor communication, poor goal alignment, and lack of focus and accountability. While all of these are internal to the group, they are still external to the individual. They are subtle signs of the environment.

So, while the term "dysfunction" can apply to both individuals and teams, please note that using EI to diagnose individual dysfunction – while possible – is not recommended. Using EI to diagnose team dysfunction, or lack of maximum team performance, is acceptable and an advanced EI application.

The EQ-i 2.0 Group Report

Below is an example of the EQ-i 2.0 Group Report.

Figure 14 - A Sample Group Report

Reproduced with permission of Multi-Health Systems (2017). All Rights Reserved. www.mhs.com

In an earlier section, I discussed the goal of balance. A Level 1 concept, the ideal profile for an individual would be balanced use of all EI skills, not high or low use in extreme fashion. Within teams, however, we need to analyze even further.

At first glance, the Overview of the Group Results suggest that the *average* EI score for the group is in perfect balance. There is a visual exercise you can do to test for balance. Start at the Total EI number, which in this case is 95, and draw a vertical line down the page, starting at the top with Self-Regard. If the profile is balanced, most scores will be close to the vertical line that was drawn. Essentially, you are flattening out the EQ-i wheel, to see if you have any bulges or divots in the wheel.

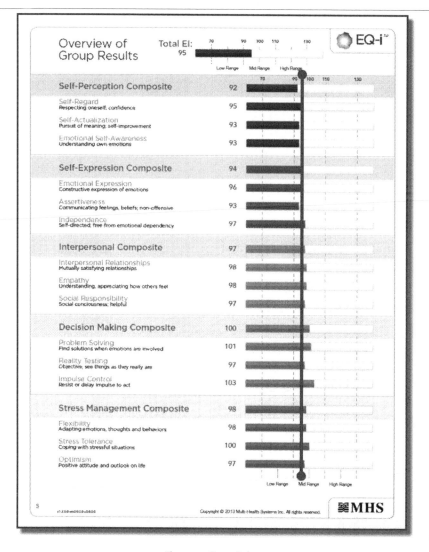

Figure 15 - Group Balance

Looking at the Overview of Group Results, we see balance at first glance. Most scores are very close to the overall score of 95. This would suggest that this team is perfectly balanced, but that assumption would be a grave mistake. Let's look at the Group Pattern Analysis, which shows the average scores in addition to the individual responses.

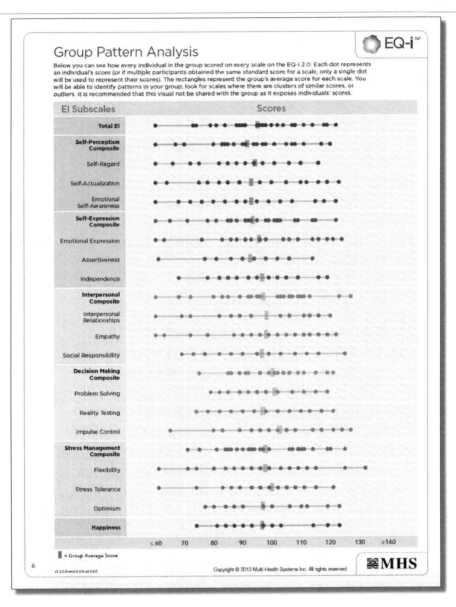

Figure 16 - Group Pattern Analysis

Reproduced with permission of Multi-Health Systems (2017). All Rights Reserved. www.mhs.com

The group pattern analysis reveals a large distance between the lower and upper ranges, and a large standard deviation, which is used to measure the amount of variation or dispersion in a data set. We can still see our vertical line, which is represented by squares on this page within each subscale. This pattern analysis is a treasure trove of data; here is how to analyze it.

Get a general idea of what the team does, if you do not know already (this should have been done during your discovery phase). This gives you an idea of how to frame your analysis. This particular pattern analysis is the EI averages of over 30 corporate litigators for a Fortune 1000 chemical company. Half of the team operated out of Europe/Asia, while the other half out of Washington, D.C. After my discovery phase, the leaders suggested that there was massive team conflict on many issues and communication was subpar (hence the main reason I suggested the Group Report).

Next, look at the dispersion of the data set. You do not need to recall your undergraduate statistics course to do this. Visual inspection and deduction is sufficient. Let's look at Assertiveness as a starting point.

Figure 17 - Assertiveness Group Pattern Analysis

Reproduced with permission of Multi-Health Systems (2017). All Rights Reserved. www.mhs.com

The square in the middle of the Figure 17 bar is the average score that you saw on the overview, and the dots represent individual response clusters from each team member. You can see that many of the team members have very high Assertiveness, most likely dominating meetings, calls, and presentations, doing so in an offensive manner that inhibits sharing of ideas and discussion. You can also see that many benighted team members are also seldom using Assertiveness, most likely resulting in silence, acquiescence, compliance, and submission, without sharing ideas or different viewpoints. So, while the result of these two extremes is an average that provides ostensible balance, in reality, the team is experiencing three psychological phenomena that are known to crush team performance.

Social Loafing

Social loafing is the phenomenon of a person exerting less effort to achieve a goal when they work in a group than when they work alone. The phenomenon was first tested using rope-pulling experiments, when researchers discovered that individuals did not pull as hard when working in a group as when they did when working alone. Many other studies since have been performed to establish the phenomenon, such as clapping and shouting experiments, as well as many others in business settings. Social loafing stems from the individual's belief that his efforts will not matter to the overall group, sending a wave of ennui through the individual team member's psyche. Often referred to as process loss, individuals will often wait to see how much effort others exhibit before exerting their own effort (sucker/aversion effect), or lower their amount of effort to match the perceived overall group effect if it is lower (attribution and equity). In short, with the Assertiveness dispersion, combined with the large variability in the other scores in the pattern analysis, social loafing is sure to occur.

Schippers (2014) wrote in the *Academy of Management Learning and Education* that social loafing could be buffered, and in some cases reversed, when group traits such as conscientiousness and agreeableness were high. His study examined over 200 newly formed teams and he determined that assessing the group to measure the level of desired traits and then focusing on boosting team characteristics (such as EI skill), would increase team performance, regardless of the level of social loafing that was present. Notice how the focus isn't to eliminate social loafing (the dysfunction), but instead to boost social factors that render it irrelevant (performance). Remember back to our discussion on the five perspectives, that is very important! Identify the dysfunction, but then coach to overcome via performance enhancement, not dysfunction elimination.

Groupthink

Groupthink is a psychological phenomenon that occurs within a group of people in which the desire for harmony or conformity in the group results in an irrational or dysfunctional decision-making outcome. Group members try to minimize conflict and reach a consensus decision without critical evaluation of alternative viewpoints by actively suppressing dissenting viewpoints, and by isolating themselves from outside influences.

The deviation in data points within two key subscales points out the presence of groupthink within this team of litigators.

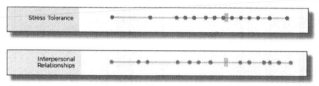

Figure 18 - Stress Tolerance and Interpersonal Relationships from Group Pattern Analysis

Reproduced with permission of Multi-Health Systems (2017). All Rights Reserved. www.mhs.com

This particular team does not tolerate stress well as a group. Low use of Stress Tolerance suggests that some members on this team will avoid stress at all costs, and that other team members thrive in stressful situations, in their minds a bit too much, so they subconsciously encourage stressful conditions (a byproduct of high use of Stress Tolerance). Combined with the dispersion of Interpersonal Relationships, this analysis suggests that some members on the team do not have the ability to form meaningful relationships emotionally, and others put too much stock in relationships, most likely at the expense of group business goals. This is a group that desires harmony, often to their detriment. Snell (2010), while investigating how to solve groupthink in healthcare facilities, wrote in the *Global Management Journal* that seeking originality of ideas creates new emotional and intellectual connections. Within teams that experience groupthink, rather than addressing the dysfunction itself, the coach should promote originality of the individuals within the group. Set up mechanisms and feedback loops to promote rewards for innovation and uniqueness and this phenomenon will cease to hinder team performance and prevent emotional connections from forming.

Group Polarization

Group polarization refers to the tendency for a group to make decisions that are more extreme than the initial preferences of its group members. Group polarization exists in all industries, from Fortune 1000, to politics, to small business. Group members who are on the minority side of a decision can easily be influenced to go with the majority. Persuasion, conformity to social norms, and differentiation are all origins of polarization. There are hundreds of studies on polarization and its existence within social psychology and the effect on team performance is well documented. Mainly, teams that have extreme personalities mixed with weak personalities, combined with a weak overall group identity, tend to be fertile ground for polarization to thrive. The group's attitude toward a situation may change in the sense that the individuals' initial attitudes have fortified and intensified after group conversation, a phenomenon known as attitude polarization. The team's Self-Actualization and Independence dispersion make this evident. The Self-Actualization analysis yields that this team lacks a true identity, because many members do not recognize what their life purpose within the team is, and the Independence score suggests that many team members are actually very dependent on others for emotional direction and identity.

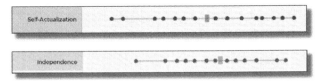

Figure 19 - Self-Actualization and Independence from Group Pattern Analysis

Reproduced with permission of Multi-Health Systems (2017). All Rights Reserved. www.mhs.com

Zhu (2013) wrote in the *Strategic Management Journal*, when investigating group polarization on corporate board decision making, that certain factors, such as lack of identity, unproductive diversity of ideas, and lack of fit within certain members, yielded decisions that were much higher or lower than the individual preferences of board members. To battle group polarization, determining emotional fit, as well as establishing a sense of identity and emotional independence, are key.

Subtle Signs

So, what does all of this tell us? The Group Report delivers to us subtle signs about the environment that are not directly observable. The directly observable behaviors would be shouting, silence, acquiescence, listlessness, apathy, and many other observable physical behaviors. The subtle signs are the emotional skills, or the high/low use of them, that create the perceptible behaviors. These subtle signs give the coach direct areas to target for improvement, but also help to create the most important thing of all: **psychologically safe spaces to communicate.** A secondary benefit is the Group Report gives the coach an idea of psychological fit for future talent. If a team is heavy or light in certain EI skills, the coach can make recommendations about future team members (if the coach has the candidate's EI profile) and envisage how well the talent will fit within the assessed team. Side note: a thorough job analysis needs to be performed before the assessment can accurately be used in selection processes, but more on that later.

The entire point of the Group Report isn't to identify the EI skill dispersion to simply put a label to the dysfunction. The real purpose is to objectively use scientific data, to elicit candid and evocative conversation with the team and team leader. Remember back to the difference between coaches and psychologists (generally speaking). Many coaches do not use assessments to debrief clients, and sessions are simply conversations based on subjective observation and judgement. The Group Report gives systematic data and insight into the team performance issues, and enables an objective, science-based conversation. Here is the advanced application methodology with the EQ-i 2.0 Group Report:

1) Debrief the main client and/or team leader on the results. They should be the first ones to view the results so they are not blindsided by the sincere conversation that is about to take place

2) Assemble the team, preferably in person at a team offsite or workshop event, and promote an environment of psychological safety

3) Set ground rules for confidential conversations. In order for the subtle signs to come to life, the team has to feel psychologically safe to speak their minds, without repercussion or consequence

4) Review with the team the social loafing, groupthink, and group polarization phenomena, if applicable

5) Review the Strategies for Action section of the Group Report, and have the teams break out into groups

6) Half of the groups should discuss the three highest subscales, specifically how to reinforce and reasons they are the highest. The other half of the groups should deliberate on the three lowest subscales, specifically why they are the lowest and ways they can be raised

Strategies for Action

| ▨ Highest Three Subscales | ☐ Lowest Three Subscales | ⬡ EQ-i 2.0 |

	Self-Regard	Self-Actualization	Emotional Self-Awareness
Self-Perception	• Being able to utilize strengths at work is related to increased engagement. Have the group identify individual/team strengths and attempt to link consideration of strengths to task assignment. • Identify the group's barriers to feeling secure and confident; work on plans to remove these barriers.	• This group may benefit from reflecting on its mission, vision, and values to reignite a stronger sense of self-worth and team worth. • Have the group brainstorm stretch goals for their short- and long-term objectives to help them see greater potential in themselves.	• Examine the reasons why certain decisions conjure up certain emotions with the group. • Have the group work on identifying the subtle cues experienced when certain emotions arise. Have them identify which emotions are helpful and under what conditions.
Self-Expression	Emotional Expression • Continue the discussion of emotions, especially ones that are harder to express. Have the group identify triggers for "bottling" emotions; discuss how to eliminate these triggers. • Create a code of conduct for sharing positive emotions; show appreciation to colleagues.	Assertiveness • Use visualization techniques to help the group see a successful, assertive outcome when interacting with others. How can they be direct and firm when necessary? • Brainstorm assertive behaviors/language that can help the group get its point across more effectively.	Independence • Continue to rely on group expertise, but not to the extent that the group can't make a decision without others' reassurance. • Help the group define where they are most independent in their project work. Are there certain times when they are less independent? Why is that?
Interpersonal	Interpersonal Relationships • Brainstorm ways this group can celebrate big milestones to foster improved relationships. • Identify teams within the organization where relationships need strengthening. What will the organizational impacts be if these connections are improved?	Empathy • Have the group identify situations where more empathy was needed. What was the impact of not being empathic? What steps will they put in place to rectify this next time? • Be attuned to body language and tone of voice to gauge emotional undertones in meetings. Role play different emotional cues.	Social Responsibility • What causes call the team to action? Are there certain initiatives that motivate better citizenship? Have the team come to a consensus on a cause they can all support. • Suggest they try to engage other teams in socially responsible behavior to spur collective action in the organization.
Decision Making	Problem Solving • Maintain an open mind to entertain all possible solutions to a problem. Have the group practice using positive emotions to brainstorm creative solutions. • Approach problems neutrally; try new ways of doing things. Practice removing emotional attachments to particular courses of action.	Reality Testing • Diagnose past decisions to examine the impact of reality testing on actual business outcomes. Where did they size things up inaccurately? What additional information was needed at the time? • Seek colleagues' perspectives on a situation to see if there is alignment in perception.	Impulse Control • Count to 10 before discussing an idea to ensure its feasibility. Have the group brainstorm other ways to keep their impulses in check, especially during meetings. • Seek colleagues' feedback before proposing a new way of doing things at work.
Stress Management	Flexibility • Ensure that proper training and resources are available to deal with change. • Brainstorm ideas with the team to arrive at solutions to cope with new developments.	Stress Tolerance • Find a confidant at work with whom the stresses of the day can be shared. • Distract yourself from challenges at work by engaging in restful pursuits (e.g., walk, bike ride).	Optimism • Fraternize with like-minded colleagues who are positive, and avoid too many interactions with negative ones. Have the group identify what circumstances cause them to be less optimistic. • Participate in spontaneous pursuits to change the routine.

Figure 20 - Strategies for Action

Master the Environment

Forecasting conditions by illuminating subtle signs is how the shinobi predicted advantage and disadvantage. The Group Report gives insight into unknown psychological and emotional elements that are an average of the EI profiles of the team members. Being aware of the changes in the environment will give supreme advantage to the team leader, who will be able to harness the potential energy of the team by accelerating passed the storming stage of group development.

– Shinobi Skill Acquired –

Ten-Mon 天文

Advanced Emotional Balance

Naginata-Jutsu is the ancient shinobi art of halberd fighting. A halberd is a spear that is combined with a battle ax. It consists of a long handle, with a short blade, but is used for medium distance adversaries. Despite having a long handle, if the halberd is used for long fighting it will leave the shinobi exposed to short range attacks because he will be defenseless, since the length of the weapon takes two hands to wield and there is no ability to also equip a shield. Despite having a short blade, if the halberd is brought in close, it will be too heavy to wield with enough swiftness to battle short-range enemies. Foes must be kept at medium distance for the halberd to be used most effectively.

. . .

EI skills are the same way. According to Bar-On (2002), it is easy to overuse and underuse many elements of the EI model, but the most effective use of the arsenal is the balanced middle. The Bar-On technical manual refers to improper high and low use as "overuse" and "underuse", but I prefer to label them as high and low use, as the term "overuse" suggests that use of the skill should *always* be dialed back. While in rare instances *high use should be tempered a bit*, the main goal of coaching should never be to initially decrease use of a powerful skill, unless that skill happens to be creating the low use of other EI skills.

The Level 1 comprehension of EI doesn't do enough to equip the coach with proper coaching techniques centered around high use, low use, and the consequences of each. Level 1 simply highlights only which EI skills affect other EI skills, not what the behavioral implications of high and low use are.

A Recap of Level 1 Emotional Balance

The Balancing Your EI section of the EQ-i 2.0 report compares scores from every subscale to three related subscales. The report generates a result for the client that shows which of the three comparison subscales is most out of balance with the current subscale being evaluated. Below is an example of the section:

Figure 21 - Balancing your EI - Level 1 Client View

Reproduced with permission of Multi-Health Systems (2017). All Rights Reserved. www.mhs.com

This simply shows which related subscales have the greatest difference, and while this is valuable information, it doesn't provide enough information for advanced EI coaching, such as high and low use implications on behavior. Coaches have to be careful not to base entire psychological profiles on these alone, since they often introduce developmental non-sequiturs and conclusions interpreted from them could be incorrect and myopic. Here is a coach's view of the same report:

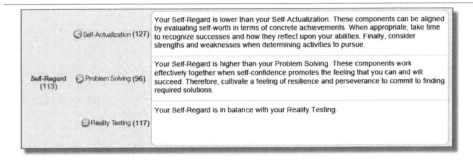

Figure 22 - Balancing your EI - Level 1 Coach's View

Advanced Emotional Balance – High and Low Use

For the purposes of advanced emotional balance, what constitutes high or low use is when the particular subscale is **more or less than 10 points from the overall EI score**. *It doesn't necessarily matter what the score of the skill itself is, it is where that skill is in relation to the overall EI score.* For example, if the client has an overall EI of 100, any composite or subscale scores that fall above 110 or below 90 can be considered high or low. But if a client has a subscale at 50, and the overall EI score is 58, the subscale is not considered low use. Refer to the graphic to highlight this point.

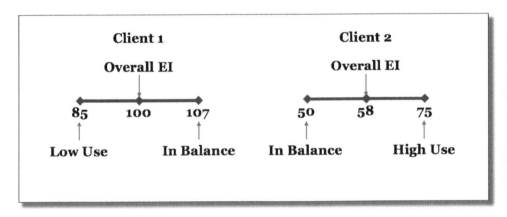

Figure 23 - In and Out of Balance

Balance is all about where the subscale scores fall in relation to the overall EI score. *Achieving advanced balance is the first phase in coaching, then raising the overall profile in unison is the second phase.* So, if the individual has some scores in the 120s and some in the 70s, the idea isn't to simply raise the 70s to the 120s. Rather, the goal should be to raise the 70s to the overall EI score and temper use of the 120s to lower that skill toward the overall EI score, *initially.* Many may wonder why we would ever want to lower the use of high EI skills, if the goal would be to eventually raise them all back up *when balanced.* The reason for this, is that the skills in the 120s, are most likely being used too much, and will actually be creating the low use of other EI skills (you would validate this through your discovery questions before proceeding). When not in balance and in high use, they are emotional crutches that allow voids to exist in other key emotional skill areas. Below is an example:

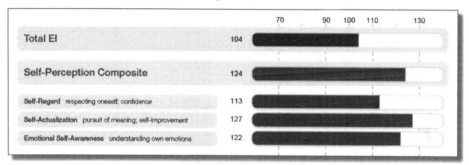

Figure 24 - EI Scores out of Balance with Overall EI

You can see from the figure above, this individual is heavily using Self-Actualization and Emotional Self-Awareness, when you factor in overall EI. If you only viewed the "Balance your EI" section from Figure 21, you would assume this client only needs to focus on Problem Solving, when in fact, the client is engaged in high use of the entire Self-Perception composite.

The advanced balance methodology is to first identify the skills that are in high and low use, discuss how to achieve emotional balance, then once balanced, work to raise all of the scores together in unison. It's like making sure the boat is level on the water before you crank up the RPM's on the engine. *Balance first, speed second.* You wouldn't want to increase boat speed if the stern was not level with the bow.

Let's review the metaphorical bulges and divots that I discussed in the Level 1 review. I'll include some stories that will highlight my experiences with these balancing acts, and provide the coaching tips needed to rebalance the client to the level of skilled tightrope performers. As always, names have been changed to protect the innocent.

Balancing Self-Perception

Figure 25 - Self-Perception Composite

Reproduced with permission of Multi-Health Systems (2017). All Rights Reserved. www.mhs.com

The Self-Perception composite addresses inner feelings and finding the meaning of life. Let's review the implications of when the subscales within this composite are out of balance.

Self-Regard is the ability for you to accept both your positive and negative attributes to maintain self-esteem, respect, and positive self-acceptance. A balanced level of Self-Regard impacts how we carry ourselves and project confidence. According to Bar-On (2013), this is the skill most associated with self-awareness, one of the core leadership development concepts that spans across all psychometric theories and coaching disciplines.

Low use of Self-Regard means that you see yourself as incompetent, inferior, or unworthy. Personal inadequacy can lead to frustration, depression, and difficulty achieving life goals. Feelings can include:

- Self-doubting
- Disrespecting oneself
- Insecurity
- Inadequacy
- Insecurity
- Low-Self Esteem

Conversely, high use of Self-Regard means that you could be narcissistic or supercilious. People engaged in high use of Self-Regard can often make others uncomfortable from talking about their own positive abilities too often, leading to difficulty in social interactions (Bar-On, 2013). Feelings can include:

- Over-confidence
- Thoughts of superiority
- Vanity
- Arrogant
- Egotistical

It is important to keep this skill in balance, or individuals may never realize their full potential or could create career derailing behaviors. Keeping Self-Regard in balance also ensures a healthy identity, as discussed in the psychological perspectives section.

Self-Actualization is an individual's ability to realize her full potential, to strive to become better, and to work toward meaningful goals and life fulfillment. This skill directly pertains to our innermost potential. It is not necessarily about performing at the highest level, but relates to our enthusiasm, energy levels, motivation, and inner excitement. Pursing satisfaction in life is one of the healthiest emotional states possible.

Low use of Self-Actualization means one has an unwillingness to set or pursue goals, or is unwilling to strive to improve performance. Low use of this skill is often associated with frustration, depression, despondency, and despair (Bar-On, 2013). Feelings can include:

- Laziness

- Unambitious
- Uninspired
- Jaded

Conversely, high use could lead to constant dissatisfaction with life or continual pursuits of quixotic missions. When one has high goals that can never be obtained, self-loathing and inner-odium can rapidly set in. Even though this skill generates emotional energy, high use can affect our Optimism and Happiness if we set goals that are too lofty and unattainable. Feelings can include:

- Constant frustration with the status quo
- Too intense during pursuit of goals
- A self-centered ambition, creating situational blindness
- An unwillingness to do any tasks that don't directly lead to a goal

It is important to keep this skill in balance, or individuals may never achieve all of life's possibilities or could behave in a way that leads to bad leadership. One of the key symptoms of depression is having nothing to look forward to.

Emotional Self-Awareness is the degree to which an individual is tuned in to inner feelings and emotions, and the ability to differentiate between emotions and their genesis. It is the ability to tell the difference between emotions that resemble each other closely such as anger or sadness. Often considered the most important factorial component of EI, this skill is connected to every other skill in the Bar-On model (Bar-On, 2013). Every psychometric that measures EI has a variation of this subscale, and most coaches *recommend that this is the first subscale score you review*, before looking at any others.

Low use of Emotional Self-Awareness means that one is unaware of where emotions come from and unclear as to their origins. In serious cases, an emotional disorder called alexithymia exists at the dysfunctional end of low use, which is essentially a complete inability to identify and describe emotions within one self. Those suffering from alexithymia are often considered immune to psychotherapy. Feelings can include:

- Emotional immaturity
- Constant surprise of others emotional states
- Denial of own feelings

- Misinterpretation of others emotions

Conversely, high use of Emotional Self-Awareness leads to over development of many feelings, which can lead to social issues and misattribution of social-emotional cues. Feelings can include:

- Self-indulgence
- Insensitivity to the needs of others
- Self-centeredness
- Over-interpretation of others emotions

It is important to keep this skill in balance, or individuals won't be able to accurately identify their own emotions as they happen nor the emotional signals of others, or they may be so involved with themselves that they may miss important emotional cues from others.

Valencia the Ambitious

I was contracted to perform executive coaching services for an Australian IT services firm, that had offices all over EMEAR, one in London, and one in Raleigh, North Carolina. I remember the excitement that I felt when bidding for this contract, thinking that I would get to recommend onsite leadership development workshops in New Zealand, the Gold Coast of Australia, and other places that I dream of retiring one day. As fate would have it, whenever we met in person, it was normally at the North Carolina office.

This organization's main purpose was selling space for datacenters. It required a unique mix of about 65% technical and 35% sales talent within most of their workforce. The company often inaccurately linked technical and sales ability together, as evident by their reward structures and corporate culture.

The best technical experts, not the best people managers, were often considered their rising leaders, so many of the budding executives had distinguished technical expertise in their fields. Each often assumed that their technical prowess would translate into becoming successful leaders of other rising engineers.

Valencia was a vibrant personality. I could often hear her laughing from all the way down the hall when I would wait for her to arrive for our coaching sessions. To this day, she is one of the only extremely "loud laughers" that I don't find bothersome. She was liked by everyone and was considered a rising star, and when combined with her unique technical ability, she was one of the first to be nominated for executive coaching by senior leadership.

Our intake session lasted more than twice as long as they normally do, because I discovered she also had interest in psychology, not just engineering, so we spent a bunch of time pouring over psychological profiles of Fortune 1000 executives, discussing the power of EI in coaching, and debating random topics such as whether ice hockey or rugby is a tougher sport. After our intake session, we set the parameters for the coaching relationship, and I set her up to take the EQ-i 2.0 assessment. With permission, I have posted part of her EI profile below.

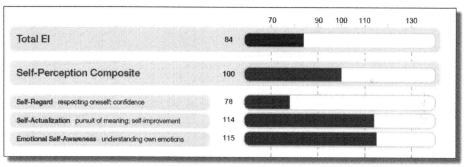

Figure 26 - Valencia Self-Perception
Reproduced with permission of Multi-Health Systems (2017). All Rights Reserved. www.mhs.com

What do you notice? You see immediately that Self-Regard is in balance with Overall EI, but the entire composite is out of balance with Overall EI, due to high Self-Actualization and Emotional Self-Awareness. Using this as a guide, I asked targeted questions during our conversations together, and through her own self-discovery, she realized that she was extremely intense in pursuit of sales goals due to her own personality and the company culture. Also, she often over-interpreted the emotional cues she got from others because she was always curious about her reputation, since she was operating at such a high level in a predominantly male environment. Being primarily a sales engineer up to this point, aggressive pursuit of sales goals could be considered a great thing, but as a leader, this could create the wrong behaviors within her team (see the Wells Fargo case of 2016 where bank workers were making fake accounts for customers, due to overly aggressive sales goals, which caused the downfall of the CEO). High use of Self-Actualization in her case would have cascaded the wrong behaviors down to her new direct reports, and over-interpreting emotional cues would have caused her to have knee-jerk reactions to her team's emotional rollercoaster that accompanied her taking charge. We were able to temper her high use of these skills, go through a targeted coaching program, and reassess after six months. By then, all of her skills in the Self-Perception composite were in balance, and her transition into the executive role was smooth. I am still pushing to have our follow up sessions in New Zealand.

Balancing Self-Expression

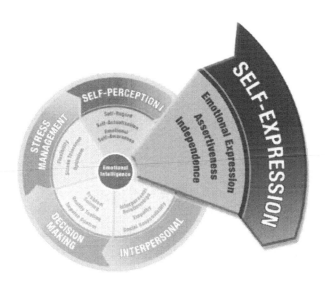

Figure 27 - Self-Expression Composite

Reproduced with permission of Multi-Health Systems (2017). All Rights Reserved. www.mhs.com

The Self-Expression composite addresses communication ability and emotional freedom. Let's review the implications of when the subscales within this composite are out of balance.

Emotional Expression is the ability to be open and communicative, while still being transparent with our moods and emotions. It consists of three key elements: the ability to express our feelings at an emotional level, at the cognitive level, and stand up for our own emotional defense (Bar-On, 2013).

Low use of this skill means that one does not communicate well at the emotional or cognitive level. Certain anxiety disorders have roots in low Emotional Expression. Feelings can include:

- Isolation
- Denial of own feelings
- Detachment

- Distrusting

Conversely, high use of this skill leads to oversharing and being overbearing. Boldness turns to rudeness, and excitement can turn to melodrama. Feelings can include:

- Emotional high jacking
- Constantly sharing too much information
- Self-indulgence
- Sharing emotions that are not relevant to the situation

It is important to keep this skill in balance, or individuals won't be able to accurately share proper emotions in the correct situations, or won't be able to connect with others on an emotional level.

Assertiveness is the ability to communicate needs and feelings in a non-offensive way, while remaining confident, yet not aggressive. Assertive people are not shy, but they are also not disruptive. This is one of the oldest skills studied, as Darwin published in 1872, *Expression of Emotions in Man and Animals*, describing Assertiveness (and Emotional Expression) as being key to survival.

Low use of this skill means that individuals feel that their contributions are not worth sharing, or are too passive in their communication style. Feelings and actions can include:

- Withholding
- Shy
- Timid
- Being a push-over
- Bashful

Conversely, high use of this skill can be construed as being too aggressive or destructive. Feelings and actions can include:

- Abusive
- Bossy
- Hostile
- Violent dispositions

It is important to keep this skill in balance, or individuals won't be able to reside in that middle space between passive and aggressive, or could miss the opportunity to really contribute to discussions, or could be considered too antagonistic.

Independence is the ability to remain self-directed in one's own thinking and to make decisions while not relying on the emotional support of others. This skill is central to free will and ensuring we are not slaves to our emotions or the emotions of others.

Low use of this skill means that one has an unwillingness to make his or her own decisions. This can lead to stress and pressure in social situations or during the management of change. Feelings and actions can include:

- Emotional dependence on others
- Clinginess
- Indecisive
- Vacillating

Conversely, high use of this skill can lead to a refusal to connect to others or consult with others during complicated times. Excessively independent individuals do not make good team members and often don't play well with others. Feelings and actions can include:

- Withholding emotions
- Isolation
- Not a team player
- Detached
- Unavailable

It is important to keep this skill in balance, or individuals won't be able to make important leadership decisions without the input of others, or leaders will not be able to build guiding coalitions during times of change management due to self-imposed emotional isolation.

Craig the Provoker

Craig always became jokingly inimical when his children referred to him as a dinosaur. A member of the baby boomer generation, he often preferred leather jackets made for bikers over formal suit coats, even in the hot California sun. Though originally from a small town in east Texas, Craig was a former university professor who taught at Stanford, and wrote a few books on leadership in startup tech environments. A book that he wrote on French and Raven's five forms of power and their applications to modern business caught the eye of a San Jose based Fortune 1000 company, and he was brought on to lead the Learning Services division for the entire organization.

When I first met Craig, though amiable, he was slow to warm up and his proclivity for introversion in social settings became quickly apparent. During my initial discovery meetings with his senior leadership, I was informed that Craig had frequently been passed over for promotion, despite his stellar work performance, due to peer feedback that he had received over the years, centering on his management style. The company considered Craig a flight risk, due to his expertise in the field and because his actual work performance was top-notch, so I was tasked with coaching Craig into a mindset that would enable him to transition to leadership and win the approval of his peers.

Getting to know Craig after a few sessions, his cleverness was obvious and our conversations were pleasant. I knew that there was something underlying within his psychological profile that was creating peer feedback that was incongruent with his engagement style. With permission, I have posted part of his EI profile below.

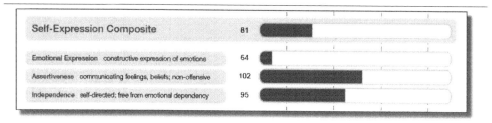

Figure 28 - Craig Self-Expression

After receiving his EQ-i results, I noticed a rare combination. Within Craig's Self-Expression composite you can see subscales that are in high and low use within the same composite, when compared to the Self-Expression composite score and his overall EI score (Overall EI was 87). Reviewing the results with Craig, I asked targeted questions and listened for hidden clues to try and discern where this rare combination came from, and how it could possibly be affecting his chances at obtaining a senior leadership position. Through self-discovery and through reviewing previous examples of when he led cross-functional teams (essentially, he led teams from a project management perspective), we revealed a management style that veiled itself within the unbalanced Self-Expression composite.

Having been a former professor, Craig liked to stimulate thought within his students using the Socratic teaching method. Essentially, the Socratic method consists of engaging in argumentative dialogue, and normally responding to a question with another question. While Craig thought that this inspired thought leadership among his project team, it actually came across as being provocative and combative.

Craig's low use of Emotional Expression led him to be detached from others and distrusting of suggestions from his peers. He elicited further discussion through the use of his Socratic teaching method, thinking that he was helping the team reach a conclusion, but it simply came across as skepticism. Combined with high use of Assertiveness, which led Craig to engage in his Socratic method in what appeared to be in an argumentative manner, Craig consistently received peer feedback that he was difficult to work with, and would needlessly provoke those whose opinions differed from his.

Craig was floored when we exhumed this reputation (we could have reached this conclusion sooner with an EQ360). We developed our coaching and development plan around raising his Emotional Expression subscale, so that others could see constructive and emotive behaviors during his management actions. We also worked on tempering his Assertiveness, so that his style wouldn't come across as overly combative. After nine months of coaching, working through development and EI balancing exercises, Craig received stellar peer reviews during the next performance management cycle, and was able to transition to senior leadership.

Balancing Interpersonal

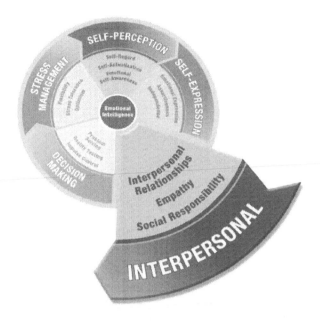

Figure 29 - Interpersonal Composite

The Interpersonal Composite addresses one's ability to develop and maintain relationships based on trust and compassion (Bar-On, 2013). Let's review the implications of when the subscales within this composite are out of balance.

Interpersonal Relationships is the skill of developing reciprocally satisfying relationships and being able to maintain them. This skill enables us to have positive social interactions and pleasant experiences in group settings. This skill is often referred to as a prerequisite to many professions and careers (Bar-On, 2013). This skill has a high negative correlation with a measure of borderline personality disorder (Bar-On, 2013).

Low use of Interpersonal Relationships means that you often isolate yourself and avoid human interactions. Those who engage in low use of this can be considered shy, introverted, or even unpleasant to be around. Feelings and actions can include:

- Being a loner
- Social withdrawal

- Cold, aloof, or "hard to get"

Conversely, high use of this skill can lead to co-dependency on others. Feelings and actions can include:

- Sharing too much information
- Unwilling to be alone
- Agitation when others don't reciprocate emotions
- Inappropriately intimate with others

It is important to keep this skill in balance, or individuals won't be able to have healthy boundaries with others and participate in mutually rewarding relationships.

Empathy is the ability to notice other people's feelings, appreciate them, and be sensitive of their implications to the social dynamic. This skill is often considered a cornerstone of social-awareness.

Low use of Empathy means the individual either lacks the ability or is unwilling to detect other people's emotional states. Those engaged in low use of Empathy are often considered untrustworthy and aloof. Feelings and actions can include:

- Inattentive
- Emotionally detached
- Selfishness
- Egotism

Conversely, high use of this skill can lead to co-dependency on others. Individuals who heavily use Empathy are considered weak managers and incapable of making difficult decisions, especially when people are involved, such as employee dismissal. Feelings and actions can include:

- Emotional dependency on others
- Conflict avoidance
- Overwhelmed by others emotions

It is important to keep this skill in balance, or individuals won't be able to connect with other people on an emotional level, or may be too heavily invested in other's emotions, to the point of sacrificing their own.

Social Responsibility is the ability to contribute to society, appreciate the greater good, or have a connection with the larger community. It involves acting in a responsible manner even when there is no direct reward in it for us (Bar-On, 2013). A study conducted in over 36 countries has shown that this skill is one of the best predictors of effectiveness at work (Bar-On, 2013).

Low use of Social Responsibility means that the individual pays little attention to larger system needs and is socially irresponsible, oftentimes developing antisocial attitudes. Feelings and actions can include:

- Social withdrawal
- Little care for the environment
- Insensitive to team needs

Conversely, high use of this skill can lead to feelings of social martyrdom. In the corporate world, it's referred to as "dying on that hill", when someone takes the fall for a cause that wasn't really worthy of martyrdom in the first place. Feelings and actions can include:

- Putting community needs above your own
- Overly committed to environmental issues
- Social subjectivity on various issues

It is important to keep this skill in balance so that care and concern for people is actively balanced with care and concern for the larger community, environment, and the greater good.

Roxanne the Good Samaritan

"Time to call Roxanne and the bloodhounds!" I would always shout, because during our virtual video conferences, her four bloodhounds loved the ringer of the telepresence machine when I called, so they would always be on video, front and center, when the video kicked on. She was a woman who loved animals, and had many dogs, cats, a cockatoo, and an Egyptian lizard called a Uromastyx. She reached out to me individually for coaching, because I had conducted an EI presentation and workshop for her chemical company a few months earlier, and she attended the seminar.

We discussed her goals at the intake call. She worked in a lab all day and felt that it was affecting her social life outside of work. Normally, I prefer to align leadership development and executive coaching services to work-related endeavors, but I liked Roxanne and she made it clear that she wasn't looking for therapy, but more "life coaching" versus executive coaching. I agreed, and of course, we started off with the EQ-i 2.0 assessment as a baseline. With permission, I have posted part of her EI profile below.

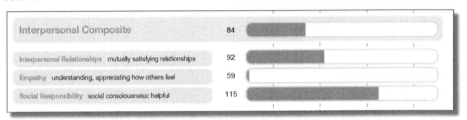

Figure 30 - Roxanne Interpersonal

Reproduced with permission of Multi-Health Systems (2017). All Rights Reserved. www.mhs.com

Like Craig, again we have the rare dichotomy of subscale scores where high use and low use exist within the same composite. Interpersonal Relationships (92) are within balance of the overall composite (84) and within the Overall EI score (86). After targeted coaching questions and self-discovery, it became evident that Roxanne had a zealous passion in promoting social issues and the greater good. Her love of animals blossomed via participation in humane societies and her heart ached every time she saw a dog in need (a big reason why she had acquired so many animals). Her work at the chemical society centered around the mission of stopping chemical pollution all over the world. Again, another worthy cause. When asked about her low use of Empathy, she did not equivocate, as her acrimony for "social offenders" (her label, which I found interesting) became abundantly clear.

She told me stories about each of the bloodhounds that she had adopted, and how each was given up to the shelter in what is referred to as an "owner-surrender", meaning that the owner simply does not want the dog anymore. In her state, the owner-surrender process consists of the soon-to-be ex-owner simply abandoning the dog in a dumpster outside of the humane society building, oftentimes under the cloak of darkness. She occasionally saw owners do this in person during the day time, and each time, she would confront the owners. She would hear sob story after sob story. Though Roxanne would become maudlin over the idea of an animal becoming homeless, she eventually became numb to the tales of individual human irresponsibility. Similarly, when her chemical society caught environmental polluters, the offenders tried to come across as martyrs or victims themselves.

This led Roxanne to develop and heavily use her Social Responsibility, because she became overly invested in the social causes of animal rescue/welfare and environmental safety. In conjunction, she developed a disdain for the individual humans that caused these tragedies, finding that she could not relate to their "victim" stories nor appreciate how they could ever feel the way that they did, to where they would have to abandon a family pet that sometimes, they had for years.

Through this discovery, we were able to reshape Roxanne's outlook on the world, by tempering the emotions associated with worldly causes, and ensuring that she didn't promote a guilty-till-proven-innocent decree on individual humans and their behaviors. She realized that her outlook toward the individual human was an insidious view that eroded her social life, and after crafting a development plan, Roxanne was able to start empathizing again. I've always loved bloodhounds, wrinkles and all.

Balancing Decision Making

Figure 31 - Decision-Making Composite

Reproduced with permission of Multi-Health Systems (2017). All Rights Reserved. www.mhs.com

Decision Making is how individuals use emotional information in the process of making decisions, and how well individuals understand the impact that emotions have on decision making. This composite also focuses on our ability to delay impulses and avoid rash behaviors.

Problem Solving governs our ability to solve problems that are interpersonal and maintains our ability to understand the impact emotions have on our decision-making processes. This subscale has two components: the ability to identify problems and then generate effective solutions, all while being aware of our emotions around the problem (Bar-On, 2013). People who use Problem Solving well are conscientious, meticulous, systematic, and do not avoid conflict. According to the US Office of Personnel Management, Problem Solving is the most important managerial competency (Bar-On, 2013). An important distinction that I always make to my coaching clients, is that this does not measure the outcomes of your problem-solving abilities, but rather how you use emotions in your problem-solving process.

Low use of Problem Solving means that individuals get overwhelmed by emotions, get stuck, or avoid problems all together. Individuals engage in conflict avoidance and often "stick their head in the sand" on many issues. Feelings and actions can include:

- Emotional ineffectiveness
- Unreliable
- Undependable
- Weak leadership

Conversely, those engaged in high use of Problem Solving can be too quick to react, and often shoot from the hip. Balanced use of this skill includes strategic planning, and those who engage in high use will often prefer to work alone since they may view others as "not on the same problem solving level." Feelings and actions can include:

- May not use conflict avoidance when necessary to do so
- Engage too quickly before thinking
- Work alone and get frustrated with lack of quick action by others
- Create groupthink within teams
- Take on more problems than they should

It is important to keep this skill in balance, so that leaders can effectively tackle challenges that need to be addressed, but also not engage in every battle that comes along. Balanced Problem Solving ensures leaders are ready to solve tough challenges, even when he is upset or emotions are running hot.

Reality Testing is the ability to remain objective during situations where emotions are involved, and not engage in fantasy or bias (we will discuss EI and cognitive bias in Part 3). Balanced Reality Testing ensures that leaders are in tune with the world around them and that they are addressing problems that actually exist, which is a cornerstone of situational-awareness.

Low use of Reality Testing means that individuals create fantasies about the work, people, and challenges around them. While these fantasies are not necessarily extravagant or extreme, they may include little fictions such as who is responsible for certain problems or imagined organizational politics. Individuals engaged in low use of Reality Testing have a hard time matching up what is experienced internally with what actually exists externally (Bar-On, 2013). Individuals who are extremely deficient in Reality Testing often experience psychosis. Feelings and actions can include:

- Being scatter-brained
- Unrealistic
- Fantasy driven
- Prone to exaggeration

Conversely, those engaged in high use of Reality Testing can lack imagination, or can lack connection to elements that she cannot physically touch, such as love or loyalty. Those engaged in high use of this skill often can be poor planners, since the future "hasn't happened yet" and is not a situation that can be engaged on a practical level. Feelings and actions can include:

- Lack of future planning
- Unimaginative
- Not creative
- Too objective

It is important to keep this skill in balance, or leaders may imagine problems and intricacies of current situations that do not exist and divert valuable resources toward quixotic missions to tilt at metaphorical windmills, or leaders will be too heavily invested in reality which will blunt creativity and long-term strategic planning capabilities within the team.

Impulse Control is the ability to resist temptation, and delay kneejerk reactions to situations where a leader would act too quickly or in a rash manner. Those who balance Impulse Control normally make carefully weighed decisions. According to Bar-On, (2013), Impulse Control is the fourth foundational cornerstone of EI (the others being Emotional Self-Awareness, Empathy, and Assertiveness), as many EI models also encompass some form of Impulse Control as a skill.

Low use of Impulse Control is often visible and destructive. Low use of this skill means that an individual has no ability to delay behaviors that could be career-ending and he can be quick to anger (a classic example is former President Bill Clinton, who wasn't able to control certain impulses and was eventually impeached for them). Frustration, impulsiveness, and anger control problems are often associated with low use. Feelings and actions can include:

- Explosive
- Short fused
- Abusive
- Lacking self-control
- Unpredictability

Conversely, those engaged in high use of Impulse Control may appear indecisive. Especially when combined with a low Self-Expression score, leaders who heavily use Impulse Control can come across as aloof, detached, or withdrawn. Feelings and actions can include:

- Unexpressive
- Overly structured
- Rigid
- Slow to act

It is important to keep this skill in balance, as Impulse Control is a key component in the ability to lead, negotiate, and execute conflict resolution (Bar-On, 2013). Balanced use of this skill ensures that emotions work in your favor, instead of against you, and that leaders can make effective decisions that are carefully weighed, but made on time.

Jon the Jack of All Trades

My favorite story about Jon, and one that is the most fitting because he was extremely intelligent, was the time he told me about his experience with the *Knowledge*. The *Knowledge of London* is the process that aspiring taxicab drivers go through in order to earn their stripes. Taxicab apprentices are required to learn every route within London, so that they can immediately respond to a passenger's request, without the need to use a map or navigation. Often considered the most demanding taxicab training course in the world, those with the *Knowledge* mention it can take around 34 months to successfully pass. If you have been to London, you will see that it is not laid out in squares like New York City, but rather it looks like someone took a bowl of spaghetti, threw it on the table, spun it around, and that leftover pattern of sauce (or gravy as my Philly clients say) became the street map. There are many unnamed streets and alleys in London, of which the majority are barely a single car width wide. When I asked him why he abandoned this quest, he simply replied, "it took up too much of my time".

Jon was part of an oil and gas company that contracted with me to perform leadership pipeline analysis by giving EQ360s to all of the high performers, or "HiPos". When it came time to work with Jon, I noticed that his reputations all had very good balance and were in line with his self-identity, but part of the verbatim analysis (the open text fields where respondents can free write in any comments about the subject) stood out to me. They all mentioned how Jon was a great problem solver, and whenever someone had any issue, big or small, Jon would be the go-to-guy. "He was a jack-of-all trades and always had the answer", seemed to be the central theme of the comments.

When debriefing Jon, he often went on wild tangents with his thoughts, displaying his expertise in many areas, telling me about the *Knowledge*, and all of the different roles he has had over the years. I still to this day think Jon would be excellent at Jeopardy. When I asked him "what is one thing you would like to improve", he quickly mentioned that he was interested in boosting his time management ability. But after looking at this EQ-i 2.0 results, it actually wasn't his time management that needed attention, but rather something else. With permission, I have posted part of his EI profile below.

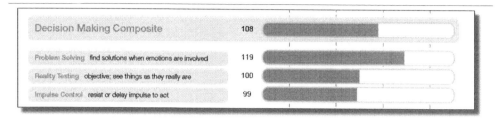

Figure 32 - Jon Decision-Making

At first glance, this seems to be in balance within the composite, but Jon's Overall EI score is 101. Now, what do you notice? He is heavily using Problem Solving. After targeted coaching and self-discovery, combined with the verbatim analysis from the EQ360, we teased out a few common themes in Jon's life. His ability to manage his emotions in reference to Problem Solving was so high, that he never turned a problem or challenge down. He owned everyone's problems that came his way, constantly sought challenges that seemed impossible, and it became part of his identity. It is the reason he is the jack-of-all-trades, because he has at some point, tried to tackle every kind of problem.

So in reality, Jon didn't have a time management problem. He simply had too many problems to manage in any given day! Sure, it gave him great experience and knowledge, but he never had time to complete any challenges. He took on too many, and his high use of Problem Solving didn't create the emotional pressure in his mind that was needed to complete the ventures, so Jon often had many open streams of work, and rarely saw projects through to completion. High use of Problem Solving led to many project starts, but very few project finishes. Luckily for him, this was easily fixable. We created a system that he used to weigh which projects and tasks of others he would engage in, and magically, his time management problem seemed to disappear. According to Jon, there are over 25,000 streets in the *Knowledge* that need to be memorized before a taxicab driver begins his 12 tests, or "appearances", with an examiner.

Balancing Stress Management

Figure 33 - Stress Management Composite

Reproduced with permission of Multi-Health Systems (2017). All Rights Reserved. www.mhs.com

Stress Management is how well individuals can cope with the emotions associated with change and unpredictable circumstances, while maintaining Optimism (Bar-On, 2013). Measures of personal resilience and toughness during times of mounting pressure are key components of this composite.

Flexibility is how leaders adapt emotions and the subsequent behaviors toward unfamiliar or unpredictable events or concepts. Those that are flexible can adapt to new circumstances without rigidity, can change their minds in the face of scientific evidence that is contrary to their own beliefs, and are tolerant and open to new processes, methods, and ideas. Flexibility is closely related to social-adjustment, and is considered by Darwin to be one of the most important skills of survival and adaptation. Organizational flexibility is often considered the most important competency for survival as well, and is one of the most highly sought after skills of new leaders, according to the US Office of Personnel Management.

Low use of Flexibility can lead to rigidity in thinking and behavior, the resisting of change, and can drastically affect survival from a career and organizational perspective (Bar-On, 2013). It also means that the individual has an inability to process new data, or change his mind or his direction easily. Feelings and actions can include:

- Rigid thinking
- Lacking curiosity
- Change resistance and avoidance
- Hesitant to take on new work

Conversely, high use of Flexibility can lead to boredom or an unwillingness to stand one's own ground when work issues conflict with personal issues. Feelings and actions can include:

- Uninterested with routines
- Inclined to start projects rather than finish them
- Hesitant to make a plan to close a project

It is important to keep this skill in balance, so that the leader can effectively lead, multitask, and adapt within rapidly changing business environments (Bar-On, 2013). Balanced Flexibility ensures that leaders can quickly and correctly respond to unexpected circumstances and challenges, remain resilient, but also balance resources and priorities in the face of many competing challenges.

Stress Tolerance is the ability to function while being in the middle of stressful situations, or facing daunting challenges head on. Balanced Stress Tolerance ensures that leaders do not get overwhelmed during times of change. People who have a well-developed Stress Tolerance tackle challenges and impending crises head on, rather than avoid them. Considered by Bar-On (2013) to be one of the essential leadership qualities, balanced Stress Tolerance measures one's ability to withstand complex conditions, constant change, and mounting pressure.

Low use of Stress Tolerance means that the leader lacks the emotional skill set that is needed to successfully approach stressful situations or organizational change. Generally, this leader also lacks confidence. Anxiety is often a byproduct of low Stress Tolerance, along with tension, irritability, poor concertation, and constant worry. Feelings and actions can include:

- Anxiety
- Agitation
- Procrastination
- Hopelessness
- Low self-confidence

Conversely, high use of Stress Tolerance means that individuals can miss stressors and dangers that exist within certain situations, and may not experience the emotional urgency needed to adequately complete the job. Feelings and actions can include:

- Unawareness of situational consequence
- Emotional disconnect
- Over-confidence
- Blind to situational danger

It is important to keep this skill in balance in order for a leader to survive in the modern business climate. According to the *Harvard Business Review*, 3 out of 4 change efforts fail. With a 25% success rate on change initiatives to begin with, having a leader with an inability to emotionally deal with change will drastically lower that percentage, and vice versa, one who engages in high use of Stress Tolerance may miss the subtle clues that present themselves that signal when a change in direction is needed.

Optimism is the ability to see the brighter side of things. Hope, positivity, and faith are all feelings that can be generated when this EI skill is in balance. Bar-On (2013) claims that there is a strong correlation between Optimism and the ability to cope with problems, and it has an important role in motivation and stress management. It is also considered a desirable management quality because Optimism contributes to corporate well-being and team functionality.

Low use of Optimism, is essentially pessimism. Feelings of depression, despondency, and gloom accompany low use. All of the feelings that accompany depression also accompany low use of optimism, and leaders engaged in low use of Optimism tend to be passive and less committed. Feelings and actions can include:

- Depression
- Helplessness
- Hopelessness

- Unmotivated
- Easily defeated

Conversely, it is possible to use Optimism too much. Much like high use of Stress Tolerance, leaders engaged in high use of Optimism can be blind to situational danger and also reality itself. Leaders tend to find positive things that do not actually exist, clouding his judgements about projects and people. Feelings and actions can include:

- Reality blindness
- Always incorrectly seeing the bright side of things
- Perpetuating unrealistic beliefs in always achieving positive outcomes

It is important to balance Optimism so that leaders can remain positive in the face of danger, but not be blind to it. According to Bar-On (2013), Optimism is strongly correlated with an ability to benefit from coaching, feedback and other talent interventions. Ensuring that the leader and team have balanced Optimism may be a vital precursor to any planned talent interventions, to ensure that the learning sticks.

Marc the Ice Dragon

Marc is a pilot for the US Air Force, based out of Anchorage, Alaska. Originally from southern California, it was always a sure bet that half of any conversation with Marc would center around the difference in weather, and how someday, he would return to 300 days a year of 80-degree sunshine. Marc is part of the Air Force that defends our borders from Russia. Whenever I would hear stories in the news about Russian fighter pilots flying mere miles within the comfort zone of USA airspace, I would call Marc and he would give me the inside scoop. His squadron would be the ones responsible to scramble, should Russia ever breach the portion of USA airspace that was considered an act of war. So, as you can imagine, the EI of these brave men and women needed to be balanced and high, in order for them to keep us from starting WWIII with an emotionally charged caprice.

I was brought in to do a leadership development workshop that centered around EI, self-awareness, and fast-twitch thinking, for the squadrons based in Anchorage. Marc was the flight commander for his unit and had been through various military leadership programs before, but wanted his unit to develop emotional toughness, given the noble task each pilot was faced with.

The workshop consisted of a 2-day facilitation, followed by individual EQ-i 2.0 Leadership Reports for each participant. Each pilot received an individual, in-person EI debrief, and provided unstructured feedback about Marc's leadership style and how it affected his direct reports. After speaking with the entire squadron about Marc's leadership style, an interesting theme began to emerge. With permission, I have posted part of his EI profile below.

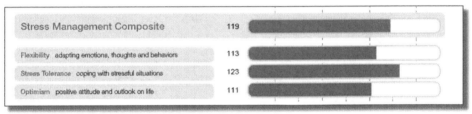

Figure 34 - Marc Stress management

Reproduced with permission of Multi-Health Systems (2017). All Rights Reserved. www.mhs.com

At first glance, this composite not only seems well balanced, but it is generally at the level I would expect to see among fighter pilots. However, Marc's Overall EI is a 105. Now what do you see? Marc is heavily using Stress Tolerance. The theme that arose from the unstructured interviews centered around the notion that Marc is a great leader and has ice water in his veins. His nickname is the "ice dragon", because he would slay many of the challenges that came his way, and never batted an eye doing so. He was heavily using his Stress Tolerance, and while this is a great skill to possess, here is what the high use created. His management style allowed stressful situations to grow and compound. As stress increased within a given situation, the level of stress began to slowly become too high for other members of the squadron. One by one, each would start to feel less comfortable, and then anxious, about the level of stress that had been reached. Only when a situation reached critical mass, would Marc step in to solve the challenge. This was because he didn't feel the same amount of stress as others, and he had made his career out of solving "difficult" challenges. What Marc didn't realize though, was that he was inadvertently emasculating his team, by constructing situations that created stress among his reports and challenges that only he could emotionally solve. Marc's high use of Stress Tolerance, while a coveted attribute for his meteoric rise in the Air Force, essentially created a team riddled with anxiety and nervousness. We were able to have a group discussion about this phenomenon, and Marc was astonished at first, but quickly saw the group's view and we were able to discuss development scenarios for him, and better communication scenarios for the squadron. I always loved doing workshops and coaching programs in Alaska; Denali national park is an awesome place to see. If you ever have the chance to go, take it.

Balancing Happiness and Well-Being

Figure 35 - Happiness Indicator

Reproduced with permission of Multi-Health Systems (2017). All Rights Reserved. www.mhs.com

Happiness as a construct isn't necessarily considered an EI skill, but rather an indicator of how well we are doing. So, while it is not a skill that can be balanced in the high and low use sense, it is important to talk about what high and low happiness convey from a well-being indication perspective.

Happiness is important for satisfaction in life, contentment, motivation, and social intelligence. According to Bar-On (2013), Happiness exists within two dimensions inside human performance, the first being motivational and the second being barometric. Happiness helps us become motivated to tackle opportunities and engage life in a proactive manner, energizing us. Happiness also gives us an indication on how well we are doing and provides a check-in on our previous performance (Bar-On, 2013). Low Happiness includes feelings of depression, gloom, worry, and social withdrawal. While not technically considered high use, individuals can be too happy. High Happiness can lead to alienation of others who are not as happy, an avoidance of things that diminish happiness, and an aversion to anything that is not considered fun. Those who have high Happiness often do not want to let go, so any person or task that does not directly contribute to the sustained Happiness might be avoided as well.

Advanced Emotional Balance Wrap-Up

This section presented an advanced application of emotional balance that can be used for individual and team coaching. It is very important to remember that the Balancing Your EI section at the bottom of each EQ-i 2.0 report subscale page, which is a Level 1 concept, is still very important for emotional health, so do not replace that concept with this one, but simply use this as the next step. Advanced balance is the concept of high and low use, and teasing out the behaviors and situations that the imbalance creates. Some coaches that subscribe to strengths-based only coaching (which I labelled as ineffective and dangerous in a previous section), will often promote high use of two or three strengths, while ignoring the rest. Hopefully this section illustrates for you why using two or three crutches and calling them strengths is a dangerous coaching method, and can often create team performance issues or serious skill deficiencies in other areas within the individual.

It is vital that you **do not** use the concept of advanced balance **to diagnose** or assign a predetermined label to an individual (as discussed in the Group Report section). Remember that the main difference between coaching and therapy is that coaches have targeted conversations and do not diagnose **individual dysfunction** (remember that group/team dysfunction is different and perfectly fine to investigate). Use the insights that you glean from advanced interpretation of these reports to ask even more targeted questions, allowing for self-discovery within your client, not coach-imposed diagnosis and conclusions.

Master the Balance

Naginata-Jutsu is still practiced today all over the world, though the ancient form has been modernized a bit. There is still much that is debated about this ancient ninja skill, as historians often discuss the exact origin of the weapon, if it was primarily constructed to defend against cavalry or foot soldiers, if it was created to give female fighters a better advantage, or if it mainly derived as an art form. Despite the debated genesis of the Naginata (the name of the weapon itself in Naginata-Jutsu), one common theme is present within all discussions. The theme of balance. The weapon should not be used for fighting too far or too close, as the advantage for the ninja disappears. Only in the balanced middle, will the shinobi truly be able to thrive. The same is for EI. Debated origins, a propensity for improper use, and a balanced sweet spot. Much like Naginata-Jutsu, mastering EI balance is a vital component of survival.

– Shinobi Skill Acquired –

Naginata-Jutsu 長刀術

Part 2 Wrap Up

So, that does it for Part 2. Part 2 consisted of what it takes to stand up a coaching practice, how to weave in psychological perspectives into your coaching and consulting, how to properly use the Group Report to identify psychological phenomena in group settings, how to interpret 360s with advanced application, and how to have targeted conversations about balance when various emotional skills are overused or underused.

These are the key points from this section that you must never forget:

- Getting certified in the EQ-i 2.0 Level 1 program is like getting your learner's permit. It is the very beginning. You must sell and work your ass off to make your new skill profitable and valuable to your organization. You are now an expert alone on an island, so you must become a self-starter.

- Each individual has multiple reputations and one identity. There is no psychological benefit to ever having these constructs merge. The main goal of advanced 360 interpretation should be to identify if the reputations are being created with purpose, and to ensure that no psychological strain exists in maintaining those reputation distances.

- Everyone coaches, advises, and counsels within a psychological perspective, whether you know it or not. You must understand what specific perspective you are driving with your questions and your end goals, or you will lead your client astray.

- Team dysfunction is not the same as individual dysfunction. Individual dysfunction is a result of: repressed memories, childhood trauma, biological factors, chemical imbalances, brain damage, and other many inconspicuous internal elements, that EI assessment cannot correct. Team dysfunction is often caused by a mismatch of personality and EI characteristics or lack of fluid conversation and effective communication. EI should not be used to diagnose individual dysfunction, but it can and should be used to identify team performance dysfunction.

- The main goal of these advanced EI concepts is not to label the client, but to give you, the coach, greater insight into how to create psychologically safe spaces for individual and team conversation. Your greatest power, is in your ability to ask targeted questions and generate self-discovery within leaders. As a coach, you are a compass and a mirror. Advanced EI concepts help you become a stronger compass and a clearer mirror.

- It is all about balance. Relying on and promoting only a few EI strengths, at the expense of others, is dangerous for the individual, the team, and the organization. Balance the skills first, make sure the metaphorical EI wheel is able to spin without divots and bulges, and then work to improve how fast the wheel spins.

Part 3

How EI can affect human cognition and decision making,
lead organizational change and craft powerful succession and selection programs

Emotional Syndromes and Configurations

Kayaku-Jutsu was one of the most effective, yet one of the most treacherous ninja skills wielded by the ancient shinobi. Kayaku-Jutsu is the skill of using fire and explosives, which includes effective placement and timing. The ancient shinobi would use Kayaku-Jutsu to demolish and distract adversaries, but since explosives were primarily used with black powder in the old days, its use was limited and only for the most skilled of shinobi.

. . .

Venturing a bit further down the psychological rabbit hole, there are many psychosocial elements that you will encounter during your EI based coaching and consulting that venture into the realm of clinical psychology and therapy. You will come across certain syndromes, emotional configurations, and psychological disorders during your conversations and talent interventions. While I cannot provide a panacea for the infinite number of disorders that you could possibly encounter, the purpose of this section is to highlight three of the most common that I have witnessed in my coaching practice. I offer guidance on a suitable method of engagement with these syndromes and configurations, and discuss how you can use these to your advantage. Much like the Kayaku-Jutsu, be careful playing with fire, it can be your greatest advantage or lead to your immediate destruction.

Disclaimer – Any emotional configurations presented are not to be used for clinical diagnosis of emotional or personality disorders discussed. The EI configurations are simply my observations collected over years of coaching and consulting, and are to be used only to guide coaching conversations, not make any clinical diagnosis. The original EQ-i contained six "Critical Items" that were designed to identify depressive conditions, psychotic states, and the potential to lose control (Bar-On, 2002). These were eventually removed so that the EQ-i could be more broadly applied to organizations. The results of the EQ-i 2.0 should be used for further discussion and probing, not to form a conclusion or diagnose emotional problems within the client. Use the following sections as guidance only for your coaching process. These configurations also assume there are no validity concerns with the results.

The Emotional Blindness of Alexithymia

Alexithymia, also known as Catalinithymia, is a disorder that inhibits the processing of emotions into words. Literally translating to "having no words for emotions", alexithymia affects both children and adults. Those who suffer from this may not have an ability to know their own self-experiences, understand the genesis of many emotions, express their own emotions, or have any real imagination. First discovered in 1976, this is classified as a deficit in emotional awareness and is thought to exist within 10% of the population. Researchers believe that it associated with autism, depression, and schizophrenia, and can affect anyone in the world.

Baughman (2011) wrote in the *Australian Academic Press* that alexithymia could have a biological component and have a correlation with EI. Her study consisted of 216 monozygotic and 45 dizygotic same-sex twin pairs who completed an assessment that measured alexithymia called the Toronto Alexithymia Scale-20. A subset of the participants also took an EI assessment, the Trait Emotional Intelligence Questionnaire. She found there was a significant negative correlation between alexithymia and EI (r = -.39), and suggested that biological factors were the link. Ghiabi and Besharat (2011) wrote in *Procedia - Social and Behavioral Sciences,* after studying 357 students in Iran, that alexithymia and EI were negatively correlated (r = -.71), and Parker (2001) found similar results when writing for the *Journal for Personality and Individual Differences,* stating the negative correlation was (r = -.72).

Short of having a coaching client take the Toronto Alexithymia Scale-20, you will have to pay attention to subtle clues during your coaching sessions to see if this could be a possibility. Having such a strong negative correlation to EI and the EQ-i 2.0 itself, the first indicator would be a low EI score. If during coaching sessions, individuals find it difficult to be imaginative or find it challenging to label emotions, alexithymia could be the culprit. Remember the goal would not be to diagnose the dysfunction, but to focus on performance. If you feel the coaching engagement is solid enough to suggest this condition, that will have to be your call, only with the preface that you are not a qualified therapist to make a definite determination (unless you are one of the few that are qualified and certified to work with vulnerable populations).

The main goal of your coaching sessions, should you encounter alexithymia, would be to focus solely on Emotional Self-Awareness. Ways that have been shown to help strengthen the ability within individuals to identify emotions are actions such as journaling, reading, dancing or other forms of expressive art, hypnosis, acupuncture, or as a last resort, psychotherapy (by someone else unless you are qualified).

EI Configurations that Might Identify Alexithymia

Disclaimer about configurations – the configurations I offer are anecdotal and based off my own coaching experience, not any official research that I have done.

In my experience delivering EI based coaching and consulting all over the world, I have encountered quite a few that have suffered from alexithymia (many have confirmed this after receiving proper diagnosis from a clinical psychologist later on). Among them, I have found that a few EI combinations, or configurations, are normally present. They are as follows:

- Extremely low Emotional Self-Awareness
- Extremely low Emotional Expression
- High Reality Testing
- Low Self-Regard
- Extremely Low Interpersonal Relationships
- Low Empathy

If you find any of your clients have similar configurations, and your coaching Spidey-sense is giving you indications of the disorder, it is worth investigating further, but tread lightly. Any emotional configurations that consist of items that are extremely low should be approached with caution.

I mention this disorder because it affects so many people - up to 10% of the population. Chances are you know a few who suffer from this. There is a lot of research on the subject of alexithymia and its relation to EI, so if this interests you and you have encountered it, check out your local library and get smart on it. If you are doing advanced EI coaching, chances are you will come across it.

"No Story" Nancy

I met Nancy through an EQ360 with a large retail organization. Oftentimes, raters of an EQ360 for a different individual will become interested in the assessment and feedback process, and reach out about doing an EQ360 of their own (I find that many of my EQ360 clients were former raters from a previous EQ360). Nancy was a regional manager for a string of high-end motorcycle stores, which made her a unique client in the sense that she was not a typical corporate manager. She led the regional sales for the company, and was responsible for individual store support, brand awareness and socialization in her region, and overall customer satisfaction and community events. She had many hats to wear within this position, and often felt that she was pulled in many competing directions, habitually faking emotional states and enthusiasm for various aspects of the job. After an initial scoping discussion, I confirmed that an EQ360 would be a valid first step in coaching and I set up the assessment.

Nancy's self-assessment was drastically lower than that of her rater groups, specifically in Self-Regard and Emotional Self-Awareness. With permission, I have posted part of her EI profile below.

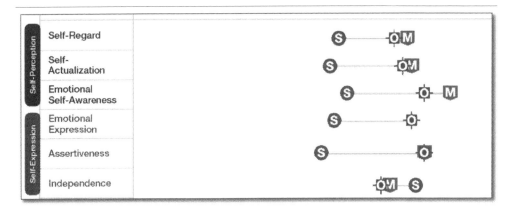

Figure 36 - Self vs. raters

After examining the results of the EQ360, we focused on her low Emotional Self-Awareness. She said "I am always asked how I feel about certain business situations, but I literally have no story to tell" (that phrase would stick with me). She would bumble through explanations and directives within situations that elicited strong emotions, despite the vacuity that occupied her emotional mind. She mentioned that she often could not find the correct words to describe how she felt, but still did a good job of hiding this vocabulary void from her peers. However, it weighed on her confidence.

I developed a plan that focused solely on developing her Emotional Self-Awareness. We implemented daily journaling strategies such as stimuli documentation, vocabulary building for similar emotions, and increased focus on words that had emotional content. After a few coaching sessions, it became apparent that it was not a lack of emotional skill or situational low use, but something else that was creating the emotional disconnect. We would continue with these strategies for the duration of our time together.

Our coaching engagement eventually ended and I didn't hear from Nancy for about eight months. She eventually contacted me again, thanking me and letting me know that the strategy of daily journaling helped her cope with her emotional abyss, and she eventually went to a qualified professional who diagnosed alexithymia. Her counselor had her engaged in group therapy where they discussed emotionally charged words and scenarios, performed creative arts, conducted various relaxation techniques, and continued daily journaling. While she no longer worked at the motorcycle company, she was much happier with life. Though we were not able to reassess with another EQ360, her overall demeanor was more cheerful, as she mentioned that she no longer had to fake her way through life, so I will assume that her EQ360 identity scores were higher. I am glad I was able to play a small role in getting her the help she needed.

I've always been a bit scared of motorcycles. I crashed one when I was in my younger and more rebellious days on Friday the 13th. Since that day, I changed my hockey number from 13 to 6, which is the number I still use today.

The Emotional Roller Coaster of the Schizoid

A schizoid, or someone with schizoid personality disorder, is someone who lacks interest in relationships, is heavily introverted, and can lack empathy, yet combines these traits with whimsical fantasies and creative thinking. Not to be confused with psychopaths, sociopaths, or those with social anxiety disorders, schizoids are more common and can be considered, for lack of a better term, watered down versions of the above-mentioned disorders. They normally abstain from violent acts, unlike psychopaths. As of this writing, there isn't a hard figure on how many schizoids could be walking among us, but I have personally run into a few in my coaching practice, and it is always an interesting encounter. For the purposes of this discussion, I will interchangeably quote research applied to both schizoids and psychopaths, as they are closely related disorders, and there is limited research on schizoids.

Schizoids are aloof, distant, cold, and are often loners. Despite the individual's ability to be a chameleon (more on that in a bit), they tend to avoid relationships and social contact if possible. The causes of schizotypal personality disorder are not yet known. Many researchers believe the cause to be genetic, though some research suggests that traumatic brain injury can also create development of this trait later on in life.

So, great, I just gave you a disorder that cannot be cured nor can be easily identified, you are probably thinking. Guilty as charged! But this syndrome is important because it becomes more prevalent as you go up the ranks of leadership, so it will be vital for you to be able to spot it when you see it.

Being a kissing cousin of psychopathology, there have been many studies on the link between psychopaths and many positions of power, from organizational managers to world leaders. Babiak and Hare (2006) wrote in *Snakes in Suits* that psychopaths (and schizoids) rise in numbers as you go up the company org-chart. Their research showed that approximately 3% of those assessed in leadership pipeline programs were psychopaths, which is well above the 1% mark of the general population. This means that the more leaders that you help develop and the higher up you consult within these organizations, the chances of you running into schizoids rises considerably.

EI Configurations that Might Identify Schizoids

Disclaimer about configurations – the configurations that I offer are anecdotal and based off my own coaching experience, not any official research that I have done.

There are precise EI combinations that signal to me, that I may be dealing with a schizoid. They align to clinical features of schizoid personality disorder as identified in the *Diagnostic and Statistical Manual of Mental Disorders*, or DSM-5. Essentially, schizoids think highly of themselves yet crave social isolation, and they are master chameleons that can fake happiness and be extremely expressive of gestures and emotions if it is necessary to blend in and not draw attention to themselves. For those that I have unscientifically identified as schizoids (they did not confirm with me my suspicions after our coaching engagements like alexithymia clients) The EI configuration is as follows:

- Extremely high Self-Regard
- Low Interpersonal Relationships
- Low Social Responsibility
- Extremely low Reality Testing
- High Emotional Expression

- High Flexibility
- Inconsistency or Positive/Negative Impression Indicator Flags

If you find any of your clients have similar configurations, and your coaching Spidey-sense is giving you indications of the disorder, do not be alarmed. Schizotypal individuals are most concerned with keeping their secret hidden, are rarely violent, and not enough is known about the disorder for treatment, coaching, or counseling. As Bateman (2015) wrote in the *Journal Series: Treatment of Personality Disorders*, the evidence for treatment of personality disorders is insufficient. As a coach, it is best to be aware of the configuration within your client, but do not press too hard for self-discovery. The schizoid is aware of their condition and has been long before they ever met you, so most, if not all, of the coaching engagement with you, is primarily a chameleon charade riddled with red herrings that are simply for the schizoid's amusement. Your best bet is to either end the coaching relationship, or go along for the ride and help them achieve their career goals, if they mention any. On second thought, as long as they are paying their bill, and you don't get too invested in the relationship, keep it going! Just know that you may be the one being analyzed, not the other way around.

One interesting finding about psychopaths and schizoids centers around the pathology in relation to EI. It used to be generally accepted that psychopaths and schizoids were deficient in Empathy, as psychopathology is characterized by emotional detachment. Ermer, Kahn, Salovey and Kiehl (2012) conducted a study called "Emotional Intelligence in Incarcerated Men with Psychopathic Traits", in the *Journal of Personality and Social Psychology*. 374 participants were evaluated for psychopathy using the PCL-R, the most widely accepted instrument to measure psychopathy, and were also evaluated for EI ability, using the MSCEIT. Remember, the main difference between the EQ-i and the MSCEIT is that the MSCEIT looks for the ability to perceive emotions. The researchers found that the correlations between the psychopaths' ability to perceive emotions and the psychopathy measures, as indicated on the PCL-R, were all close to zero. General understanding of the pathology is that psychopaths and schizoids are supposed to be lacking Empathy, yet within this study, the subjects were not missing the ability to accurately perceive emotions in the MSCEIT. This suggests that psychopaths and schizoids do not actually lack Empathy. Though further research is required to be definitive, it is now believed that psychopaths do perceive emotions accurately in others, but they are not affected by them, or frankly, just do not care. Psychopaths can be highly motivated to manipulate others, and being able to perceive emotions in others is a key component of this. This is consistent with my personal experience. When I encounter a schizoid, I do not find that their Empathy is very low. Notice how I did not mention Empathy scores in the configuration, because I have encountered one or two that have had fairly normal Empathy scores.

While there is no specific way to coach someone out of the disorder, Babiak and Hare (2006) mention a few ways that you can help the organization avoid costly mistakes and the damage schizoids can do. They recommend:

- A well-developed internal succession program
- A strong focus on tangible results that are verifiable
- A structured interview process that helps illuminate moral and ethical characteristics among new candidates

In this instance, while it would be unethical to report to anyone that you are working with a schizoid, you could try and pivot your role from an individual coach to an organizational consultant, and start working with other leaders to help the organization with the above-mentioned steps.

I mention this disorder because it affects so many people, up to 3% of the leader population. Chances are you know a few who suffer from this. There is a lot of research on the subject of the psychopaths/schizoids and the relation to leadership, so if this interests you and you have encountered it, check out your local library and get smart on it. If you are doing advanced EI coaching, chances are you will come across it, especially at the C-level.

Lawrence the Lonely

Lawrence was a middle manager of a multi-national company that sold Human Resources software which helped other organizations streamline repetitive and mundane HR processes. I was brought in to consult with this organization on the development of a leadership pipeline that identified, developed, and prepared top talent to make the next organizational step to Director.

Coaching clients fall into one of two buckets. Those that seek out coaches and are really into it and those that only go through coaching because they were "volun-told" to do so, usually because coaching is part of a larger program or development need that was identified by a manager. Both buckets of clients come with their own advantages and disadvantages. Clients that seek out coaching are often more receptive to coaching and assessment, but can sometimes not follow through with development if the coaching experience doesn't marry up with their built-up preconceived notion of what the coaching experience should have been. Clients that do not seek out coaching but attend due to other factors, are generally slow to adopt the feedback or open up during discovery, but usually have the most to gain from coaching since their expectations are much lower. Lawrence was part of the latter bucket.

Lawrence went through an EQ360 like all of the other leadership pipeline participants and scored extremely high in areas of Interpersonal Relationships and Social Responsibility (which is opposite of a typical schizoid profile). Rater scores were equally as high. This didn't cause any concern until I noticed two distinct things – his Positive Impression Indicator score was a 5, and the verbatim analysis at the end of the EQ360 had a common theme from raters that described Lawrence as isolated, unavailable to direct reports, emotionally detached, yet extremely expressive at times. These do not invalidate the assessment, but are always areas of caution when interpreting the results.

The challenge with this report was that the organization did not want to offer the participants of the leadership pipeline ongoing coaching (only the ones that successfully completed the program would be given this opportunity to help with the transition), so I only had one time to debrief with Lawrence on the results. Since I didn't receive permission from Lawrence to discuss the themes of the debrief or share an anonymized version of his results, I will share generalities. Lawrence began the debrief in character, sticking to the persona that the EQ-i results portrayed. During discovery, I highlighted the verbatim comments and immediately saw a shift in Lawrence. He mentioned that some could construe his disposition as aloof and cold, because he recently had a death in the family and wasn't coping well (he didn't mention this when asked at the beginning of the debrief if there was anything that may have affected how he took the assessment). His demeanor changed for the rest of the debrief, switching from a highly gregarious social butterfly to despondent and somber. Initially, I felt that the debrief led to more questions than answers, and afterwards, I strongly suggested that we continue coaching if his department's budget would allow for it. He thanked me, agreed that additional coaching would be beneficial, and said he would reach out as soon as he secured funding. I never heard from Lawrence again.

Reflecting back on my notes, and piecing together other various tidbits of feedback, I can only speculate that I was most likely dealing with a schizoid who was trying to hide his condition and remain in the shadows. One thing that unscientifically confirms my reflection is that Lawrence would mention that he loved to day dream excessively, his office was decorated with comic book characters, and he had a huge fondness for animals. All are telltale signs of the presence of a schizoid.

The Emotional Destruction of the Machiavellian

A Machiavellian differs from the psychopath in a few ways. Even though Machiavellianism, Psychopathy, and Narcissism create the "Dark Triad" and the three personality traits often overlap in many areas, there are a few key differences between Machiavellians and schizoids/psychopaths. Jakobwitz (2006) wrote in the *Journal of Personality and Individual Differences*: "Narcissism is characterized by grandiosity, pride, egotism, and a lack of empathy, Machiavellianism is characterized by manipulation and exploitation of others, a cynical disregard for morality, and a focus on self-interest and deception, and Psychopathy is characterized by enduring antisocial behavior, impulsivity, selfishness, callousness, and remorselessness." While there are many shared traits between the three in the Dark Triad, the main difference is that while psychopaths and schizoids can be manipulative, they prefer social isolation. Machiavellians on the other hand, thrive on the mistreatment of others and on being politically deceptive. They employ cunning tactics for personal gain and self-interest, often at the expense of others. The term itself dates back to 1469, and many monarchs were thought to possess this trait. There has been extensive research on Machiavellianism in the workplace over the last 40 years, but very little is known about its connection to EI.

Some of you have most likely encountered the workplace bully. Kessler (2010) wrote in the *Journal of Applied Social Psychology* that there is a high degree of positive correlation between Machiavellianism and bullying, abusive supervision, and counterproductive workplace behavior. Machiavellians never show humility, constantly show arrogance, would rather be feared than loved, are often unethical and immoral and love to surround themselves with sycophants and lickspittles. An easy way to distinguish between the schizoid and the Machiavellian is the former would rather never be discovered, only manipulates when necessary, and does so in a covert manner. The latter believes they possess scintillating wit, wants the world to see their power, and they overtly engage in deviant behavior.

Some organizations actually attract Machiavellians since many of the behaviors they exhibit are desirable from an organizational goals perspective. Kroger (2015) wrote in the *Academy of Business Research Journal* that corporations can be Machiavellian magnets, because "Machs" are often better competitors, negotiators, project managers, and strategists. What they lack in people management ability, they make up for in certain tactical abilities. That means that you as the leadership coach, will often encounter scenarios where the organization and culture attract Machiavellians, the leadership says publicly that their deviant behavior is unacceptable, not warranted, and needs to be coached, yet corporate goals and business outcomes drive the aberrant behavior. Oh, what tangled webs we weave! In coaching engagements where I am brought in at the behest of senior leadership to coach unwilling or uninterested managers, or to help analyze a toxic company culture, a Machiavellian is almost always in my midst, and more often than not, the company culture itself is what attracted them in the first place.

EI Configurations that Might Identify Machiavellians

Disclaimer about configurations – the configurations that I offer are anecdotal and based off my own coaching experience, not any official research that I have done.

There are precise EI combinations that signal I may be dealing with a Machiavellian. Machiavellians think highly of themselves, think very little of social norms and organizational ethics and they are master manipulators that can be extremely expressive of gestures and emotions, if it is necessary acquire what they want. Petrides (2011) performed a study in the *Twin Research and Human Genetics Journal* that investigated the relation of EI traits to the Dark Triad. The study findings are fascinating and in line with my personal experience. Using the TEIQue (Trait Emotional Intelligence Questionnaire) to measure EI, and the MACH-IV to measure Machiavellianism, they found:

Across the Twin 1 and the Twin 2 data, Machiavellianism showed its strongest negative correlations with adaptability, impulsiveness, relationships, stress management, self-motivation, empathy, happiness, optimism, and with the emotionality, self-control, and wellbeing factors. (Petrides 2011)

This is consistent with the EQ-i 2.0 profiles of those whom I unscientifically have identified as Machs (unlike with alexithymia, Machs did not confirm their status with me after coaching). The EI configuration is as follows:

- Extremely high Self-Regard
- Low Interpersonal Relationships
- High Social Responsibility
- Extremely low Reality Testing
- High Emotional Expression
- Low Assertiveness
- Low Optimism
- Low Empathy
- Low Stress Tolerance
- High Flexibility
- Inconsistency or Positive/Negative Impression Indicator Flags

If you find any of your clients have similar configurations and your coaching Spidey-sense is giving you indications of the disorder, there actually may be cause for alarm. In my experience, Machs feel that they are never wrong and assume they can control any situation. Coaching is supposed to foster self-improvement through psychological safety and client vulnerability. Machs never like to feel vulnerable. On the low end, you will be manipulated into thinking that your coaching is having an impact. On the high end, the Machiavellian will do everything in his or her power to remove you from the organization. I have heard many coaches speak of times that they were ousted from organizations, and when I hear the exit story, it normally sounds like they ran into a Machiavellian. This is a good reason to ensure that you have solid legal contracts before doing work, your coaching method follows an ethical standard, and you take the proper notes in case any accusations arise.

Everything is not lost if you run into a Machiavellian though. Quite the contrary, this should be viewed as a great opportunity. Within change management methodology, there are ideas of creating urgency and guiding coalitions, to help create and sustain organizational change. Part of this is the practice of creating or identifying your "Change Champions." Machiavellians make excellent champions. Advanced coaches can appeal to the Mach, because unlike schizoids who wish to remain in the shadows, they want to take over the world (I always think of Pinky and the Brain when I say "take over the world"). If you can help Machiavellians accomplish their goals, all of their destructive power can work in your favor. Assuming their deceptive ways already gained them political clout within their organization, a Mach-turned-champion will help your reputation positively spread like wildfire within the organization. Remember when I said that coaching meant you were a compass and a mirror? Use that mirror to show the Mach an even better version of themselves, and point them in the direction of achieving their goals even faster, and you may successfully weaponize the deceptive powers that they possess.

Mach 4 Miko

Miko and I used to play roller hockey together in the cul-de-sacs and tennis courts of Northern Virginia back in middle school. Ice hockey was not that popular back then because the Washington Capitals weren't that good, so roller hockey was what the local kids played. We kept in contact over the years, and he brought me the biggest change management challenge that I have ever faced – technology implementation within the Federal Government. Miko was a director of IT and the agency he worked for was looking to bring online over 100 digital processes that would replace outdated analog processes that were used by over 70,000 workers, some for over 30 years. As you can imagine, the culture that was ingrained was not one of rapid change.

I've always known that Miko would sellout his grandmother if it meant his position could improve a smidge. He was a fast-talking and tough negotiator, always looked for the weaknesses in others, and rarely let someone win in anything that was considered competitive (I couldn't count how many times Miko got unnecessary penalties in roller hockey games). When Miko learned that my main focus while studying psychology was Emotional Intelligence, you can imagine the never-ending laughter that ensued. That was until, I told Miko that he was a Machiavellian. Miko would eventually take the Mach-IV test of Machiavellianism, and his score would confirm my suspicions. I'll tell you what I got on the Mach-IV assessment if you give me a glowing book review. See what I did there?

Miko owned it and actually reveled in it, eventually embracing the nickname given to him by his peers of "Mach 4" (a combo of his newly discovered label and his fast-talking style). Miko took the EQ-i 2.0 assessment as part of the change initiative that I was leading, and his results confirmed EI characteristics of "high-Machs". With his permission, I have posted part of it below.

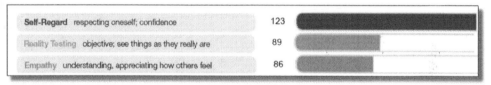

Self-Regard respecting oneself; confidence	123	
Reality Testing objective; see things as they really are	89	
Empathy understanding, appreciating how others feel	86	

Figure 37 - High Machs

According to Lewis Schiff (2013) in *Business Brilliant: Surprising Lessons from the Greatest Self-Made Business Icons,* there is an enormous disparity between self-made millionaires and those within the middle class, when it comes to the definition of acceptable business and wealth-building behavior. According to Schiff, over 90% of millionaires claim that exploiting weaknesses in others during negotiations is necessary, while only 24% of non-millionaires believe so. Of the millionaires, 80% say that always coming out on top is vital (31% for non-millionaires), 77% do not have any problems with business confrontation (13% for non-millionaires), and 78% directly claim that Machiavellian behaviors are essential to wealth (17% for non-millionaires).

Miko was a prime example of all of these statistics, and it was most likely a major factor of his professional success. Miko embraced the role and we implanted him as the change leader for the digital steering committee of this large-scale IT change effort. Despite 30 years of entrenched processes, labor union negotiations, massive IT implementations, and multiple site-readiness assessments, Miko was able to help me lead the change effort from an internal perspective, mainly in part to his many Machiavellian attributes. Luckily, he was one of the few Mach's that embraced the persona and the label, though oftentimes, many Mach's will not. As stated before, Mach's can be your change champions or your worst enemy. Luckily, I had some decent rapport with Miko after saving his bacon all those years during our hockey battles.

Emotional Syndromes and Configurations Wrap Up

This section provided the top three syndromes I have encountered in modern business. Within each, an emotional configuration and an advanced coaching method was presented. In summary, when you find that a client may suffer from an emotional disorder, you can:

- Promote greater Emotional Self-Awareness and other cognitive methods
- Pivot toward the organization and consult on how to minimize impact
- Turn them into your greatest champion

If any of these disorders interest you and you are looking for follow up reading, I suggest the *Psychodynamic Diagnostic Manual* (PDM) or the *Diagnostic and Statistical Manual of Mental Disorders* (DSM). Both will have detailed methods for accurately identifying many of these disorders scientifically.

Mastering the Art of Fire

Kayaku-Jutsu is the skill of using fire and explosives, which includes effective placement and timing. Considered an advanced technique for the shinobi, proper use of this skill could determine victory or defeat in an instant, due to the overwhelming power and volatile nature of this skill. Much like the Kayaku-Jutsu, encountering emotional syndromes and configurations during your coaching and consulting should be addressed with caution. Mastering the psychological techniques will ensure that your "fire" includes effective placement and timing, and that your coaching sessions remain powerful and successful.

– Shinobi Skill Acquired –

Kayaku-Jutsu 長刀術

Emotional Intelligence, Heuristics and Cognitive Bias

Perhaps one of the most recognizable skills of the shinobi in ancient lore, that is often characterized in modern depictions of the ninja, is the skill of stealth movement. The Shinobi-Iri, directly translating to stealth movements and enemy camp entering methods, was the skill of staying hidden, escaping unnoticed, and moving in the shadows. The ninja learned special ways of walking to move silently, and trained endlessly to cover long distances by running. The masters of the Shinobi-Iri could access areas that were inaccessible to others, and do so without enemies ever knowing they were there.

. . .

One of the questions that arises most often when asked about my sundry educational background is "what made you transition from finance to psychology"? One of my first roles out of college was working for a management consulting firm doing financial program control. Our team was responsible for keeping contract spend on plan, and reporting the variance of planned costs versus the actual costs to the program managers. We would prepare financial reports, cost/benefit analyses, ROI studies, and other metric-based presentations for senior leadership, with a recommendation on what to do next. Over time, I began to notice that leaders would take our financial recommendations, cogitate for a bit, and then make business decisions that went against hard data and financial recommendations. I started to understand that organizations were simply collections of people, and those people made judgements about business direction that were often subjective and at odds with hard data. I recognized that individual psychology was just as important, if not more so in business decision making as finance, data, numbers, and reports. Much like the skill of Shinobi-Iri, there are hidden and stealth processes at work that operate in the shadows of our brains that sway organizational direction more than anything else.

Israeli psychologists Amos Tversky and Daniel Kahneman, two of the most brilliant psychologists of the modern era, began to study decision-making processes in the 1970s referred to as heuristics. The term heuristics translates to simply any approach to learning or problem solving. In the psychology world, heuristics normally refer to mental heuristics, or shortcuts, that individuals use to make decisions quickly and easily, sometimes sacrificing accuracy and perfection. Our brains create mental shortcuts from experience, acquired knowledge and other methods, and these heavily affect our ability to make decisions. Since the application of advanced EI principles is to help leaders make better decisions through self-discovery, helping leaders understand how EI affects the unique decision-making processes that their brains have developed over their years of experience will be vital.

In this section, I discuss heuristics, bias, and how to battle them with EI. There are many heuristics that exist in the realm of psychology and it is important to note that heuristics themselves do not need to be addressed during coaching. Psychological heuristics are the mental shortcuts that ensure we do not have to perform a full analysis on every decision we encounter daily, and they normally work to our benefit under most circumstances. Only when the mental shortcuts lead to systematic divergences from logic, statistical probability, or rationality, do they lead to cognitive biases, which should be addressed in EI coaching. Before diving into the different biases I have encountered, I list the top few heuristics that are most prevalent and what biases normally result. If you find that you constantly encounter heuristics and biases in your coaching practice, I recommend reading the books by Kahneman to get smart on the subject.

Anchoring Heuristic – The tendency to rely too heavily on the first piece of information we hear. This can lead to the cognitive bias known as Focalism.

Availability Heuristic – When individuals make judgements based on how easy information comes to mind. This is probably the most common heuristic and can lead to hundreds of different biases, such as memory error, social, and behavioral biases.

Representative Heuristic – When individuals compare information they receive to current mental prototypes. This can lead to asymmetric and memory error biases.

Contagion Heuristic – When individuals view something as having contacted something else that is contaminated, the original object is contaminated. Such as when food touches the ground we assume the food is no longer edible. This can lead to decision-making, belief, behavioral, or social biases.

Scarcity Heuristic – When individuals place more value on an item based on its availability alone. This can lead to systematic biases.

Affect Heuristic – When individuals use emotional response as a major contributor to decision making. This can lead to decision-making, belief, or behavioral biases.

The key aspect about heuristics is that they are unique to the individual, because they have been acquired and hard-coded over an entire lifetime of empirical knowledge, direct experiences, social norms, and inimitable individual journeys. These heuristics operate in the shadows of our psyche, usually working to our advantage. When these processes fail us, they lead to cognitive bias.

According to the *Handbook of Evolutionary Psychology*, a cognitive bias refers to a systematic pattern of deviation from logical judgment, where an individual draws inferences about other people, groups and situations in an illogical manner. A subjective reality is created from their perceptions, which in turn dictates the individual's behavior. Thus, "cognitive biases may sometimes lead to distortions in perceptions, erroneous judgments, illogical interpretation, or what is broadly called irrationality" (Haselton, Nettle & Andrews, 2005). While developing leaders for organizations all over the world, I have come across hundreds of cognitive biases that have decreased the performance of individuals and teams, led to bad business decisions and created failed change efforts. Much like the previous section, I offer the 21 most common biases that I have encountered, what the EI configuration looks like, and some coaching tips on how to battle them. Like the previous section, these are based on my subjective observations over years of coaching. The EI configurations are not meant to diagnose any clinical disorders, only to drive more powerful coaching conversations.

The Same Disclaimer – Any emotional configurations presented are not to be used for clinical diagnosis of the emotional or personality disorders discussed. The EI configurations are simply my observations collected over years of coaching and consulting, and are to be used only to guide coaching conversations, not make any clinical diagnosis. The original EQ-i contained six Critical Items that were designed to identify depressive conditions, psychotic states, and the potential to lose control (Bar-On, 2002). These were eventually removed so that the EQ-i could be more broadly applied to organizations. The results of the EQ-i 2.0 should be used for further discussion and probing, not to form a conclusion or diagnose emotional problems within the client. Use the following sections as guidance only for your coaching process. These configurations also assume there are no validity concerns with the results.

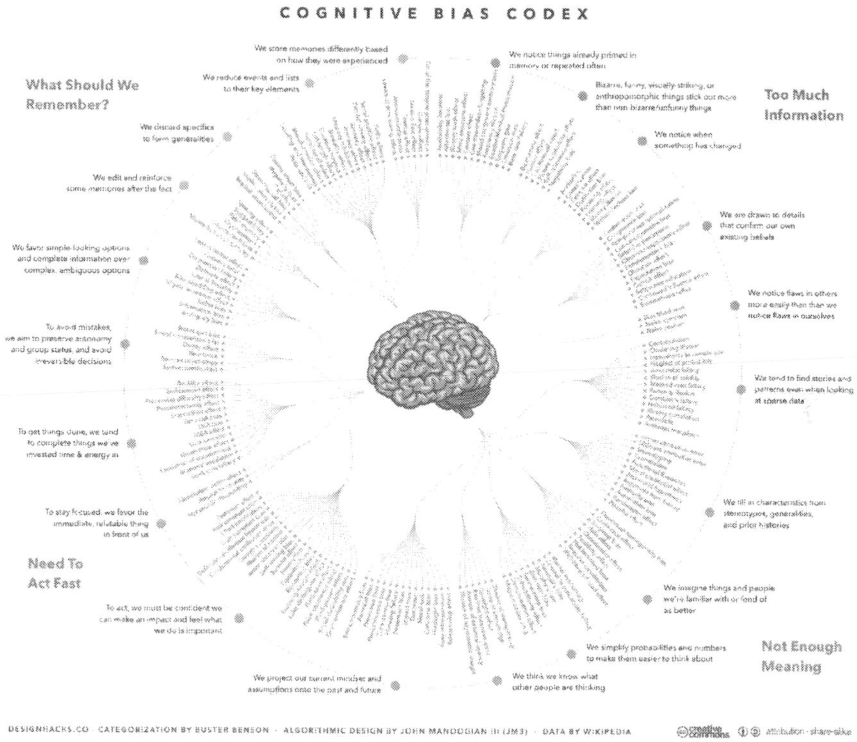

COGNITIVE BIAS CODEX

What Should We
Remember?

We store memories differently based
on how they were experienced

We reduce events and lists
to their key elements

We discard specifics
to form generalities

We edit and reinforce
some memories after the fact

We favor simple-looking options
and complete information over
complex, ambiguous options

To avoid mistakes,
we aim to preserve autonomy
and group status, and avoid
irreversible decisions

To get things done, we tend
to complete things we've
invested time & energy in

To stay focused, we favor the
immediate, relatable thing
in front of us

Need To
Act Fast

To act, we must be confident we
can make an impact and feel what
we do is important

We project our current mindset and
assumptions onto the past and future

We think we know what
other people are thinking

We notice things already primed in
memory or repeated often

Bizarre, funny, visually striking, or
anthropomorphic things stick out more
than non-bizarre/unfunny things

Too Much
Information

We notice when
something has changed

We are drawn to details
that confirm our own
existing beliefs

We notice flaws in others
more easily than we
notice flaws in ourselves

We tend to find stories and
patterns even when looking
at sparse data

We fill in characteristics from
stereotypes, generalities,
and prior histories

We imagine things and people
we're familiar with or fond of
as better

We simplify probabilities and numbers
to make them easier to think about

Not Enough
Meaning

DESIGNHACKS.CO · CATEGORIZATION BY BUSTER BENSON · ALGORITHMIC DESIGN BY JOHN MANOOGIAN III (JM3) · DATA BY WIKIPEDIA · attribution - share-alike

Figure 38 - The Cognitive Bias Codex, which shows over 180+ biases. Cognitive biases can be organized into four categories: biases that arise from too much information, not enough meaning, the need to act quickly, and the limits of memory.

161

The Illusion of Asymmetric Insight — "I know you but you don't know me". This is a social bias that falls under the attribution bias category. Attribution biases refer to cognitive biases where systematic errors are made when people try to find reasons for their own behavior or the behavior of others (Kelley, 1967). The Illusion of Asymmetric Insight makes it seem that **you know someone far better than they could possibly know you**, and also assumes that **you know someone else better than they know themselves.** This applies to groups as well, where a group feels it knows outsiders far better than outsiders could possibly know the group.

This bias leads to misunderstanding important groups like customers and stakeholders. It leads individuals to believe that customer and stakeholder needs and challenges are already known, or that "I know what you need more than you know what you need". Rather than offer true solutions that are based on an objective customer qualification process, the wrong products are pushed onto the customers based off incorrect information produced by the bias (remember the section on proper sales techniques). *End results often include loss of sales, decreased team performance, and lower customer satisfaction.*

This bias normally occurs when the individual has low self-awareness and consists of:

- High Self-Regard
- Low Reality Testing

Over 90% of the leadership development plans I have created where someone is experiencing the Illusion of Asymmetric Insight bias, this combination of emotional skill use is the culprit. In this instance, the EQ360 assessment is the best weapon to battle this bias. Use the results of the EQ360 to generate self-awareness and to craft a development plan that involves careful reduction of Self-Regard (confidence) while simultaneously boosting Reality Testing (seeing things objectively). In my experience, the key difference between middle management and executive leadership is the level of self-awareness that the individual possesses, and an EQ360 can maximize self-awareness and help the middle manager battle the Illusion of Asymmetric Insight bias.

The False Consensus Effect — Another attribution bias, this refers to the idea that **most people think that his or her ideas, beliefs, and values are considered normal, and that the majority of people agree with them.** This leads to a perception of consensus, and incorrectly creates overconfidence, leading to:

- High Self-Regard
- Low Emotional Expression
- Low Impulse Control

This leads to incorrect decision making, false assumptions, and is one of the top enemies of Change Management.

When managers assume that his or her beliefs are in consensus with others in the group, specific details or decisions are glossed over or go undiscussed. Many employees will often not challenge management decisions in the discussion stages, but will offer passive resistance during deployment and change management stages if the program direction is one they are not in agreement with. The end result is a failed change effort, and management is dumbfounded as to why, claiming all along that "everyone agreed to the decisions", when in reality, they never truly confirmed if that was true.

In this instance, the Workplace assessment and general psychological strategies can be deployed to ensure the culture is a "psychologically safe" environment to proactively voice opinions. The False Consensus Effect creates an environment where differing opinions are discouraged, so being aware of this bias ensures it doesn't silently perpetuate change resistance and groupthink.

In addition to high use of Self Regard (confidence) and low use of Emotional Expression (constructive expression of emotions) and Impulse Control (resisting the impulse to act), the Workplace assessment will likely reveal that the individual is also engaged in low use of Empathy (understanding how others feel) and Social Responsibility (social consciousness), so creating a development plan based on balancing these skills is essential.

- High Self-Regard
- Low Emotional Expression
- Low Impulse Control
- Low Empathy

- Low Social Responsibility

It is one of the few biases where the emotional configuration consists of five out-of-balance emotional skills. In addition to self-assessment, creating feedback loops in the form of frequent and informal check-ins, or comfortable conversations, helps battle this bias by promoting feedback and psychological safety. Best-practice is two check-ins per week, no more than five minutes long if verbal and no more than three sentences if written.

Focalism – Also known as Anchoring, this is a decision-making bias where individuals are **overly-reliant on the first piece of information that they hear or put too much importance on the event that happens first.** This leads to incorrect decision-making and sub-optimal negotiation results. Skilled negotiators and car salesmen often exploit this bias by using it to influence someone else's value on an item. For example, if a car salesman wants to sell you a $40,000 car, he may show you a $60,000 car first. Suddenly, the $40,000 car doesn't seem so expensive. Negotiators will offer an initial price for an object or a base salary as an opening action, knowing that it will frame the rest of the discussion. Dietmeyer (2004) wrote an article called "Strategic Negotiation: A Breakthrough Four Step Process for Effective Business Negotiation" in *Kaplan Publishing*, where he illustrated that initial offers have a much stronger influence over the outcome of the negotiation than later counteroffers. Results of the study show those who anchored the negotiation process had significantly better results. Katz and Sosa (2015) wrote an article for *Conflict Resolution Quarterly* highlighting the importance of EI within skilled negotiators. Even in scenarios where the negotiation is distributive (win-lose), or integrative (win-win), and the relationship between the parties ends at negotiation end or continues on, there is a common EI pattern present within individuals that do not anchor successfully and fall victim to this bias. The following is the most common EI configuration present within those who succumb to this bias:

- Low Emotional Self-Awareness
- High Emotional Expression
- Low Assertiveness
- High Flexibility

- Low Reality Testing

McElroy (2007) conducted a study and wrote in *Judgement and Decision Making* that IQ and cognitive ability do not have an effect on anchoring but that personality traits, specifically openness to new experience, does have an influence. This aligns with my experiences of those engaged in high use of Flexibility, which is essentially being too open to new experiences due to boredom or lack of ability to stand one's ground during stressful situations.

In this instance, generating self-awareness should be the key focus to reduce the effects of Anchoring/Focalism. The Workplace assessment, along with a specific coaching method, can generate the self-awareness needed within the client to battle this bias. Best-practice is to ask questions that guide specific event recollection within the client, centered around times of negotiation and purchases. Tease out the underlying emotions that he or she experienced when buying something that drew emotional power, such as a house or a car. Work diligently to help them label every emotion they can recall during the purchasing/negotiating process, and your client will start to see a theme emerge from an EI perspective that most likely will match the EI configuration that I listed. Only then, will they be able to battle this bias in future negotiations, when their Emotional Self-Awareness kicks in and they sense similar emotions developing.

Bandwagon Effect – This is a decision-making bias that is related to groupthink, where **an individual's tendency to believe something increases with the number of others that believe the same.** Individuals will give more weight to the number of subscribers of an idea rather than their own rational decision making processes, resulting in group ineffectiveness and irrationality. One of the most famous works on this topic was a book written by Charles Mackay in 1841 called *Extraordinary Delusions and the Madness of Crowds*. Mackay highlights the bandwagon effect with many notorious tales of irrationality. Most notably was the Dutch Tulip mania, which was a time during the Dutch Golden Age where contract prices for tulip bulbs reached exorbitant levels and then suddenly collapsed. The price of tulip bulbs eventually rose to that of 10 times the annual salary of a skilled craftsman, simply due to the bandwagon effect run amuck in early seventeenth century Europe. The bandwagon effect compounds when group decisions and positions are easily observable, like in politics or public companies. The following is the most common EI configuration present within those who succumb to this bias.

- High Empathy
- Low Assertiveness
- High Flexibility
- Low Stress Tolerance
- Low Independence

Individuals with this particular configuration often feel the collective emotional power of the group, and have FOMO (fear of missing out). The high use of Empathy and Flexibility can render the individual feckless. Combined with a lack of ability to communicate his or her position and an inability to battle stress, individuals take on the position of crowds. An allusion to the *Extraordinary Delusions and the Madness of Crowds*, James Surowiecki wrote in his book, *The Wisdom of Crowds*, that the many can actually be smarter than the few, if the crowd possesses certain criteria that align to EI skills. He wrote that key criteria that crowds must possess are diversity of opinion, independence, decentralization, and aggregation. Essentially, when a crowd uses the EI skills of Assertiveness and Independence, they are able to flip the script and the collective many can be wiser than the lone few. Surowiecki (2004) also highlighted when crowds failed to be more intelligent, suggesting that homogeneity, centralization, division, imitation, and emotionality create the bandwagon effect. These align directly to the EI configuration listed for this bias.

In this instance, a Group Report can identify if a particular team is deficient in these skills. Analyze the Group Report to look for the patterns listed, and then dive into the individual assessment results to identify those who are contributing to the group psychosis. The best coaching principle for this scenario is to promote psychological empowerment and safety. During a team performance workshop, preferably in-person as opposed to virtual, organize the team into sub-groups to discuss the results of the Group Report and introduce the bandwagon effect concept. Promote psychological safety and ensure that the leaders endorse this message. Once the team is able to start having conversations without retaliation, you will be able balance the skills in the EI configuration through targeted group debriefs.

Confirmation Bias – This is a belief and behavioral bias that is the tendency for individuals to **seek out and only remember information that validates one's preconceptions.** Referred to as a systemic error of inductive reasoning, this bias becomes amplified when deeply emotional beliefs are involved, such as in politics or religion. This generates a poor listening ability within individuals, as conversations become more about seeking affirmation rather than information. This bias may be one of the oldest biases known, as Greek historian Thucydides wrote in *The History of the Peloponnesian War* around 431 BC that "for it is a habit of mankind to entrust to careless hope what they long for, and to use sovereign reason to thrust aside what they do not fancy." The bias has also been referred to in the *Divine Comedy*, by Francis Bacon in his philosophical works, and by Russian novelist Leo Tolstoy. Many studies have examined the effect of this bias in finance, law, psychology, health, politics and science.

In my coaching practice, I have come across this bias more than any others, though the EI configuration is one of the least specific. The most common pattern consists of:

- Extremely Low Emotional Self-Awareness
- Low Flexibility

Many leaders who experience this bias are normally very rigid in their ways, and lack an ability to identify their emotions, where the emotions come from, and the slight nuances between them. As the coach, you will need to disinter scenarios from the client's past where she has felt strongly about a particular polarizing viewpoint. Ask about times when they heard information that was counter to their chosen belief, and then help them generate the self-awareness within so that they recognize that simply hearing opposing information is what essentially caused the internal paroxysm.

Clients with low use of Emotional Self-Awareness are some of the most difficult to coach for one main reason. Self-Awareness is one of the EI cornerstones according to Bar-On (2013) and many other EI skills cannot develop without this skill. When a client lacks Emotional Self-Awareness, combined with a rigid decision-making process, the end result is a fertile ground for confirmation bias to thrive. Neurologist Anthony Damasio (1994) wrote in *Descartes' Error* that emotions are not a luxury, but rather essential to our buying behaviors and thinking, and that all rationality required emotional input. Emotions create our preferences from which we choose our products, and logic later substantiates and validates the purchase. Some studies have shown within fMRI neuro-imagery that when consumers evaluate brands, the emotional centers of the brain fire substantially more than the information processing regions.

Similar patterns hold true when affirmation-seeking confirmation bias is present, in that emotions (which the client is unaware of due to low Emotional Self-Awareness), drive hard stances on issues and the facts are cherry picked later to affirm that belief. Much like most of your coaching conversations and engagements, this bias can only be battled through self-discovery within the client. Any of the assessments can accomplish this but I have primarily used the Workplace report and targeted questioning to detect this bias and then crafted a development plan that was dedicated to raising Emotional Self-Awareness first, before focusing on anything else.

Conservatism Bias – Considered an extension of Focalism, this is an information processing bias which refers to **the inclination of individuals to overweigh older information and discount newer information, and continue that belief into future activities.** A famous example of this bias was the slow adoption of the fact that the Earth was round. Though Isaac Newton described the Earth as an ellipsoid in this seventeenth century work, *Principia*, the debate over the spherical Earth dates all the way back to Pythagoras in 500 BC. The idea that the Earth was flat was hard to let go of for many centuries, and many still did not believe it until sailors like Ferdinand Magellan and Christopher Columbus actually sailed the waters. The main difference between Conservatism and Anchoring/Focalism is that this bias is a continuation of belief that extends into future activities and is not contained by a singular event. Similar to Focalism, the following is the most common EI configuration present within those who succumb to this bias:

- Low Emotional Self-Awareness
- High Emotional Expression
- Low Assertiveness
- High Flexibility
- Low Reality Testing

The main difference between coaching to eliminate Focalism and coaching to eliminate Conservatism is that Focalism normally is contained to specific events, such as negotiations or purchases, when Conservatism is an ongoing behavior that permeates other activities, such as views on people, places, companies, finances, etc. Coach to eliminate Conservatism in the same manner as you would Focalism (using the Workplace assessment and targeted questioning), just ensure that you steer focus toward ongoing efforts and beliefs, as opposed to only overweighing information presented first.

Information Bias – This is a cognitive bias where **the individual assumes that more information is always better.** Sometimes referred to as "analysis paralysis", this bias delays action and decision within the individual. This is a common bias that I encounter within leaders of all industries and is normally accompanied by the following EI configuration:

- Low Problem Solving
- Low Independence
- High Flexibility

Leaders that suffer from this bias are often unable to use emotions effectively in their decision-making processes resulting in inaction. Combined with a high use of Flexibility, individuals do not feel the emotional pressure to make decisions quickly, yet also lack the Independence needed to make decisions on their own. In my coaching practice, I always promote the idea that "finished beats perfect", coined by the French Enlightenment writer Voltaire, to try and promote action and growth. This bias creates scenarios where the opportunity cost of the additional analysis exceeds any benefits that could be gained from the new information, or essentially, the situation has come to a point where no additional information could create a better outcome.

Much like the Conservatism bias, this particular predisposition has a storied history, and has appeared in Shakespeare's *Hamlet*, in Winston Churchill speeches during World War II, and within corporate strategy books dating back to the 1960s (Kennedy, 2006). Perhaps the most famous example of "analysis paralysis" is Aesop's fable of the *Fox and the Cat*. While discussing methods of escape should the hunters come, the fox boasts that he has many methods of escape and the cat claims she only knows of one. Once the hunters ultimately arrive, the cat escapes the one way she knows how, while the fox ponders all of the ways he can escape, and is eventually caught while still in the decision-making process.

Psychologist Barry Schwartz devised the term "Paradox of Choice", where he discusses how increased choice or seeking superfluous information leads to paralysis, anxiety and indecision. His research suggests that overthinking or overanalyzing kills creativity, lowers performance on highly cognitive tasks, destroys will power, and creates unhappiness. I have used the Workplace assessment to identify the EI configuration, but the best way to identify this bias is with the EQ360, as this will give you clear insight into the difference between their decision-making identity and reputations. The most effective coaching methodology for someone that suffers from this bias is to infuse within them the power of deadlines. Being able to self-create deadlines, clients combine this with public accountability to force decisions even in times of discomfort. Make sure that you don't over promote fast decisions however, as I have seen clients quickly become addicted to swift decision making and go from "analysis paralysis" all the way over to "extinct by instinct", which is when someone makes a fatal decision via gut-reaction alone.

Ostrich Effect – This is a belief and behavioral bias **when individuals avoid information that is perceived to be negative**. Predominantly found within behavioral finance, the bias refers to when investors purposely avoid negative financial data. Even though it is an urban legend that an ostrich will bury her head in the sand to avoid danger, the term for this bias still pertains to those who purposely avoid negative information, hoping that self-imposed blindness to the situation will cause it to evanesce.

The EI configuration for this bias is unique and I find it to be rare within executive leadership. Generally speaking, this bias seems to be prevalent among newer managers within low stress environments. The EI configuration is as follows:

- Low Problem Solving
- High Optimism
- High Independence

Leaders within low stress environments often do not feel the emotional pressure of organizational decision making, resulting in low use of Problem Solving. Combine this element with a high use of Optimism, the managers feel that they can simply bury their head in the sand and everything will turn out OK once they arise. High use of Independence is also present, as these managers often exhibit a freedom from the emotional pressures of others that allows them to feel safe while buried in the sand. Being related to Confirmation bias, the most effective coaching mechanism for this is the EQ360. The individual is most likely unaware that he or she is perceived as an ostrich and engages in self-imposed situational blindness, so the verbatim analysis will be essential in helping the leader become self-aware. If you sense during your intake that your client may be susceptible to this bias, while setting up the EQ360, write in specific questions asking the respondents about how the subject responds during situations of increased pressure or when a binary decision needs to be made. The verbatim analysis will be essential to illuminating this behavior to your client, who is most likely unaware that they engage in this bias.

Curse of Knowledge – Omnipresent within technical environments, this bias refers to **the tendency of individuals to assume that everyone around them has a certain amount of knowledge.** A cognitive bias, those who suffer from this "forget" what it is like to not know something and are unable to effectively communicate with those who do not know what the individual knows. This is one of the biggest drawbacks within organizations that promote the best technical expert or engineer to the leadership ranks. Newly minted people managers, who are by promotional pathway designated the smartest of the workers, are in positions where they now need to lead a team. Deviating from direct knowledge application and diverting toward delegation, the new manager will get frustrated when delegated tasks are not completed to satisfaction and he often forgets that subordinates might not know all that he knows.

A common EI configuration for this bias is as follows.

- Low Reality Testing
- High Self-Regard
- Low Empathy
- Low Interpersonal Relationships

When I consult companies on the best way to design leadership pipeline and manager onboarding programs, this one bias is always in the forefront of my mind. New technical-experts-turned-managers will understandably have high Self-Regard, due to their recent promotion, which serves as vindication for their lifelong dedication to their technical craft. This leads to a low use of Reality Testing, where the new leadership responsibility clouds judgement and realistic thinking. Managers will push Empathy and Interpersonal Relationships to the side, still relying on technical expertise to accomplish the team goals, rather than focus on leadership and people management. All of my onboarding programs will have an assessment of self-awareness for technical leaders, ensuring that they are well-equipped to understand that technical expertise does not always translate to effective people leadership. In your coaching practice, design your onboarding programs and succession plans around promoting awareness of the gap in people leadership ability that commonly exists within technical leaders. Create training material that reminds new leaders of how there are varying levels of knowledge within the new team, and also promote psychologically safe conversations between the new team and team leader. Follow up with a Group Report in 6 to 12 months to ensure that safe conversations are taking place, and that the leader hasn't become unaware and surrendered to the *Curse of Knowledge*.

Empathy Gap – A cognitive bias where **individuals underestimate the effect that visceral drives have on our own attitudes and actions.** Those who suffer from this bias have a difficult time differentiating between their own emotions and the perceived emotional states of others, often resulting in poor articulation of others feelings on the low end and completely misreading situational attributes and behavioral origins on the high end. Remember, Empathy is the skill of recognizing how someone else feels, and the ability to articulate the description of that feeling to others, with respect. If someone is simply engaged in low use of Empathy alone, he or she would not be able to recognize or articulate. Those that suffer from the Empathy Gap take it a step further and inadvertently attribute their own personal state to others and find it difficult to comprehend those that are currently experiencing different emotional states.

Carnegie Mellon University psychologist George Loewenstein conducted a study in 2003 where he tested the "hot-cold" Empathy Gap within university gym students. Two groups of students – one who hadn't started exercising and the other who was at the end of their workout – were asked to read a story about hikers who got lost in the wilderness. The study facilitators asked each individual about which feeling would be worse between hunger or thirst. Those who had just finished their workout and were feeling the state of extreme thirst, were much more likely to say that thirst was a worse feeling than hunger, as opposed to the group who hadn't started working out yet. Those who experience this bias, not only cannot relate to how others feel that are experiencing other emotional states, they carelessly project their own feelings onto others. In leadership, this generates a recognizable EI configuration, which is as follows:

- Low Empathy
- Low Emotional Self-Awareness
- Low Reality Testing
- High Assertiveness

In coaching, this is an important bias to be aware of. Empathy and Emotional Self-Awareness are the cornerstones of EI, and this particular bias happens to consist of low use of both. The Empathy Gap bias extends past low use of Empathy alone because those who suffer from this not only cannot understand how others feel that are in different emotional states, but assume their current emotional states are diktat and they erroneously apply it to business situations. An EQ360 is essential in this situation, because the results will most likely show wildly varying reputations. At first, this will confuse the client, because he will be unaware of the wavering reputations. Like with most syndromes and biases that lack in Emotional Self-Awareness, boosting this skill first will be paramount. It will be up to you as coach to use the results of the EQ360 to show how the varying reputations are a result of different emotional projections driving distance between the rater groups. Work to increase Emotional Self-Awareness, drive situational awareness with the reputation distance, and then slowly introduce the concept of the Empathy Gap, allowing for the client to self-discover individual instances where he may have unconsciously imposed visceral drives onto the unwilling. Luckily, I haven't found this bias to be very common, as those in leadership rarely perpetuate low use of both Empathy and Emotional Self-Awareness. However, I have found this to be most prevalent in workplace bullies and those who have an authoritarian leadership style.

Framing Effect – A cognitive bias where **choices are influenced by the way the information is presented** to the individual. Aldert Vrij wrote in his book *Detecting Lies and Deceit,* about a scenario where study participants were shown a traffic accident and then asked questions about the incident. One group was asked about how fast the cars were going when they "contacted" and another group was asked about how fast the cars were going when they "smashed". Those who were asked about the cars smashing, reported higher speeds. In addition, even though there was no glass breakage in the video, those asked about glass breaking who were in the "smashed" group, reported 32% higher that they remember glass breaking. The way the question was framed, changed the actual memories of study participants (Vrij, 2008).

This bias is important to recognize because it makes leaders susceptible to impressionable peers and direct reports. Like I discussed earlier, decisions within organizations are rarely made solely based on objective hard data, and subjective factors often play a major role in leadership decision making. Leaders who are susceptible to the Framing Effect, might be easily manipulated by Machiavellians and schizoids, so developing leaders around effective and objective decision-making will be vital. A common EI configuration is as follows:

- Low Reality Testing
- High Empathy
- Low Independence
- Low Problem Solving

Leaders who suffer from this bias are often accused of "listening too well". High use of Empathy, combined with low use of reality testing and independence leads to overly acute listening of nuances and word reflections. While leaders believe they are being punctilious, in reality they are overweighing words within communications and reframing the entire conversation around certain words. I have found this to be especially ubiquitous in virtual environments, where the majority of directives and communications are written. Think about how you yourself read emails. You most likely read emails from others, replicating in your brains the voice you hear them speak, in the tone you hear them speak. All too often, that tone and voice reflection is influenced by the last correspondence we had with the individual. If you had a bad encounter with your boss, you will most likely read subsequent emails with a bit of disdain, since written correspondence does not have an updated voice reflection that accompanies it. There is also a tendency to read written correspondence more than once. This leads to misappropriation of words that were most likely not given much thought by the original author.

One of the best ways to battle this bias is to first establish the EI configuration via a Workplace report, then work with the client to understand what influenced decision making after reading a directive, such as an email or memo. Explain the Framing Effect (most clients I've worked with had never heard about it), then walk back through examples of recent decisions and see if the individual can recall specific words or phrases that influenced that decision. If specific words can be recalled, chances are, they accidentally let those words frame the context of the correspondence. This is a self-awareness bias that is usually easily dismantled, once the leader is aware of its presence. Eliminating this bias will ensure leaders are making sound decisions that are not rooted within random framing of information intake.

IKEA Effect – Derived from the furniture retailer, this cognitive bias is **when individuals place a much higher value on items that they assembled themselves**, regardless of actual end state value. This becomes important in modern business because there is a revolving nature to organizational projects, especially in publically traded companies. Many items of value, such as engineering endeavors and IT projects, are often created by individuals on rotation, meaning that they are brought in to address a specific challenge, and then rotated off to another part of the business. Those that suffer from the IKEA Effect will often feel that items she created are much more valuable than those created by others, solely because of the fact that she created them. This is important in management, specifically within projects that fail. I have noticed that leaders who are susceptible to this bias have difficulty letting go of projects that have failed. While no second thought would be given to other failed projects, ones that were created and assembled by the leaders I coach are often given much heavier weight than others. Conversely, there is a tendency to look at products that "weren't created here" and assume they are of lessor value, simply because the current team did not create it. A common EI configuration is as follows:

- Low Reality Testing
- Low Independence
- Low Flexibility
- High Self-Actualization

This configuration is characterized by an unwillingness to be objective, a lack of ability to be emotionally independent of others, a rigid management stance, and a pursuit of goals that are unrealistic. Those who can't let go often believe that her legacy will be affected, and Self-Actualization is heavily used, meaning that she will try to ensure that every work stream ever started by her results in success. A Workplace report will help you identify this bias, along with targeted questions during the discovery phase that focuses on times that the leader was unable to let go. Allowing the leader to self-discover that letting go is much more productive then trying to save all project orphans, will do wonders for the leader in terms of personal development. In my experience, this is one of the easiest biases to identify and coach the client out of, because historical project success is normally considered binary. The client will quickly see that there is no merit or value in harping in the past, and that no everlasting reputation comes from individual project failure (or success).

Allais Paradox and the Certainty/Pseudocertainty Effects – This paradox refers to a breach in decision theory and contains the Certainty and Pseudocertainty Effect biases. The Allais Paradox is named after French Economist Maurice Allais who served as a major inspiration to Kahneman's eventual work in cognitive bias. He described in a 1953 paper that **an individual's decision making can be inconsistent with expected utility theory** (the theory that individuals will choose the course that results in the highest expected utility or outcome). To describe the paradox, consider the following, where participants are asked to choose between the following scenarios:

Experiment 1: Choose between:

A) $1 million for sure

B) 10% chance of receiving $5 million, 89% chance of receiving $1 million, 1% chance of receiving nothing

Experiment 2: Choose between:

C) 11% chance of receiving $1 million, 89% change of receiving nothing

D) 10% chance of receiving $5 million, 90% chance of receiving nothing

The expected value for option A is $1 million and for option B is $1.39 million. As expected, most participants chose option A within experiment 1, despite the lower overall mathematical value. Kahneman and Tversky would eventually label this the Certainty Effect where people tend to prefer certain outcomes despite higher value in a different scenario, even if the risk of no value is as small as 1% (Kahneman & Tversky, 1979). This suggests that people give extra value to scenarios that are totally absent of risk. In experiment 2, if similar decision-making processes as experiment 1 were followed, participants would prefer option C, but in the study, most participants chose option D. In the first experiment, the less risky choice was preferred over a higher expected utility, while in the second experiment, a higher expected utility ($0.11 million expected utility in option C and $0.50 million expected utility in option D) was preferred over the less risky choice (Allais, 1953). Allais essentially proved that decision making under risk violates the expected utility hypothesis. This is what Kahneman and Tversky labelled the Pseudocertainty Effect, where although people prefer certainty over uncertainty, if the scenario is described or approached differently, individuals will prefer or ignore the uncertainty that was previously rejected in a preceding scenario. In multi-stage decision making, those falling victim to the Pseudocertainty Effect bias often reject the uncertainty of previous scenarios or decision stages when evaluating a later stage, which was evident when those who chose option A then subsequently chose option D. The Allais Paradox proved that humans do not always act in the best interest of maximizing utility or minimizing risk, and that decision-making processes can align with certainty or uncertainty, depending on perceived risk, how the question is framed (Framing Effect), and of course, the EI of the decision-maker.

Koçaslan (2014) wrote in the Journal of *Neuroquantology* in a paper called "Quantum Interpretation of Decision Making Under Risk" that those who experience irrationality, or behave in a "different reality", often make different decisions under risk than others. This means that IQ, personality, and decision-making theories such as the expected utility hypothesis, do little to predict how one will make important decisions while under risk, because decisions are often made before risk is assessed in our rational brains. EI however, can irradiate irrationality and help those that exist within different realities generate the needed self-awareness to realize that they may be falling victim to this paradox and the biases that dwell within it.

As a coach, you should keep this paradox in mind if the leader tells you during discovery that he has received feedback describing an erratic or unpredictable decision-making style, and direct reports are often confused as to project direction or the company vision, since direction seems to "change" often. In this scenario, an EQ360 is vital to discovering the existence of this paradox and the Certainty/Pseudocertainty Effects. Combined with the feedback of possessing a fitful decision making style, you will most likely discover competing reputations that vary wildly across rater groups, and a common EI configuration is as follows:

- High Decision Making
- High Independence
- Low Emotional Self-Awareness
- Low Impulse Control

Leaders with this EI configuration find it too easy emotionally to make decisions and often do not feel the emotional pressure that comes from risky decisions. Combined with an inability to delay those decisions, the Allais Paradox has an environment to thrive. Leaders will often be independent of the emotions and input from others, while simultaneously lacking in the emotional awareness to realize it. Like with all other configurations that contain low use of Emotional Self-Awareness, raising this EI skill is paramount and should be considered your first coaching task. Have the leader keep a decision diary for an agreed upon timeframe, and when they are jotting down important decisions that involve risk, make sure they also capture what emotional factors led to that decision. During each coaching session, discuss the decisions in the diary, the perceived risk of the decisions and what emotions led to them, and any outcomes of those decisions. Also, ensure that each session contains dedicated time to discuss the reputation distances and investigate any cognitive dissonance or unintended reputation distance, as discussed in the Advanced 360 Interpretation section.

Actor-Observer Bias & the Fundamental Attribution Error – This is a social bias that refers **to the tendency for individuals to make different attributions depending on whether they are the actor or the observer** in a given milieu. The actors often overemphasize the influence of the environment and underemphasize the influence of internal characteristics, like personality, in any given situation, but reverse the attribution and overemphasize internal trait influence and underemphasize environment when they are the observer. Essentially, those who suffer from this bias will consider situational forces when attributing their own behaviors, but will overly focus on the internal traits of others when attributing other people's behaviors (Baumeister & Bushman, 2014). This bias is often considered one of the central barriers of effective communication. The Fundamental Attribution Error simply refers to the external behavior attribution only, where the individual overemphasizes trait-based explanations and underemphasizes environmental-based explanations for determining causes of behavior (essentially only the "observer" component). When someone applies the actor-observer bias toward an entire group or team, it is then referred to as the ultimate attribution error.

Malle (2006) published in the *Psychological Bulletin* a study titled "The Actor-Observer Asymmetry in Attribution: A (surprising) Meta-Analysis." This study was a meta-analysis on 173 published studies that examined the actor-observer hypothesis, and Malle determined that the asymmetry only held when the actor was highly idiosyncratic. His meta-analysis determined that there was not enough evidence to prove the commonality of the bias across workplace environments; it only appeared within situations when individuals behaved erratically.

One area of talent management that I see this bias run amuck is within performance reviews and rating systems. Many companies struggle with performance rating systems and it is becoming trendy for many organizations to completely eliminate the archaic practice that rose to prominence during the times of American vaudeville. The reason is because modern organizational research is determining with increasing efficacy that organizational fit and environment is a key component of individual and team performance. Leaders that suffer from this bias often overly attribute poor performance from team members to internal factors, while ignoring psycho-social factors. Unfortunately, getting organizations to ditch or revamp the entire performance review process is almost impossible, but developing the EI within leaders to remove idiosyncratic attributions is achievable.

I tend to prefer the uniqueness and peculiarity of idiosyncratic behavior; it just makes the world and the workplace much more interesting. So, when I encounter this particular bias, the focus isn't to eliminate the oddities, but to generate awareness of the bias that complements the quirks. A common EI configuration is as follows:

- Low Reality Testing
- High Independence
- Low Emotional Self-Awareness
- Low Social Responsibility

Leaders with this configuration often do not have a strong sense of emotional self or the emotions associated with external reality, which is essentially the core component of this bias. Combined with an ability to not rely on others for emotional stability and an absence of directing emotional energy toward the larger system, leaders with this combination often find themselves falling victim to this bias. Since the majority of individuals I coach who suffer from the actor-observer bias are leaders, a Leadership report is the best method to battle this bias. Much like the Workplace report, the emotional profile generated will provide enough information when combined with targeted questioning and discovery to determine if this bias is present, and the additional intelligence from the Leadership report will help target your coaching questions toward specific tendencies that the leader has in performance rating. The focus should be on the leader's biases and rating behaviors that result from the idiosyncrasies, not removing the idiosyncrasies themselves.

Halo Effect – This cognitive bias is a specific type of confirmation bias that was coined by one of the original discoverers of emotional-social intelligence, Edward Thorndike. He discovered that **an observer's overall impression of an individual, brand, or company, affected other unknown traits about the subject.** Thorndike introduced the term in his 1920 article "A Constant Error in Psychological Ratings", where he discovered that when military officers rated individuals, ratings were too high and too even with special qualities that started the trend in the rating. In other words, when an officer rated a solider high initially in a particular area, such as leadership, character, intelligence, etc., the subsequent ratings all benefited from the symbolic halo of the individual. Dion, Berscheid and Walster (1972) later investigated the relationship between physical attractiveness and the halo effect, publishing a study called "What is Beautiful is Good" in the *Journal of Personality and Social Psychology*. Students at the University of Minnesota were asked to view pictures of individuals who were considered attractive, average, or not attractive, and then asked to judge along 27 different personality traits and predict certain life outcomes and social attributes. The study participants overwhelmingly attributed better ratings to those that were deemed physically attractive. The beautiful people were considered to have more socially desirable traits, have more success in life, have happier marriages, and command higher salaries. In essence, the symbolic halo created by the initial physical attractiveness skewed the subsequent ratings for the individual. Though not as many studies have investigated the reverse, the horn effect refers to when an observer has an initial negative predisposition about something the subsequent ratings will have a penchant for the negative.

Much like the actor-observer bias, the halo/horn effects are still prevalent today within organizational performance rating systems. Because of these biases, first impressions are more important than ever, because those impressions can affect the individual's performance ratings, salary increases, and career trajectories, while she is under the same manager. Swider, Murray, and Harris (2016) conducted a study on initial impressions and published their findings in the *Journal of Applied Psychology*. They confirmed much of the extant literature on the topic of first impressions and found that the pre-interview stage of rapport building, even within highly structured interviews, had more influence over the final interview scores than any of the actual interview content. The study authors even go so far as to suggest that rapport building should be removed from the interview process entirely, because of the weighty influence of the first impression and the lasting effects created. Essentially, once the halo or horn is in place, it is tough to alter perceptions. This bias leads to faulty hiring decisions and indecorous performance ratings. A common EI configuration for leaders that suffer from this is as follows:

- Low Reality Testing
- Low Emotional Self-Awareness
- High Empathy

Leaders that suffer from this bias will often not be tuned into the emotional reality of many situations, leading to incorrect performance attributions and labelling. The low use of Emotional Self-Awareness leads individuals to become unaware of the origin of many emotions, incorrectly attaching imprints from rapport building or first impressions to assumed levels of skill. The key distinction of this emotional configuration among other biases is the high use of Empathy. Leaders will often feed off of the emotional positivity that is felt during rapport building or first impressions, and seek to multiply that reciprocal emotional euphoria by prolonging the emotional response. In essence, the leader feels good because the person she is interacting with feels good, and the leader's emotional brain becomes conditioned to find ways to perpetuate and replicate the emotional high, and incorrectly attaches the emotional response from the first impression to all subsequent meetings and interactions. Like most biases, a Workplace report and a direct dedication to raising Emotional Self-Awareness are key to battling this bias. If you suspect that your client may have a predilection for first impressions, try to acquire performance rating data from his or her direct reports, and ask targeted questions that line up historical experience with the performance rating data. It will be fairly easy to enlighten your client that she suffers from the halo effect, if you can show them how their impressions guide their performance ratings.

Bizarreness Effect – The bizarreness effect is a memory bias that refers to **the tendency for individuals to remember bizarre material over common material.** An important distinction is that the bizarre information itself does not enhance memory, but that the information itself is essentially more distinguishing, meaning that the encoding of the sensory input is easier. McDaniel and Einstein (1986) wrote in the *Journal of Experimental Psychology: Learning, Memory, and Cognition*, that bizarre images were more easily accessed than common images by memory, indicating that significant mnemonic enhancement can be derived from bizarre imagery. However, their findings did not advocate that memory is best facilitated by making imagery as bizarre as possible, meaning that there is no positive correlation between heightened levels of bizarreness and speed of memory recall. Rather, bizarreness and common imagery is binary, meaning that once an item is deemed bizarre by an individual, no increased bizarreness yields any faster memory recall. McDaniel and Einstein updated their findings a decade later in a study called "The Bizarreness Effect: It's Not Surprising, It's Complex". They discussed how bizarre items contradict expectations within an individual and create a startle response. That startle response stimulates additional mental processing functions and increases cognitive load, enhancing the encoding processes in the sensory cortexes and increasing memory creation functions in the hippocampus. Depending on the memory retrieval method of each individual, bizarre imagery is more "hard-coded" than common imagery due to the increased cognitive load used to process it, and the distinctiveness of the imagery combined with the added startle response component, allows for faster recollection in order-based retrieval strategies.

This bias is important because it exists on the opposite side of the spectrum of the halo effect. The halo effect initially deals with first impressions, the bizarre effect deals with lasting impressions. This bias affects how others will remember us, long after we are gone. There is a famous axiom in organizational change and project management, that is "whenever we wanted to persuade our staff to support a particular project we always tried to break their hearts." The bizarre effect, is one of the cognitive biases that venture over to the dark side of EI.

Until now, you probably assumed that EI was all about the power of good, but it has a dark side, and those individuals who are highly emotionally intelligent know how to wield the power for sinister and malevolent agendas, and the bizarre effect is one of the most used methods. One of the most influential leaders in recent memory spent years studying the emotional effects of his own body language, carefully crafting specific hand gestures and speaking mannerisms that allowed him to become a mesmerizing and spellbinding public speaker. He would practice his hand gestures for hours in front of mirrors and focus groups, asking about the different emotions that slight tweaks in gestures created. He would use the bizarre effect in his movements and his messages to use the power of emotions to sway a nation of people. That leader was Adolf Hitler.

Since that time, many researchers and historians have researched how world leaders and politicians use the dark side of EI, as discussed earlier in the Machiavellian section. Sometimes referred to as the awestruck or dumbstruck effect, researchers at the University of Cambridge discovered that when a leader gave an inspiring speech, filled with emotion that had bizarre characteristics, the audience not only was able to recall many more parts of the speech, or more specifically, how they felt during certain times of the speech, but that there was likely less scrutiny of the overall message.

Of course, the bizarreness effect isn't only used for evil. Many attribute the effectiveness of Martin Luther King Jr.'s speeches to his mastery of emotive discourse, and many organizational leaders consistently use bizarre imagery to break people's hearts in an effort to persuade. The reason is because the limbic system comprises of a few major brain functions, such as the amygdala and the hippocampus, that are responsible for memory formation. Initially, the hippocampus works in conjunction with sensory processing regions dispersed in the outermost layer of the brain called the neocortex to form the new memories. When a memory is initially created, the hippocampus rapidly combines this information into a single memory, indexing information from the sensory processing regions. This is why damage to the hippocampus by injury or neurodegenerative disorder produces anterograde amnesia, which is the incapacity to form new memories. The hippocampus can no longer retrieve mnemonic information collected in the neocortex. So essentially, all memory formation happens here. We also know that the amygdala performs a primary role in the processing of memory, decision-making, and emotional reactions, so essentially, emotions and memory formation happen in the same place since the amygdala and hippocampus are roommates! This is the scientific reason that people will always remember how you made them feel, while rarely remembering what it is you say. For this bias, it isn't one you coach someone out of doing it (they know they are doing it and using it to their advantage), you coach others how to identify it and not be susceptible to it. Those who are susceptible to the bizarreness effect often possess a specific EI configuration, which is as follows:

- Low Reality Testing
- Low Problem Solving
- Low Independence
- High Empathy
- High Interpersonal Relationships

Leaders that suffer from this will often feel the emotions that are purposely being emoted and feel disproportionately connected to the individual creating the effect. Being unable to use the emotional skills associated with realistic thinking and emotional individuality, the leader who suffers from this effect will often feel passionate after a public speech or performance. A Workplace report will reveal this configuration, and the proper coaching technique consists of establishing patience within the client. As the coach, it will be important to identify specific emotional triggers that cause certain courses of action within your client, and installing a pause before those triggers within your client's decision making process. Simple, yet effective, measures of controlled breathing or counting to a predefined number (like 10 or 100), are effectual in slowing down decision-making processes in order to allow enhanced cognition to take place. Also, establishing a system of checks and balances, such as encouraging the client to have an accountability partner, will ensure that certain courses of action can be delayed and decided upon after the bizarreness effect has abated.

Humor Effect - In a 2007 article titled "Current Directions in Psychological Science", researchers discovered **that humor can moderate and counteract the effects of mental exhaustion**, and that humor could provide energy and relief in situations of enmity or rancor (Baumeister, 2007). To test this theory, researchers conducted a study and gathered 74 students and asked them to perform mentally exhausting tasks that consisted of finding every occurrence of the letter "e" within a two-page text and crossing it out. Some students were then randomly assigned to watching a video containing humorous material or non-humorous content. Following the video, the students were asked to complete an unwinnable game. The students who watched the humorous content before the unwinnable game, demonstrated twice the persistence of the other group (Cheng & Wang, 2014). Cheng and Wang concluded in their paper "Examining the Energizing Effects of Humor", written in the *Journal of Business and Psychology*, that humor was important in energizing others to do tasks that were not considered desirable.

From a memory perspective, humorous items are more easily remembered than non-humorous items, due to the increased cognitive load and processing time that the hippocampus endures. The emotional arousal caused by the humor creates a more memorable experience, aligning with certain elements of the bizarreness effect. Those who are master manipulators of these two biases will oftentimes create experiences for others that are both bizarre and humorous.

This is a particular bias that leaders should use to his or her advantage, when the team's animus toward certain business outcomes cannot be avoided. Rather than trying to avoid this bias, leaders can wield this bias toward a utilitarian outcome. But first, it is important to understand that there are many differing theories of humor. Some of the top theories are:

- Relief theory, which posits that humor is created when psychological tension is reduced.
- Superiority theory, which describes the notion that humans laugh about the misfortunes of others.
- Incongruous juxtaposition theory, which claims that humor is perceived at the moment of incongruity between concepts and real objects in any given situation.
- Script-based semantic theory, which essentially is the portrayal of a punch line after a given dialogue.
- Computational-Neural theory, which is a timing based humor which is added to situational ambiguity.
- Ontic-Epistemic theory, which asserts that laughter is a response to cognitive impasse.
- Misattribution theory, which claims that humans actually do not know why something makes them laugh.
- Defense mechanism theory, which states that humans laugh in response to disarming stressful situations.
- O'Shannon humor theory, which is a combination of multiple theories and posits that humans laugh depending on context, information, awareness, and inhibitors.

Since humor is often considered a good thing, I often do not coach clients to become immune to humor or to stop using humor within work functions. Rather, I encourage clients to embrace humor in their daily lives and seek out leaders who are masters of this art. Since there are many theories and models of humor, leaders who can successfully wield humor often have a specific EI configuration, which is as follows:

- High Optimism
- Balanced Assertiveness
- Balanced Empathy
- High Self-Regard

Leaders who masterfully wield this bias are often overly optimistic, yet have their assertive and empathic skills in check. Anyone who uses humor to deescalate situations and deliver bad news, are often overly confident, but in this scenario, it isn't necessarily an undesired configuration. An EQ360 will often reveal this bias, because the individual results will show the above configuration, and the verbatim section of the EQ360 will allow for tailored feedback on this area. If you suspect that your leader uses the humor effect, write in a few questions that ask the raters to specifically identify the leader's diffusing techniques, and see if the bias reveals itself. Unlike other biases, I believe that this one is necessary and important in leadership, and should be identified and encouraged within more leaders in the workplace, as long as the humor is performed well. Brooks and Bitterly (2017) wrote an article in the *Wall Street Journal* titled "Why it Pays Off to be Funny at Work – Usually", that humor can come across as performance enhancing when done well, but can offend and alienate people when done poorly. Humor done well can burnish an individual's image and empower teams, because people communicate more effectively when they can joke with one another. Brooks and Bitterly cite research which shows that sarcasm boosted creativity and that humor among groups also created an environment that fostered greater support and more constructive criticism. When a series of studies at University of Pennsylvania's Wharton School on presentation style and the inclusion of humor were conducted, it was found that the use of humor also demonstrated more confidence and intelligence. However, within situations where a serious tone was desired, such as within a customer service function, humor was considered off-putting and non-serious, resulting in lower reviews of customer service experiences. Essentially, humor is normally a great thing in the workplace, as long as it's done well and in the right environment.

Zeigarnik Effect – This memory error bias refers to the notion that **people will remember unfinished or uncompleted tasks better than completed ones.** First discovered by Bluma Zeigarnik in 1927, she first studied the effect after her professor, famous psychologist Kurt Lewin, noticed that a restaurant server could better recall unpaid orders, but then lost the memory recall once the bill had been paid. Essentially, Zeigarnik discovered that once a task is started, a specific task-tension in the brain is created and does not dissipate until the task is completed. If the task is interrupted, the task tension remains, making cognitive recall easier. Nicholas and Cohen investigated the Zeigarnik effect on decision making, publishing a paper in the *Journal of Judgement and Decision Making* called "The Effect of Interruption on the Decision-Making Process". In the experiment, participants were asked to complete a set of four different gambles. On half of the attempts, the participants were interrupted with a different task, and with those participants, a cost was incurred. The interruption increased the time and amount of information needed to make subsequent decisions, and the results were consistent with the idea that participants were able to recall the pre-interruption information easier, while the task was yet to be completed (Nicholas & Cohen, 2016).

Essentially, this bias has two very important implications for leadership and decision making. First, those who multitask and juggle many projects simultaneously, require extra information to reach the same decision making point than those who do not multitask, due to the lasting task-tensions from the uncompleted tasks that require extra cognitive processing power. Multitasking has been shown to reduce overall performance and effectiveness, as Judd (2015) wrote in the *Australasian Journal of Educational Technology* that multitasking negatively impacted students' learning and the ability to manage and complete competing tasks.

Second, managers who have many direct reports, will often be able to recall those individuals who always "appear busy", better than those who complete work in a timely manner. So, while being busy does not equate to being productive, managers who suffer from this bias will be able to more easily recall the work efforts of the busy versus the completed efforts of the productive, leading to misattributions in performance ratings and overall praise.

Leaders who suffer from this bias have unfortunately been conditioned over time to believe that frantic busyness or visual frustration while performing work functions equates to productivity, because they, and others, can more easily remember all of the tasks that have yet to be completed, better than those that have since been completed. From an organizational perspective, it is obvious why this bias can be dangerous. Leaders who suffer from this bias often have a specific EI configuration which is as follows:

- High Problem Solving
- High Flexibility
- Low Stress Tolerance
- Low Emotional Self-Awareness

Individuals with this configuration will be prone to more starts than stops, lack the ability to manage the stress that accompanies unfinished projects (which is why more dedication and attention is directed toward them), and also lack the emotional awareness needed to realize they are being affected by the bias. If your client suffers from this bias, a Workplace report will be sufficient to identify the configuration, as well as targeted questioning around stack ranking of team members. In my coaching practice, I encounter this bias frequently when I am brought in to examine why certain managers misattribute performance rankings to team members that is incongruent with the overall team or leadership impression. Through targeted questioning, ask the client about his best team members, and see if a theme develops that highlights a rating style that has a predilection towards the busy versus the productive. Like with any bias that encompasses low Emotional Self-Awareness, first work to increase the use of this skill, then illume the bias by showing the client a pattern of performance rating misattribution that historically favored the busy versus the productive.

Primacy Effect – Another memory bias, the primacy effect **is the notion that individuals will better recall primary information over subsequent information.** Similar to anchoring, information that is presented first has a better chance of recall than information presented later on. This is a major decision-making bias, that has shown to drastically affect important organizational objectives and even court cases. Pennington (1982) discovered that witness testimony order affected verdicts, discovering that more guilty verdicts were delivered when the strongest witnesses for the prosecution were presented first rather than last (Pennington, 1982). Nahari and Ben-Shakhar (2013) wrote a paper called "Primacy Effect in Credibility Judgements: The Vulnerability of Verbal Cues to Biases Interpretations" in the *Journal of Applied Cognitive Psychology*, finding that credibility judgements were affected by the order of the information presented to the study participants. Much like with court trials, the researchers determined that information that is presented first heavily affects the eventual outcome or judgement, as that prime information is used to make initial impressions, and all interpreted information that followed formed a basis to substantiate that information. Many other biases, such as confirmation, anchoring, first-impression, etc., have a genesis within the primacy effect, however there is a clear demarcation between primacy and focalism. This bias is different than focalism/anchoring (a decision-making bias) because it is a memory recall bias. Once the decision is made it ventures into focalism. It is an important distinction because memory recall can affect behaviors and judgement, without an official decision ever taking place. Many of us act and behave in certain ways, using information that we recall to guide those behaviors, even if we never come to a definite conclusion about that information.

Even though they exist within different bias classes, they can be identified and coached the same way. The following is the most common EI configuration present within those who succumb to this bias:

- Low Emotional Self-Awareness
- High Emotional Expression
- High Flexibility
- Low Reality Testing

Use the Workplace assessment to discover the configuration and use targeted questioning to discover this bias. My favorite coaching technique if I suspect this bias is to run a mini, yet unscientific, experiment. Show your client a list of numbers at the start of your coaching session that are out of order, with more memorable numbers occurring toward the end. For example, your list could be 9, 2, 7, 47, 200, 666, 99. Subjectively speaking, 666 should be more memorable than 2 or 9. Conduct your coaching session as normal, then at the very end, ask which numbers were recalled. If the initial numbers were recalled over the latter, yet more identifiable numbers, your client could suffer from this bias. Through targeted questioning, ask about different times that judgements and important decisions occurred, and determine if those judgements were substantiations of initial information that was presented on the subject.

Fading Affect Bias – This bias refers to the phenomena where **information that is associated with negative emotions is forgotten more quickly than information associated with positive emotions.** Much like the bizarreness and humor effects, it is well established that emotions have extreme power over memory recall. This bias is important because it is a natural tendency for humans to recall positive images of one self, rather than negative images. Walker and Skowronski (2009) wrote in the *Journal of Applied Cognitive Psychology* that Fading Affect Bias, or FAB, has a particular function within healthy brains to induce individuals to be positive when reflecting inward, and protect individuals from extreme prolonged sadness from events such as the death of a loved one. Technically referred to as a bias because it leads to misattributions of memory recall due to emotional tagging of the event, this is a healthy bias that should be present and encouraged in all humans. FAB is at odds with Freudian theory, which derived that repressed memories of conflict often drove many behaviors later in life and had lifelong staying power. FAB is often associated with grit, resilience, human adaptation, and perseverance.

This bias is important to highlight because it applies to social groups and teams as well, not only individual memory recall. Aligning with the cognitive perspective of psychology, practicing positive reinforcement of thoughts, while eliminating negative self-doubt and self-talk, ensures that a healthy environment is created that allows FAB to flourish. Walker and Skowronski (2009) determined that social support mechanisms, such as correctly practicing cognitive psychology techniques within social settings, showed that events with high audience diversity and events that were shared with many other listeners showed stronger FAB. In other words, the more people who experienced the positivity, the more positivity that was created. This aligns with the cognitive and humanistic perspectives of psychology, and leaders who are superior at promoting FAB often have the following EI configuration:

- Balanced Emotional Self-Awareness
- Balanced Emotional Expression
- Balanced Assertiveness
- High Optimism
- High Well-Being

Unlike other biases, it should be a part of every coach's process to encourage positivity, under the guidance of FAB. Walker and Skowronski (2009) associate FAB with motivation and a hopeful outlook on the future, both of which are important elements that successful leaders should promote within their teams. With your clients, use the Workplace or Leadership report to determine the EI configuration, and then set one of your coaching goals toward achieving the desired EI pattern while promoting actions that increase positivity among teams. It is important not to avoid negative events/news or encourage leaders to only align with strengths and positivity. The key takeaway is that a leader should prefer to promote positivity over negativity in her leadership style, not using fear or conflict to motivate but rather hope and inspiration.

Illusion of Transparency – Relating to the illusion of asymmetric insight, this social bias is the tendency for people to overestimate how much their current mental state is known to others or how much the mental states of others are known to the individual. A well-known experiment that highlights this bias is to tap out the beat to a song that everyone would recognize if they knew what song was being tapped. For example, tap out the rhythm to "Happy Birthday" or "We Wish You a Merry Christmas", and as you tap it, you can hear the song in your head, clear as day. If you were to ask others what song you were tapping, that you can distinctly hear in your head, only 3% of those asked will actually guess correctly (McRaney, 2010). This bias has implications in public speaking performance (the speaker assumes the audience knows how nervous he is), negotiations (one side feels that all of their cards are on the table), and team performance (leaders assume that team members know what the leader wants done). Garcia (2002) wrote in the *Journal of Business Psychology*, in a paper titled "Power and the Illusion of Transparency in Negotiations", that low power individuals feel more transparent than do high power individuals within the negotiation, even though no actual power difference existed initially. The low power individuals felt that their intentions were more known, thereby creating a self-fulfilling prophecy that they lacked power, which would eventually come true during the course of the negotiations. This is also true in public speaking. Those who suffer from this bias assume that the audience knows how nervous the speaker is on stage or where the speaker messed up a particular part of the speech. This assumption creates more anxiety and mistakes, thereby self-fulfilling the prophecy that did not originally exist. Savitsky & Gilovich (2003) wrote in the *Journal of Experimental Social Psychology*, in a paper titled "The Illusion of Transparency and the Alleviation of Speech Anxiety", that the illusion played a key role in self-exacerbating the nature of speech anxiety, and that being aware of the bias improved the quality of the speaker's performance, from both the speaker's view and the audiences view. As a means to alter speech anxiety, the authors suggest Cognitive Behavior Modification, or CBM, which focuses on identifying and eliminating dysfunctional self-talk and understanding that our behaviors are often outcomes one's own self-verbalizations. Venturing into the realm of clinical psychology, CBM is used to treat those with panic disorders, agoraphobia, and other anxiety disorders, eliminating the thought patterns that counteract recovery behaviors. Corey (2012) wrote in *Theory and Practice of Counseling and Psychotherapy* that one could change thoughts and behaviors, while also avoiding detrimental behaviors, via a three-phase process: self-observation, beginning new self-talk, and learning new skills. If we extrapolate that process from the clinical realm and extend it to performance coaching, that three-phrase process lines up with using EI and the cognitive perspective of psychology to generate powerful performance implications for our clients that can help them eliminate this bias. Create self-observation by administering the Workplace or Leadership report, use the results of the assessment to help the client begin new self-talk, and solidify the new skills with a coaching plan or EI growth graph. This is one of the few biases where a clinical method is recommended for a non-clinical setting, due to the powerful anxiety this social bias creates within leaders. Most leaders that suffer from this bias often have the following EI configuration:

- Low Emotional Self-Awareness
- Low Independence
- Low Reality Testing
- Low Stress Tolerance
- High Self-Actualization

Leaders are often unaware of how this bias affects them, are extremely dependent on the acceptance of others in a social sense, have a distorted view of the reality of the situation, and often do not emotionally tolerate stress well. A unique aspect of this configuration is that the client will often have high Self-Actualization and lofty life/career goals, which is most likely one of the reasons they are in a position of negotiating or public speaking in the first place. The anxiety stems from having goals that may seem unreachable, creating the apprehension that is allowed to mentally flourish due to the specific EI configuration listed. Coach the client through the CBM process, and watch them become a masterful orator.

Mastering the Art of Stealth

There are many aspects to human behavior that are stealthy, hidden, go unnoticed, or operate in the shadows. The ninja learned special ways of walking to move silently, and the masters of the Shinobi-Iri could access areas that were inaccessible to others, and do so without enemies ever knowing they were there. By understanding how cognitive heuristics and mental processes create bias, the modern-day shinobi can recognize the internal decision-making levers that drive modern business. Using EI to battle cognitive bias is a powerful method of performance improvement for your client, and mastering Shinobi-Iri means that the coach can access influential aspects that often operate in the shadows.

– Shinobi Skill Acquired –

Shinobi-Iri 忍び入り

Emotional Intelligence and Leading Change

Within the Shinobi-Iri skill, there is a subset of distinct methodologies that help the shinobi move silently to achieve missions, infiltrate covertly and escape undetected, and remain invisible while gathering intelligence. Nyukyo No Jutsu refers to the correct use of timing when deploying shinobi tactics in order to maximize chances mission success. Correct timing was of the utmost importance and the shinobi would often only get one attempt at success. Each movement had to be perfectly timed if the shinobi wanted to ensure a prosperous outcome.

. . .

When it comes to leading organizational change at a very high level, efforts normally break down into two categories: technology and talent. Almost all change initiatives involve deploying new technology, changing business processes, reallocating budgets, or some other type of transformation that involves varying degrees of technology. The most common form in today's environment involves the purchase of a new technology system, where a new solution is procured and the receiving organization (RO) braces for technology change. However, 3 out of 4 IT transformation projects fail (Kotter, 2012). This is because most focus on technology, very few focus on talent.

The typical organizational change effort normally consists of three distinct stages: the decision, the resistance, the adoption. The decision is essentially the leadership decision. This can be a directive, an IT procurement or purchase decision, a re-org, or any decision by senior management that something needs to be changed. The resistance is the first reaction of other leaders and the rank and file when the decision is made public. Resistance can be curiosity, fear, anxiety, or general interest. The key here is that whether positive or negative, the organization as a whole is not ready to accept the change, which is defined as change resistance. Lastly, the adoption is the roll out of the change effort, where the users, stakeholders, customers, and others are required to change daily work functions to incorporate the new technology. The effort within this stage is focused on accelerating consumption of services and fully utilizing the new system. EI will help maximize chances of success within each stage.

The Decision Stage

The decision stage is best addressed using the coaching techniques discussed in the previous heuristics and bias section. Cote and Yip (2012) conducted a study called "The Emotionally Intelligent Decision Maker", and concluded that individuals with higher levels of EI can correctly identify which events caused certain emotions (Emotional Self-Awareness), and determine which of those emotions were not relevant to the decision that currently needed to be made (Decision Making), thereby leading to more effective decision-making overall. Researchers from the University of Toronto extended this research by looking to see how sitting in traffic affected the decision-making ability of leaders. Essentially, a stressor (traffic) created anxiety within leaders, and the researchers wanted to determine how that affected the ability to make investment decisions once the individuals arrived at work. They concluded that the investment decisions had much more to do with the anxiety that was created during the unrelated event of sitting in traffic than the facts of the investment scenario in low EI individuals. Those who had high EI, were able to make decisions that were more fundamentally sound, despite still experiencing the anxiety that was caused by the effect of sitting in traffic (University of Toronto, 2013). Using EI to battle bias, irrationality, and compartmentalize unrelated emotions, ensures that the leader has the decision-making skills that will allow her to kick-start a positive change effort.

The Resistance Stage

The first step to minimizing resistance is to *prime the organization for change*. This ensures that we do not run into insurmountable change resistance and maximizes our chances of project and program success. Harvard Professor John Kotter's 8-step process for leading change is world-class, and consists of a repeatable framework that organizations all over the world have used to create and lead successful change. It consists of: creating a sense of urgency, building a guiding coalition, forming a vision, enlisting a volunteer army, removing barriers, generating short term wins, sustaining acceleration, and instituting change (Kotter, 2012).

The first two steps are the most important, because it involves an assembly of people and will be the time when you need to move those people, emotionally. In order to prime the organization for the upcoming change, steps 1 and 2 are vital building blocks to the change effort, and getting people to move quickly will be key.

As a change management consultant, you can wield EI effectively in steps 1 and 2 to prime the organization for the upcoming opportunity and to lay the foundation for a prosperous change. As discussed before, according to the Bar-On model of EI, the Interpersonal Composite within the EQ-i 2.0 assessment "includes Interpersonal Relationships, Empathy, and Social Responsibility. This facet of EI measures one's ability to develop and maintain relationships based on trust, articulate an understanding of another's perspective, and act responsibly while showing concern for the organization" (Bar-On, 2002).

Figure 39 - The Interpersonal Composite

Reproduced with permission of Multi-Health Systems (2017). All Rights Reserved. www.mhs.com

As a recap, Interpersonal Relationships refers to how skilled one is in developing and maintaining mutually satisfying relationships based on trust and compassion. Empathy is recognizing and understanding how someone else feels, and includes the ability to articulate that understanding in a respectful way. Social Responsibility involves acting responsibly, having social consciousness and showing concern for the larger organization.

But remember, it's all about balance. The idea isn't to simply "raise" the use of these skills within the change leader, as high use of these EI skills can often be just as detrimental as low use. You can use the EQ-i to assess the proposed change leader, or if possible, members of the guiding coalition or change effort. Balanced Interpersonal Relationship ability gives a change consultant the ability to bond quickly with others, which will be vital when priming the organization for change.

Individuals with low Interpersonal Relationship skill are often isolated from others and are considered socially withdrawn, cold, unfriendly, hard to like, or are hard to get to know. These characteristics prove detrimental when trying to build a guiding coalition, since oftentimes that step involves trying to convince others of an unrealized vision, which might prove difficult if the change leader isn't well liked or understood.

Conversely, individuals engaged in high use of Interpersonal Relationship skill can be too free or disclosing of personal data, too demanding of disclosure from others, co-dependent, or unwilling to work alone. Starting change management efforts can often be lonely at the beginning, and personal walls will erect quickly within others once change plans start to become socialized, so being too expectant of disclosure from others can shut down eventual change champions before the change leader has an ability to add them to the coalition.

Having balance in Interpersonal Relationship skill ensures that everyone feels that the change is begin done *with* them and not *to* them, and ensures that the vagueness that accompanies the start of the effort doesn't create walls in others that are insurmountable to the change leader.

Balanced Empathy ability generally leads a change leader to be sensitive, aware, and appreciative of how other people feel, which will be vital when rooting out oppositions of change within individuals in steps 1 and 2 of the process.

Individuals with low Empathy skill are often inattentive, uncompassionate, selfish, or self-centered. These characteristics make creating a sense of urgency and creating a guiding coalition impossible if others feel that the change leader is only attempting institutional change for egocentric reasons.

Conversely, high use of Empathy skill includes emotional dependence, dishonesty derived from holding back bad news, conflict avoidance, or a dysfunctional attachment to other people's emotions. Building a guiding coalition requires change leaders to be attentive to others' needs, while being firm and honest about the upcoming change. Oftentimes, upcoming change means bad news and possible conflict for someone or some group, and being too empathetic can lead to a withholding of vital information out of fear of hurting others.

Having balance in Empathy skill is vital to creating and sustaining a guiding coalition, and ensuring unbiased communication throughout the opportunity.

Balanced Social Responsibility is the ability to keep in mind the welfare of the larger organization during the change effort, which will be fundamental when creating urgency for the upcoming change, to portray that the change effort isn't at odds with larger organizational goals.

Individuals with low Social Responsibility skill are often unencumbered by rules or group expectations and often are insensitive to others' needs, socially irresponsible, and pay little attention to the organization or surrounding environment. This can lead to the development of a change plan that is on an eventual collision course with larger organizational goals.

Conversely, those engaged in high use of Social Responsibility skill sometimes act like a martyr and may put organizational needs ahead of the current change initiative, be overly sensitive to others' needs, or could derail the change effort at the first instance of conflict with organizational goals.

Having balance in Social Responsibility ensures that the change leader doesn't cannibalize existing organizational goals with the upcoming change effort, but also doesn't sacrifice the change effort at the first sign of larger organizational tension.

The change leader will become the focal point of the business transformation, and it will be up to the change leader to make critical and timely decisions and communicate effectively to all levels of the stakeholder map. Developing the EI within the change consultant, with an assessment such as the EQ-i 2.0, will ensure that the practitioner is equipped to deal with the stress and reactions of the opportunity. Much like a first impression, most change efforts only get one chance to get it right, and with over 70% of change efforts failing, priming the organization for the upcoming change with EI, dramatically increases the chance of change success by ensuring that steps 1 and 2 of Kotter's model get off to a perfect start, minimizing the chances of change resistance.

The Adoption Stage

JB Wood wrote in his books *Complexity Avalanche* and *Consumption Economics*, that there is this tendency to think that the massive deployment of technology is the end goal, when in reality, it is the starting gun. It used to be that technology providers would sell some massive human resources system to a company, that had millions of features, turn it on, and say good bye. There was no focus on accelerating consumption of that technology, no focus on enablement, no focus on the psychological aspect of change, nothing! What happened was that companies would spend millions of dollars on a platform that 99% of the workforce barely utilized to its full potential. He referred to this as the "consumption gap", which resulted from technology becoming more complex and a declining focus on talent and enablement. The consumption gap creates a growing chasm, that blocks effective change, among other things.

Officially, a lack of resources is the most common reason that 3 out of 4 IT projects fail, however, a deeper dive finds that it isn't a numbers problem, it's a people problem. There is often very little effort dedicated toward enabling the organization, and the people within it, to accept the change. The RO not only needs training on the new technology, but it also needs to be equipped with the emotional ability to receive the change.

People do not like change for a variety of reasons — having to learn a new job role, worry about job security, fear of reorganization, etc. When fear sets in, employee engagement and worker productivity drastically declines. This is oftentimes the reason why budgets blow through the original pre-deployment predictions; financial analysts didn't account for fear-induced-productivity-decline, that creates a phenomenon called "The Valley of Despair".

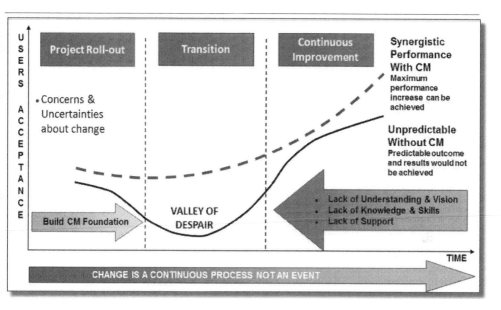

Figure 40 - The Valley of Despair

This is often caused because of a lack of understanding and vision, skills, and support. All three of these can be addressed by EI and minimized by emotionally intelligent leaders and change champions. Technology implementations must also be accompanied by workforce enablement around the stress of managing change, reduction of the stress of pending uncertainty, and a contagious optimism that keeps morale high. The Bar-On model of EI can do just that.

As a recap, the Stress Management Composite within the EQ-i 2.0 assessment "is comprised of Flexibility, Stress Tolerance, and Optimism. Collectively, this facet of EI addresses how well one can cope with the emotions associated with change and unfamiliar or unpredictable circumstances, while remaining hopeful about the future and resilient in the face of setbacks and obstacles" (Bar-On, 2002).

Figure 41 - The Stress Management Composite

Reproduced with permission of Multi-Health Systems (2017). All Rights Reserved. www.mhs.com

Flexibility is how well one adapts emotions, thoughts, and ultimately behaviors to circumstances that are unpredictable or unfamiliar, like a new technology deployment. Stress Tolerance is how well one copes with difficult situations, ambiguous scenarios, and stress due to lack of clarity, and how well one believes that he can influence situations in a positive manner. Optimism is an indicator of one's positive attitude and measures how well one remains hopeful and resilient, in the face of oncoming setbacks. But, remember it's all about balance! Like in the resistance phase, the idea isn't to simply "raise" the use of these skills within the change leader, as high use of these emotional intelligence skills can often be just as detrimental as low use. You can use the EQ-i to assess the proposed change leader, or if available, all members of the organization. Balanced Stress Management ability gives the organization the ability deal with the emotions that come with uncertainty, unpredictability, or massive change.

Individuals with low Flexibility have an inability or unwillingness to take in new data or change direction easily, which can result in rigid thinking, lacking curiosity, change resistance, or slow efforts when starting new projects.

Conversely, individuals engaged in high use of Flexibility can be prone to more starts than finishes, a reluctance to closure, or becoming bored and/or predictable too easily.

Individuals with low Stress Tolerance will not be able to handle the change, as he will be anxious, agitated, feel hopeless/helpless, lack self-confidence, or procrastinate due to fear.

Conversely, individuals with high Stress Tolerance might not be able to see legitimate stressors that require attention, might not be invested in the outcome of the change effort, be emotionally disconnected, or be overly-confident.

Individuals with low Optimism will be pessimistic, depressed, self-defeating, and have a negative outlook on the change effort.

Conversely, individuals with high Optimism might be blind to project dangers and critical paths, have unrealistic beliefs and assume the change will occur regardless of effort, or see opportunities that do not really exist.

Learning about the upcoming technology will be important, and accelerating consumption of future services is dependent on adequate tools training. However, if the project fails before you reach productivity mountain, all of the tools training in the world will not matter. Ensure that your workforce is emotionally and psychologically equipped to not only manage the upcoming change, but to *lead* the change. Assessing the EI of individuals and teams, with the EQ-i 2.0 individual or Group Report, is a great way to determine the best change management strategy when it comes to your people. Before you configure the technology, enable the talent.

EI will help leaders become aware of decision making styles and the biases that may have lasting impact on strategic decisions and purchases, help minimize resistance and prime the organization for change by essentially accelerating stages 1 and 2 of the Kotter methodology for change leadership. EI will also empower your organization and its leaders to be emotionally and psychologically equipped to accept the upcoming change, deal with uncertainty, and avoid the valley of despair.

Mastering Change

The ancient shinobi used Nyukyo No Jutsu to ensure correct use of timing to enter the enemy stronghold. Having the right equipment, agents, and battle plans, were all worthless without following precise timing that maximized chances of success. When it comes to leading change efforts within organizations, using EI to enable decision-making ability, prime the organization for change, and create psychologically safe environments to accept the change, will ensure that timing of the change effort is correct and that the chances of failure are minimized.

– Shinobi Skill Acquired –

Nyukyo No Jutsu 忍び入り

Determining Psychological Fit

Another skill within the subset of Shinobi-Iri, Nyudaki No Jutsu was often considered the trickiest of the infiltration techniques. Rather than rely on timing, distraction, or discovering weak points, this skill refers to determining psychological characteristics of the enemy to gain advantage. The modern-day ninja can use EI to determine psychological functions of individuals to determine organizational fit, aid in employee selection, and help with leadership succession planning.

. . .

American management consultant Peter Drucker once said "the ability to make good decisions regarding people represents one of the last reliable sources of competitive advantage, since very few organizations are very good at it". There is an abundance of extant literature on the subjects of psychometrics and the relation to job selection and succession planning, and some assessment providers even have dedicated assessments for these topics.

Selection

The overarching concern with every other job-fit assessment is that they are either aptitude or personality based, which are both considered static elements of humans. Essentially, if a job candidate does not possess a subjectively pre-defined innate ability to perform a task, or does not contain the correct mix of natural personality traits, many selection assessments would tell organizational decision makers that the candidate is not, nor ever will be, right for the job. This leads the organization to continue searching for candidates who were simply born with the configuration that they are seeking, and leaves job seekers with no chance to prove that they could be the best candidate for the position after all. Many organizations miss out on great talent utilizing this practice. But, as we know by now, EI is dynamic and measures a set of skills in a snap shot in time. Blank (2008) wrote in the *Employee Relations Law Journal*, in a paper called "Selecting Employees Based on Emotional Intelligence Competencies: Reap the Rewards and Minimize the Risk", that employers have traditionally used applications, resumes, and interviews to select employees, and these factors may predict average performance in a job but they do not identify who outstanding performers are. Standardized aptitude and intelligence tests have been found to disproportionately disqualify applicants of specific classes, creating disparate or adverse impact, which the Equal Employment Opportunity Commission defines as a selection rate for any race, sex, or ethnic group at less than 80% of the rate for the group with the highest selection rate (Blank, 2008). However, hiring managers and employers can justify adverse impact if they can show that the selection criteria is valid. According to Blank (2008), the law recognizes three types of validation.

1. Criterion validity, which is a statistical relationship between scores on the selection process and job performance.
2. Content validity, which shows that the content of a selection process is representative of bona fine occupational qualifications, or BFOQs, of the job.
3. Construct validity, which shows that the measurement of underlying human traits map to important job characteristics.

Personality assessments run the risk of identifying mental disabilities, which render them illegal in the selection process. In the court case of Karraker v. Rent-A-Center in 2005, a federal appellate court ruled that the most widely assessment of psychopathology, the Minnesota Multi-Phasic Personality assessment, or MMPI, screened out persons with disabilities, and could not lawfully be used as a selection tool. EI assessments identify skill, not dysfunction, so the risk of inadvertently identifying a disability and disqualifying the candidate are zero.

There are many reasons to implement an EI competency-based selection process. First, many studies have shown that EI competencies are predictive of high performance within work functions. Second, individuals with high EI represent less legal risk. Studies have shown that workers with high EI exhibit less of the bad behaviors that plague organizations, such as theft and sexual harassment (Blank, 2008). A trained I/O psychologist or human capital consultant can perform a job analysis, which identifies the job functions, skills, knowledge, attributes and abilities that are vital for success. Competencies can then be matched to the job functions and a job description can be developed. Behavioral interviewing techniques along with structured interviews can be combined with EI assessment to select candidates that have the core EI functions necessary to excel in the position.

Herpertz, Nizielski, Hock, and Schutz (2016) wrote a research article titled "The Relevance of Emotional Intelligence in Personnel Selection for High Emotional Labor Jobs", and determined that an applicant's ability to regulate emotions predicted performance in group exercises, and EI assessment should be a core component of the selection process for jobs that have increased cognitive load.

Organizations can use EI to select employees, even when the EI profile isn't a precise match, because EI assessments can provide information that applies to immediate psychosocial fit and provide an onboarding roadmap for the employee and the organization, that frames the 30-60-90 day plans. Let me give you an example.

David the Independent

I once consulted for a Fortune 500 organization within the software technology space that specifically dealt with IoT, or the Internet of Things. In addition to the technical and educational skills that were necessary for the position, the organization needed to make sure that the candidate possessed the correct use of EI skills that were needed to flourish in a high-pressure environment that had requirements that changed daily and lead a global team of engineers that followed the sun (a global workflow model where specific tasks are passed around to different worksites every day based on time zones). The organization had tried to use personality assessments in the past, but often found that those that possessed the subjective personality traits determined to be necessary from a previous job analysis, often did not possess the necessary skills and experience needed for the job. The company could never find the right match because the job analysis (done by a previous consultant) determined that someone who ranked high in Extraversion and Traditionalism would be the best fit for the company, but most of the best IoT engineers that were drawn to this field were often introverted and thrived on breaking traditional norms and barriers.

I conducted a new job analysis that consisted of ditching the personality based assessment and replacing it with the EQ-i 2.0, while also using the Group Report to measure the EI of the current team, leading me to clues about the current culture, what EI skills were in abundance, and which were currently lacking within the current team. After a discovery phase with leadership and discussing the results of the Group Report, I determined that an individual with the following EI configuration would have the highest chance of success in the current environment:

- Low Social Responsibility
- High Independence
- High Problem Solving
- Low Reality Testing
- High Stress Tolerance

Essentially, the ideal hire would best operate within this organization if he or she did not care about breaking traditional norms, had a high degree of emotional freedom from others, was able to skillfully use emotions in the decision-making process, was wildly creative, and could tolerate the emotional pressures that came from the IoT industry. After sitting in on roughly 10 interviews, administering the EQ-i 2.0 assessment and debriefing the results, we finally met Dave.

Dave possessed all of the ideal work experience, technical skills, and education that would traditionally predict successful performance in the role, but was a mismatch on two key elements of the EI profile delivered by the job analysis (high Social Responsibility and low Independence). With this information, the interviewers were able to target specific instances within Dave's past to determine if this mismatch should be of concern during the next round of interviews. Essentially, he had formerly come from an organization where promoting Social Responsibility was a core value of the company. The company also emotionally encouraged the reliance of others to complete daily tasks due to a system of checks and balances, constant feedback loops and a flat organizational hierarchy. Basically, he constantly had to rely on the feedback of others to complete his work.

While a traditional personality or aptitude based selection assessment would have created enough doubt about Dave around psychosocial fit, using the EQ-i 2.0 provided us the roadmap to success. Dave was hired and we designed an onboarding program that consisted of a 180-day ramp up period that was a blend of on-the-job learning and EI skill development. The onboarding program consisted of reinforcing the current EI skill set he possessed, learning to temper the use of Social Responsibility, and acquiring the necessary emotional skills needed to develop a high level of Independence. The program consisted of weekly coaching sessions, EI-based exercises, tracking development on EI growth graphs, and culminating with a EQ360 at the 180-day mark. Using the EQ-i 2.0 as a selection assessment matched up the right talent for the position, and gave the organization the perfect roadmap to ensure a successful onboarding for their vital position.

Much like with bias, managing change, and other aspects of EI development, it is all about balance, not trying to blindly raise all EI scores to the max. In some instances, low EI scores can actually be more desirable. Remember, low scores simply mean low use of the skill, which can be a function of the job or company culture. For example, if a company was looking for individuals who would make the best bill collectors, the organization would most likely not look for someone that had high use of Empathy. If a company needed wildly imaginative or creative ideas, the ideal candidate would not have high Reality Testing. A job analysis and EI based selection process can determine all of these aspects, and ensure that candidates that have the highest chance of success are recruited for the position, all while minimizing the legal risks that come along with aptitude and personality assessment selection methods.

Succession Planning

Easter and Brooks (2017) discussed the keys needed for effective leadership transition in *People and Strategy*, concluding that creating a stable foundation within the organization is important to ensure a smooth transition of power. Secondly, they highlight that in order for a leadership transition to be successful, the employees must be engaged, as engaged employees will provide support to the interim leader and help mitigate the inevitable disruption. Their research shows that companies that do not focus on employee engagement during transitions can lose up to 30% of current business and that the lack of support can lead 46% of new executives to underperform. In my own doctoral research, I discovered that the EI of a manager does have a positive correlation to employee engagement, even within virtual environments (manager-employee relationships where there is little or no face-to-face interaction). In my study, a Spearman correlation analysis revealed that there was a significant, positive relationship between Overall EI of managers and EE of virtual workers ($\rho = .226$). Therefore, if EI is related to employee engagement, and engaged employers provide for more successful leadership transitions, it is obvious that every succession plan should have a solid foundation based in EI principles.

There are many reasons to have an EI based succession plan. Most companies have a succession planning document, but many of them aren't operational, because they are not dynamic programs that consistently identify and groom potential leaders, they are simply static lists with a few names slotted for the top spots. A succession plan needs to be a program that aligns talent management activities, the company vision, and employee engagement efforts, to create development opportunities for potential leaders to hone skills and remain futureproof. There are a few fundamental issues that companies need to investigate while crafting a succession planning program.

Identifying the high-potentials. It will be rare that organizations have someone who is a perfect fit for the top roles, so some grooming and coaching will be needed. The Leadership report can be used to identify who the high-potential employees are, and provide a roadmap of which skills need to be raised in order to maximize chance of success in the new role.

Internal versus external. It is the tendency of company boards to first look outside the company for a new leader, since developing leaders internally takes effort and money, and the allure of an outside viewpoint can be exciting. But a 2012 study by a professor at the University of Pennsylvania's Wharton School determined that external hires were 60% more likely to be fired or let go and 20% more likely to leave on their own, than those hired internally. Outside hires also cost more, and perform worse. This makes it vital that a company's initial preference should be to look inward, but only if a succession planning program is in place that develops the desired leadership qualities.

Diversity. When organizations have no succession plan, or even succession plans that are personality assessment based, the general result is that leaders look for new leaders that are exactly like them. Using EI as a base for succession planning ensures that traits aren't used to craft ideal candidate profiles, but EI configurations instead. To date, there is no correlation to EI configurations and race, gender, or specific classes, unlike personality and aptitude assessments.

Many organizations even use succession planning software to help create programs that are designed to help companies identify, develop, and track talent for future leaders. A robust software system will include a suite of tools that allow the organization to have an active succession planning program. Some of the most important features of a valid tool are: dashboards that allow you to highlight key positions for succession planning, follow high-performers in their career progression, report on employee skills and experiences, appraise individuals and groups on competency based criteria, allow human resources to assign competencies to key performance metrics, display multiple talent profiles, benchmark employees, identify retention and flight risk employees, create development plans for high-potentials, calculate bench strength, historical performance data integration and management, display candidate comparison tools that can adjust for job-specific criteria, and allow for career research opportunities. Many of those features are dynamic and should be matched to a dynamic list of competencies, such as EI, rather than a static list of personality traits. A succession planning roadmap that incorporates EI should follow three distinct phases.

Design. Rather than simply have a torpid list that is rarely updated, a succession plan should invest heavily in the planning stages. As a talent management consultant, you should help the organization determine the depth of the talent pool, and if it should include executives, managers, or everyone, and if that pool should focus on high-potential employees or a possible wider pool. After the depth is determined, perform a job analysis that determines the skills, experience, and competencies needed for the key roles, and use the EQ-i 2.0 Workplace, Leadership, and Group reports to bench mark key roles or teams. If necessary, now is when you should decide if the organization could benefit from an HR software package that includes succession planning and EI competency mapping.

Act. Assess all current employees within the identified talent pool by analyzing performance reviews, and use the EQ-i 2.0 to identify any EI skill gaps that may need to be addressed for future roles. Perform structured interviews to determine each employee's career goals, and create various training, mentoring and leadership programs based off the gap analysis and career goals of the workforce. From those programs, track progress of skill gap closure, and start to generate a short list of top candidates for each position that falls under the succession plan.

Evaluate. Since leadership vacancies are often abrupt and without warning, it is important to keep top talent primed to pounce, should the opportunity arise. This involves not only keeping the talent skill set up to date, but also keeping the talent. Potential leaders with newly acquired skills become more desirable to other companies, and if a leadership vacancy doesn't open soon, they become flight risks. This stage of succession planning is a mix of art and science, as it will be important to keep skill sets current and gaps closed, while still maximizing employee engagement within the organization. While this seems like a counterproductive exercise – to train people for leadership positions only to increase their chances of leaving if a position does not open up – a famous conversation between a fictitious CFO and CEO highlights the importance of this step.

CFO: "What happens if we train them and they leave?"

CEO: "What happens if we don't, and they stay?"

Sarah the Successor

I once consulted for a regional credit union that often would lose key talent to other larger credit unions or to larger banks. This credit union was considered a starter job in this particular industry, and had built a fabulous college recruitment program that always brought in the best talent from university students who majored in finance, economics, and business. Employees would learn the skills of banking through rotational job programs that were designed to give each individual well-rounded and diverse banking experience, and managers were almost always home grown and promoted from within.

Being a regional credit union with a limited number of local branches, there were only a few executive positions within the corporate office. When these college graduates reached a branch manager position, there was a major stepping stone between that position and that of senior leadership at corporate, and the credit union found that many managers, some who have spent their entire careers since college, moved on to other institutions. This created a dynamic where most of senior leadership comprised of external talent that did not start at the bank, but the rest of the talent pool were all employees that were born and raised within this credit union. Essentially, the credit union was great at attracting and developing talent, just not retaining talent at the higher levels.

I was brought in to create an active succession plan that would extend the success of the talent acquisition program. After meeting with senior leadership, it was determined that I needed to implement the *Design, Act, Evaluate* process, and install EI feedback loops and assessments to baseline talent profiles and determine skill gaps. Fortunately, most of the employees had well documented employee experience histories and performance reviews, since most of their careers were spent within the same company. We needed to determine why talent was leaving.

One of the most powerful discovery tools you can have in your arsenal is the exit interview. An exit interview is simply a structured interview where you ask the individual why they are leaving, what could have been done to make them stay, and if there is any feedback they would like to provide to the organization as a final thought. I love exit interviews because of the candor you will experience from the individuals. Through a series of managers that left while I was contracted and some former managers that had already left but agreed to meet with me, I was able to craft a pretty clear narrative. As expected, many of the leaving managers mentioned how a lack of upward mobility at the credit union was a major factor, there was a hidden theme that emerged that ended up being a more powerful reason that most managers left.

Part of the college recruiting process that made the union so attractive was the fact that the credit union was heavily involved in the community and promoted Social Responsibility. This appealed to top talent who also wanted to make a difference in the community, as the credit union branches aspired to truly be "neighborhood banks", often sponsoring food drives, community events, and local marathons. This became an identity for most branch managers, as that position was the one responsible for community outreach and advocacy. Since most of the executive leadership was brought in externally and did not develop this home-grown identity of Social Responsibility, and the corporate headquarters was located in an office park rather than a neighborhood, senior leadership never focused on community events and rarely engaged in Social Responsibility. Branch managers did not want to wait for positions to open, only to then be in a position where their core values and EI skills could not be met.

I validated this with the use of the EQ-i 2.0 Leadership and Group reports. The assessments results confirmed that branch managers and teams had high use of Social Responsibility as individuals and teams, and corporate leadership had low use of this skill. Being identified as a necessary element of talent retention via the exit interviews, I implemented a succession planning program that incorporated exercises that individuals could perform on their own to keep use of Social Responsibility high, and made suggestions for senior leadership to implement social programs at the executive level that aligned with EI competencies and skills that promoted Social Responsibility.

Sarah had been with the credit union since she was a teenager (she interned there her college junior and senior year summers), and had a position waiting for her when she graduated from a local university. Working her way up the ranks and eventually to branch manager, Sarah began to have the feelings that so many before her experienced, and could not decide if it was time to leave. She was one of the first to go through the new succession planning program, which was focused on identifying her career goals, skill gaps, EI profile, and banking competencies, and aligning it with possible open positions in the future. As predicted, her Social Responsibility was high, but her Independence was low.

- High Social Responsibility
- Low Independence

This meant that she did identify with the high Social Responsibility that the credit union promoted, but also heavily relied on the emotions of others for decision making. She would be a prime candidate to leave if she didn't have others around her that promoted the high Social Responsibility. After going through the initial program, her employee engagement increased. This, combined with developing a plan to keep Social Responsibility high, was enough to get her to stay at the organization, despite the long wait time that was expected for a spot to open up. We kept her skills up to date as time passed, the program kept her engagement high, and after 13 months, a position opened up at corporate which she was identified as the top potential candidate for. Last I heard, she was in the process of trying to use her new position to relocate the corporate office closer to a neighborhood, so that senior leadership could also espouse the mission of being a neighborhood bank. Before my engagement with the credit union was over, she mentioned to me in passing, that the succession plan was one of the main reasons she stayed.

Mastering Psychological Fit

Nyudaki No Jutsu was often considered the trickiest of the infiltration techniques. Rather than rely on timing, distraction, or discovering weak points, this skill refers to determining psychological characteristics of the enemy to gain advantage. Essentially, the skill set of the ninja would not matter if it wasn't psychologically advantageous to strike. Modern day ninjas can apply this skill to psychosocial fit within organizations. Measurement of skills, abilities, aptitude, and personality are not enough, as talent, technology and the organization all need to psychologically and emotionally match. At the highest levels of leadership, when differences in talent are miniscule, dynamic EI skills and the gaps identified during competency and job analysis, are the best methods of creating supreme advantage.

– Shinobi Skill Acquired –

Nyudaki No Jutsu 忍び入り

A Sword That Can Only Cut Once

The ancient shinobi were masters of Cho Ho, which is the ninjitsu art of espionage. Methods of successful intelligence gathering and surveillance were mastered, as information served as the shinobi's greatest weapon. Shinobi would devise new ways to locate and recruit spies, turning former enemies into friendly agents, creating the ultimate competitive advantage.

. . .

The battle for top talent gets fiercer every day between corporations. Digital technology trends develop at a quicker pace than ever before, and organizations need to be agile and swift when responding to constantly changing customer demands and global trends. A popular area of focus for many companies is on the generation known as Millennials.

The Kids Aren't All Right

Technically defined as any person reaching adulthood in the early 21st century, a Millennial is someone born between the early 1980s and late 1990s. Millennials are a popular target for corporations because they are the first generation to grow up with the Internet, and generally possess technology abilities that organizations desperately need to sustain competitive advantage globally.

Millennials are considered the largest generation yet and the most ethnically and racially diverse. They dominate social networks, aspire to make a difference at work, and will be 50% of the workforce by 2020, and 75% of the workforce by 2030 (DeVaney, 2015). Millennials came to career prominence during a time of war, have the highest amount of student loan debt in history, and started their careers during the Great Recession. The amount of technology innovation and creation that occurred during the Millennials' lifetime, is considered to be more than all of human history before it combined.

According to DeVaney, this has created a strong sense of Social Responsibility among the population, as social change has always been the zeitgeist of the Millennial era, economically and politically. DeVaney (2015) describes Millennials as entitled, optimistic, civic minded, close to family, values work-life balance, and impatient, in contrast to Generation X who she describes as self-reliant, adaptable, cynical, and resourceful. There is a profusion of extant literature on Millennials in the workplace, but much of it has one fatal flaw. Most literature that provides tips and tricks on dealing with Millennials over-generalizes the effect that the unique combination of technology innovation and environment had on molding the Millennial mind, and assume most, if not all, Millennials behave in a similar manner. Give it a try – use your favorite search engine to look up "Millennials in the workplace", and you will see article after article that generalizes all humans that fall into this age range, citing socioenvironmental factors as internal drivers for specific workplace behaviors. Millennials, just like all other humans, cannot be generalized by age range. While upbringing and environment do have an impact on emotional and social development, EI combinations within individuals still remain one of the most inimitable aspects relating to human behavior. If you truly want to attract Millennials and sustain competitive advantage within your company, it is important to understand how different generations vary in a general sense, but blanket approaches to talent management and recruitment will yield underwhelming results.

Recruiting Spies With EI

Every employee that works at a company, was previously an employee of another company (except those fresh out of school, of course). Essentially, all recruiting and talent acquisition is really corporate espionage. Organizations convince top talent to leave competitors and join the other side. Using EI can create massive competitive advantage when recruiting spies from other organizations.

I was asked to develop a talent acquisition strategy and onboarding program where the main goal was to attract top Millennial data science talent. The talent profile for most data scientists in this effort was "early in career", meaning that they were either currently in college or still within the first few years of their corporate life. I came into the program when a change in direction was needed after a slow start to recruiting. The talent acquisition consultants before me performed the necessary job analysis and job description creation, but used general Millennial data to frame the recruiting strategy. There were four main themes that drove the recruiting efforts:

1) Millennials will only stay for two years
2) They want a coach, not a boss
3) They only want to work on big projects
4) Work-life balance was most important

The company, thinking they were being edgy and distinct, instructed internal college recruiting coordinators to market the idea to Millennials that this company was one where it was all about fun, the politically hierarchy was flat, they didn't have to waste their time with little tasks, and anyone could work from home anytime they wanted to. While these themes seemed to do well from a marketing perspective, using those themes to drive retention and onboarding after the talent was hired was a disaster. Millennials were attracted at record numbers, only to leave with an equally blistering pace once they arrived. HR was dumbfounded as to why this was happening.

Overarching themes and population generalizations can be great for marketing, as evident by the recruiting numbers, but once the talent arrived, no specific onboarding program tailored to the specific needs of each individual was ever created. Exit interviews from the talent that swiftly left revealed that most felt a depersonalization once they arrived at the organization, but each cited very specific reasons for leaving that seemed to lack any general theme. Essentially, each one had his or her own reasons for leaving, due to specific challenges that were experienced during the onboarding. What was missing, was a tailored approach that contained the core overarching themes that attracted them there, and unique onboarding attributes that were malleable and customizable for each individual.

The 70/20/10 Model

In the 1980s, the Center for Creative Leadership created the 70/20/10 model, which is a commonly used formula for training professionals in development and learning, but is also used for onboarding new talent. Originally, the model dictates that 70 percent of knowledge is obtained through on the job experience, 20 percent from interactions with peers, and 10 percent from formal education. This model has stood the test of time, and is used in many onboarding frameworks globally. The challenge, is that sometimes these three development areas breakdown, onboarding is unsuccessful, and talent vacates the organization. Remember that learning, memory, and retention are all affected by emotions, and each individual has a unique emotional profile. The only way the success of this model can be sustained is by adding EI to the development model and installing targeted EI coaching.

70 percent of the learner's development should come from hands-on experience. It enables employees to discover job-related skills, make decisions, interact with peers, and discover what challenges the actual job will contain. While this learning curriculum can be general for all of the talent that has been on-boarded, the unique challenges that each new hire will face will be drastically different. Much like in university classes where every student in the auditorium is receiving the same lecture, some may grasp the material well while others my stumble. The reason is because each individual, despite being a part of the same age demographic, will possess unique emotional and personality challenges that uniquely affect memory, retention, focus, and learning. When new hires perform hands-on learning in the 70 percent portion of the model, an EI profile must accompany each learner, so that the onboarding program managers can tweak subtle aspects for each learner to maximize effectiveness.

I administered the EQ-i 2.0 to each new hire and reviewed their profile with them and their immediate manager (with the new hire's permission of course). We were able to show that some of the new hires tolerated stress well when others didn't, some used emotions heavily in decision-making processes when others didn't, and some were assertive enough to speak up when something was not understood in the material when others were not. Knowing the emotional challenges of each individual, allowed the onboarding managers to tailor subtle nuances of the program delivery to each individual, which maximized learning and retention.

20 percent of the model is learning through coaching, mentoring, collaborative learning, social development, and peer interaction. Essentially, new hires learn how to be good corporate citizens, work and communicate in teams, and develop a network that will help promote career aspirations.

Using the results of the EQ-i 2.0, each new hire was able to understand strengths and weaknesses in social settings. Some were able to receive feedback easily, while others were not accustomed to it. Some were able to develop relationships easily, while others came across as more withdrawn. Rather than penalize the ones who were more introverted or socially inept, the program was able to be altered a bit to help those who lacked certain social skills receive extra development and coaching.

10 percent of the model comes from professional learning, such as courseware, books, events, or other academic sources. Opposite of the 20 percent section of the model, the new hires that excelled in this area were the socially withdrawn and isolated individuals, while the social butterflies often struggled in this part of the learning model since it required learning all alone. Understanding who learned best in secluded situations was important to understand when evaluating the results of this phase.

Using the EQ-i 2.0 to augment the talent acquisition strategy for this organization, we were able to attract and retain top Millennial talent. It may seem daunting to specifically customize general aspects of onboarding and learning curriculum for each individual, but that isn't necessarily the idea here. The main goal is to bolt on the EQ-i 2.0 to the existing curriculum to determine the current use of emotional skill within each individual, so that onboarding managers can know which new hires needed extra focus in certain areas. Think of it as "white glove service" onboarding.

EI is a Blade That Can Only Cut Once

While it is always important to document lessons learned when involved in coaching and consulting projects, it is important to always remember this one unequivocal fact:

EI profiles are a snapshot in time

Because of this, EI profiles are essentially blades that can only cut once. Results from previous efforts can guide general decision making, but no coaching, consulting, or development plans should take place unless there is a specific EI profile in place that is a current, valid, and reliable snapshot in time. This ensures that erroneous programs aren't created based off of data that might not be accurate. For this reason, it is imperative to use EI to target unique development outcomes instead of using it to produce general training programs or strategy themes, because EI profiles are unique to individuals, even across various demographic characteristics, such as age, gender, or race. In my own organizational research, one area that I investigated was the relationship of the EI of managers and employee engagement (EE) in virtual work environments. I wanted to see if the EI of a manager translated across the virtual realm and had any impact on how engaged employees were. Specifically, I investigated the relation of Overall EI, the Self-Expression composite, and the Interpersonal Composite, to employee engagement. In my study, I found that there was a statistically significant relationship between Overall EI and EE ($\rho = .226$), Self-Expression and EE ($\rho = .224$), but not Interpersonal and EE ($\rho = .012$), in virtual environments. If I only looked at Overall EI and ubiquitously applied the theme that "EI affects EE in virtual environments" and built programs around developing Overall EI, that would have been a mistake, because a deeper dive found that the Interpersonal composite had no relation to EE within this study. I also found another interesting tidbit, hidden deep within the Self-Expression and EE relationship.

Using a statistical test called Levene's test for equality of variances, I found that there was no significant difference between gender groups within the correlation of Overall EI to EE and Interpersonal to EE, but a difference between group means was discovered within Self-Expression and EE. When separated by gender, the correlation between EE and Self-Expression among males was (ρ = .250) and in females was (ρ = .071). Here is a table for your reference:

Spearman's rho	Self-Expression	Correlation Coefficient	1.000	.071
		Sig. (2-tailed)	.	.700
		N	32	32
	Pulse Score	Correlation Coefficient	**.071**	1.000
		Sig. (2-tailed)	.700	.
		N	32	32

a. Gender = F

Spearman's rho	Self-Expression	Correlation Coefficient	1.000	.250
		Sig. (2-tailed)	.	.065
		N	55	55
	Pulse Score	Correlation Coefficient	**.250**	1.000
		Sig. (2-tailed)	.065	.
		N	55	55

a. Gender = M

The results of my study showed that a male manager's Self-Expression did have an effect on EE within virtual work environments, but Self-Expression had no effect within female managers. A follow-up to this study showed that employees at this company, viewed similar expressive behaviors differently when those behaviors came from a male versus a female manager. If I had created development programs under the general theme that Self-Expression development led to increased EE, male managers would benefit from this training, while female managers would not. I was able to use EI to specifically pin point what development initiatives would work for one population but not another, ensuring that company dollars and employee hours were not wasted. When I investigated why the Interpersonal composite had no effect on EE, when previous extant literature on the relationship between EI and EE in non-virtual realms showed that there was a relationship, I discovered that it was because Empathy did not translate over virtual meetings unless all participants were using a web camera. Once this was discovered, an initiative was put in place to mandate the use of webcams in all meetings for a pilot study, and the organization saw the relationship between the Interpersonal composite and EE strengthen after 6 months (from $\rho = .012$ to $\rho = .201$).

Master the Recruitment

The ancient shinobi used varying techniques to attract, retain, and develop spies that were stolen from other clans. The shinobi used the talents of the new acquisitions to develop battle plans, sustain competitive advantage, and stay ahead of rivals. Understanding that this type of espionage was a two-way street, it was important for shinobi not only to use techniques that initially attracted new spies, but kept those spies within the clan. Practicing Cho Ho, shinobis were able to understand that specific recruitment strategies were to be used to maximize attraction and retention of each individual spy, depending on the circumstances that would appeal to that spy. Mastering this concept will ensure that you are able to recruit the spies you need to win, regardless of the individual circumstances surrounding each encounter.

– Shinobi Skill Acquired –

Cho Ho 戸隠流

The Battle Continues

Tai Jutsu was the ancient art of unarmed combat. Normally considered a final step, the shinobi would descend onto the battle field after all other ninjitsu skills had been exhausted. The shinobi prepared for battle through spiritual refinement, acquiring knowledge through disguise, impersonation, strategy development, and stealth entering modes. Clans would conceal battle plans, refine weapon techniques, and engage in battle through the use of spying, espionage, and attacks from afar. Once the ninja saw the battle drawing toward the apogee, the shinobi would engage in hand-to-hand combat, only when the chances of battle success were fully maximized. Tai Jutsu was the most unpredictable aspect of the battle, because it required the ninja to be the closest to his enemies. However, use of this skill was the only way the battle could continue and eventually be won.

. . .

We are just starting to scratch the surface on how EI and psychology can be applied to organizations to create positive outcomes. Many incorrectly believe that EI is only used for leadership development, which is the furthest from the truth. Remember, EI is dynamic and considered a use of skill, so matching up various combinations of skill use to organizational goals is an infinite arena of possibilities, waiting to be discovered.

Every day, the research on the relationship of EI to a vast number of business variables continues. To give you an idea of the wide applicability of EI to modern business, here is a list of research titles from the last five years alone, compiled by the Consortium for Research on Emotional Intelligence in Organizations:

- *Utilization of emotional intelligence traits by public school superintendents in the state of Arkansas.*
- *Finding the right fit: Using organizational culture and emotional intelligence in the lead pastor search process.*
- *Examining first-line managers' leadership practices, emotional intelligence, and workplace spirituality in the manufacturing industry.*
- *An examination of the relationship between emotional intelligence and transformational leadership of Texas superintendents.*
- *Online education, emotional intelligence, and interpersonal skills for the 21st century workforce.*

- *The influence of interpersonal and intrapersonal self-regulatory variables on performance outcomes of counseling interns.*
- *The impact of gender and emotional intelligence on career commitment among senior undergraduate hotel management majors in Taiwan.*
- *A new mixed model measure of Emotional Intelligence.*
- *The relationship between a leader's self-perceived level of emotional intelligence and organizational climate, as perceived by organizational members.*
- *The relationship between emotional intelligence of a leader and employee motivation to job performance.*
- *Leader emotional intelligence and workgroup engagement: A quantitative correlational study.*
- *Unique competencies required for female leadership success in the 21st century.*
- *The relationship between the emotional intelligence of secondary public school principals and school performance.*
- *Fight or flight, stay or leave: The relationship between emotional intelligence and voluntary turnover.*
- *A correlational study of emotional intelligence and project leadership.*
- *Differences in emotional intelligence and team cohesiveness in men's and women's community college athletic teams.*
- *Employee retention during a leadership change.*
- *Leadership development as a relational process: A grounded theory investigation of leader experiences.*
- *A study of emotional intelligence levels of abilities of project management practitioners.*
- *The relationship between emotional intelligence and job satisfaction among nurses at a community hospital setting.*
- *Emotional intelligence and performance of civilians in federal government.*
- *Cognitive distortions and gender as predictors of emotional intelligence.*
- *The impact of intervention methods on emotional intelligence.*
- *A correlational study of emotional intelligence and successful sales performance in Puerto Rico.*
- *The relationship between emotional intelligence and leadership practices of human services administrators.*
- *Examining the ability of emotional intelligence and work location to predict job satisfaction.*
- *The role of a leader's emotional intelligence and how it relates to employees' motivation and job satisfaction.*
- *Emotional intelligence and community healthcare productivity.*
- *Teacher emotional intelligence and the quality of their interactions with students.*
- *A quantitative study of the relationship between emotional intelligence and virtue ethics in accounting professionals.*
- *Examining the relationship between emotional intelligence of accountants and job satisfaction.*
- *Emotional intelligence as a predictor of a sales manager's sales performance.*

- *Examining teacher burnout using emotional intelligence quotients: A correlational study.*
- *The relationships among master's level counseling trainees' training level, emotional intelligence, and psychophysiological correlates of emotion regulation during a simulated counseling interaction.*
- *Exploration of the project management practitioner's emotional intelligence competencies.*
- *The relationship between thinking styles and emotional intelligence: An exploratory study of retail managers.*
- *Emotional intelligence: A quantitative study of the relationship among academic success factors and emotional intelligence.*
- *Emotional intelligence and the transformational leadership of female nonprofit leaders.*
- *Emotional intelligence and leader-member exchange: Do emotional competencies matter?*
- *Medical providers' emotional intelligence: Relationships with patient satisfaction and treatment adherence.*
- *An examination of emotional intelligence and leadership competencies among Black and White female middle managers.*
- *The relationship between emotional intelligence of principals and the overall organizational climate of public elementary schools.*
- *The moderating effect of emotional labor on the relationships of emotional intelligence and adjustment with managerial job performance.*
- *A correlational study: Elements of emotional intelligence and leadership among technology leaders.*
- *Emotional intelligence, emotional competency, and critical thinking skills in nursing and nursing education.*
- *Examining emotional intelligence and transformational leadership within US army national guard leaders.*
- *The relationship between teachers' emotional intelligence and attrition intention.*
- *Emotional education: A case on the perceptions of secondary school teachers' emotional intelligence leadership training.*
- *Determinants on mechanism of emotional marketing: Emotional intelligence, perception of emotional labor' action, efficacy and customer' coping strategy on customer satisfaction.*
- *Compassion fatigue and emotional intelligence in physicians.*
- *Human resource professionals' perceived effects of leader emotional intelligence on employee commitment at colleges and universities.*
- *Emotional intelligence in medical laboratory science.*
- *The relationship between emotional intelligence, self-efficacy, and clinical performance in associate degree nursing students.*
- *A mixed methods study exploring the relationship between servant leadership and emotional intelligence.*

- An investigation of the relationships between emotional intelligence, engagement, and performance.
- An examination of virtual teams: Exploring the relationship among emotional intelligence, collective team leadership, and team effectiveness.
- The relationship between team emotional intelligence and team interpersonal process effectiveness.
- Exploring the emotional intelligence of obstetrics and gynecology medical residents.
- Using emotional intelligence as a leadership strategy to make good leaders great.
- An exploratory qualitative study of the relationship between an educational leader's emotional intelligence and effective teams.
- A study of emotional intelligence and service ability among North Carolina mental health professionals: Implications for research and practice.
- Quantitative correlational study: Emotional intelligence and project outcomes among Hispanics in technology.
- The role of emotional intelligence skills in the academic achievement of students pursuing associate degrees at a south Texas college.
- The relationship of ethical behavior in the workplace to emotional intelligence and perceived leader integrity.
- Emotional intelligence associated with accountability of individual corporate board of directors: A quantitative study.
- Quantitatively studying the relationship between emotional intelligence and leadership competencies in health care.
- Emotional intelligence and nursing student retention.
- The relationships among emotional intelligence, gender, coping strategies, and well-being in the management of stress in close interpersonal relationships and the workplace.
- Understanding the factors that affect project managers' development and use of emotional intelligence in managing project stakeholders.
- The relationship between emotional intelligence and decision-making style among healthcare leaders in Iowa.
- Emotional intelligence and conflict resolution styles: Implications for United States National Guard leaders.
- The relationship between emotional intelligence of school principals and their ability to identify the strengths or talents of a member of their leadership team.
- A qualitative phenomenological study of emotional intelligence: Effects of stress on small business leaders.
- Impact of emotional intelligence on leadership effectiveness, success and job satisfaction.
- Emotional intelligence in Indian executives.
- A study of emotional intelligence, thinking styles, and selling effectiveness of pharmaceutical sales representatives.
- Emotional intelligence: A key to improving federal chief information officer management.

- *The relationship between emotional intelligence and communication apprehension in job fair attendees.*
- *The relationship among emotional intelligence and leadership styles of law enforcement executives.*
- *A comparison of emotional intelligence and leadership styles among Texas public school principals.*
- *A study of personality, emotional intelligence, social maturity, and job performance among nurses in rural east Texas.*
- *Exploring impacts of emotional intelligence, gender and tenure on sales performance among hospice sales professionals.*
- *A study of the relationship between emotional intelligence and individual performance in an inbound North American call center.*
- *An explanatory study: The relationship of emotional intelligence, organizational culture, and performance ratings.*
- *The relationship of certified flight instructors' emotional intelligence levels on flight student advancement.*
- *The relationship between emotional intelligence and leadership effectiveness among sponsored research administrators.*
- *Impact of therapist emotional intelligence on psychotherapy, and, relevance of therapist emotional intelligence for psychotherapy.*
- *Humor and emotional intelligence: A correlational study of leadership. Examining the relationship between emotional intelligence and leadership styles of U.S. Navy senior enlisted leaders.*
- *Applying positive leadership principles to an investigation of organizational stress in military units and the benefits associated with providing leaders with emotional intelligence social awareness.*
- *Examining job satisfaction, emotional intelligence, and servant leadership: A correlational research design.*
- *An emotional business: The role of emotional intelligence in entrepreneurial success.*
- *A correlation study of emotional intelligence and behavioral style of bio-pharmaceutical industry District Sales Managers.*
- *The relationship between principal's emotional intelligence quotient, school culture, and student achievement.*
- *The relationship between emotional intelligence and leadership practices among physicians.*
- *Beyond the scoreboard: Examining the effects of emotional intelligence and coaching efficacy on the transformational leadership of collegiate coaches.*
- *Emotional intelligence in charter school principals and student performance.*
- *Impact of training intervention on emotional intelligence in health care administrators and physician leaders.*
- *Effects of the TM technique on anxiety, emotional intelligence and trust: Implications for supply chain management.*
- *Retail managers' situational leadership style and emotional intelligence.*

- *Examining the relationship between emotional intelligence and counterproductive work behaviors with a food service sample.*
- *Emotional intelligence and educational leadership: Measuring the emotional intelligence of educational leaders and their corresponding student achievement.*
- *Organizational excellence: A study of the relationship between emotional intelligence and work engagement in process improvement experts.*
- *Emotional intelligence and burnout among teachers in a rural Florida school district.*
- *The emotional intelligence of general counsels in relation to lawyer leadership.*
- *Emotional intelligence, career decision difficulties, and student retention: A quantitative study.*
- *An examination of leadership styles and emotional intelligence with behavioral healthcare service providers in a healthcare organization.*
- *Is the emotional intelligence of secondary school principals correlated with the job satisfaction or performance of their teachers?*
- *Exploring Impacts of Emotional Intelligence, Gender and Tenure on Sales Performance Among Hospice Sales Professionals.*
- *A Study of the Relationship Between Emotional Intelligence and Individual Performance in an Inbound North American Call Center.*
- *Organizational Excellence: A Study of the Relationship Between Emotional Intelligence and Work Engagement in Process Improvement Experts.*
- *The emotional intelligence of general counsels in relation to lawyer leadership*

This list is just a few over the last couple of years; I am sure that a more exhaustive search would yield even more literature on EI research. Many thanks to the wonderful scholars who continue to discover the power of EI within individuals and organizations.

Areas of Future Focus

Where we go from here is the most important discussion topic. Hopefully, the concepts in this book have elevated your understating of the applicability of EI to various scenarios and the power behind finding statistically significant relationships between EI and desired business outcomes. While I have provided an advanced view of how EI currently applies to modern business, I want to get you thinking about the future of EI. These are some of the latest and most important areas of study on emotion that are shaping the future of emotional and social intelligence research. Each of these future focus areas are fascinating.

The Hippocampus and Future Thinking - Researchers at the Boston University Medical Center have recently discovered that the hippocampus, historically known for its role in memory formation, actually plays a large role in shaping future events (Palombo, 2016). Originally published in the *Cerebral Cortex* journal, researchers investigated the brain's capacity to imagine future events, and the role that the hippocampus and emotions had in shaping future scenes. Considered a cognitive ability, the ability to think about the future is believed to have a profound impact on our present. Using fMRI scans, researchers compared the brain activity of healthy adults while they were imagining the future. The researchers then asked questions of the participants pertaining to present events or future imagined scenarios. They found stronger activity in the hippocampus when participants imagined a future scene. Research in this area is still in the early stages, but to think that EI can actually shape one's future thinking opens a wide range of potential possibilities, coaching avenues, and organizational research. It is under the category of "mental time travel", which is the act of mentally projecting oneself into the past and future. How cool is that?

Emotional Intelligence as a Clinical Diagnostic Tool – I have spent the majority of this book highlighting why EI should not be used for clinical diagnosis of individual disorders. It is because the research on the subject has been finite and inconclusive. That is until now. Researchers at the University of Georgia looked at those with Borderline Personality Disorder, or BPD, and discovered new research that indicates this disorder may have to do with lowered brain activity in emotional centers of the brain that are responsible for Empathy. Originally published in the journal of *Personality Disorders: Theory, Research, and Treatment,* researchers conducted a study with over 80 participants and asked them to complete the Five Factor Borderline Inventory, which determined the degree of BPD within each individual. Using fMRI scans, participants were asked to complete empathetic tasks, and the researchers found that those with more BPD traits had lower areas of empathetic brain function than others (Haas, 2015). The study showed that BPD is a continuum, rather than binary (previous research suggested that you either had BPD or you didn't). Haas (2015) found that individuals that had trouble processing emotions, specifically Empathy, had decreased neural activity in two parts of the brain: the temporoparietal junction (TPJ) and the superior temporal sulcus, the two areas of the brain most important in processing Empathy. The TPJ incorporates information from the thalamus (the section of the brain that regulates consciousness and sleep) and the limbic system, processing information related to moral decisions. This area of the brain plays a major role in theory of mind (the ability to attribute mental states to oneself and different states to others). Damage to this area has also been shown to produce out-of-body experiences (Haas, 2015). The TPJ is also known to play significant roles in other disorders, such as amnesia, Alzheimer's and schizophrenia. His findings suggest that developing EI can actually reverse troubling personality disorders such as BPD, or be used to treat other mental disorders.

Other research published in *Biological Psychiatry* claims that there is a middle ground between neurotic and psychotic disorders, and suggested that emotional dysregulation was responsible for specific limbic system structures which may heighten the intensity of negative emotions, creating an inability to regulate emotions. This creates a scenario where the brain is unable to cope with overly emotional situations, causing posttraumatic stress and mood disorders (Ruocco, 2013). Imagine if EI could treat personality disorders and mental disease. This would create a major paradigm shift in the treatment and prevention of mental illness.

Communicating with Animals Through Emotions – I am a huge dog lover. I think that dogs are one of the greatest gifts to mankind, and researchers at the University of Lincoln have discovered that dogs can recognize emotions in humans. Albuquerque (2016) claims that dogs form abstract mental representations of positive and negative emotions, rather than displaying conditioned behavior previously thought by behavioral psychologists. The researchers wrote in the journal *Biology Letters* that dogs spent significantly longer looking at facial expressions that matched certain emotional states of humans, indicating that dogs can differentiate between emotions and facial cues. Albuquerque (2016) claims that dogs have the capacity to internally categorize emotional states, suggesting that dogs can recognize emotions in humans and other dogs. From my personal experience, I have to believe this is true. Sometimes I feel that my dogs know me better than I do. But imagine if emotion was the Rosetta Stone that finally unlocked the ability to speak to animals. That would change the world.

Empathy and Violent Video Games – Full disclosure, I was a total video game nerd growing up. I was a world video game champion in 1995. My parents thought that video games would fry my brain, but little did they know that some of the most avid gamers of the 1990s would eventually become some of the best surgeons and fighter pilots of today. A consistently debated topic that exists today is the link between violent video games and anti-social behavior. Many believe that school shooters or home-grown terrorists are partly conditioned to engage in violent behavior due to hours spent playing first-person shooter type video games. In a recent study published in *Frontiers in Psychology*, researchers investigated the short-term and long-term effects of playing video games on Empathy. The researchers used fMRI scans to compare the neural response of non-gamers and gamers when shown emotional and empathetic images, and revealed no difference in measures of aggression or empathy between the two groups (Szycik, 2016). Their research suggests that any behavior that results from violent video games is either short-lived or non-existent. Further research in this area is certainly required, but initial findings suggest that environmental cues do not affect empathetic brain function, and that imbalanced individuals who commit heinous acts of violence derive their impulses from elsewhere.

Love is Blind – Research from Washington University in St. Louis has found that couples are clueless when it comes to spotting when their partner is hiding emotions. Eldesouky (2016) found individuals often underestimate how often a partner is suppressing emotions, even in the best of relationships. Publishing their study in the *Journal of Personality*, the researchers found that women see their partners in a more positive light than do men. They also discovered that if someone is generally more emotional, their partner thinks they are less likely to hide emotions (Eldesouky, 2017). Essentially, even the best of couples hide deep down emotions, by overly expressing surface level emotions. Knowing that EI can be used to hide deeper emotions, is a double-edged sword. Research in this area suggests that EI is multi-layered within individuals, and further research in this area can seek to quantify the different layers of EI within us and how those different layers interact and create behaviors on the surface level.

Emotionally Intelligent People Can't Spot Liars – People who rate themselves high in EI tend to overestimate their own ability to spot when someone is lying. Published in *Legal and Criminological Psychology*, researchers asked 116 participants to self-report EI, and then watch videos of 20 people from around the world pleading for the safe return of a kidnapped loved one. In some videos, the person was a family member, and in others, the person was the individual responsible for the kidnapping. The participants were asked to rate the believability and sincerity of each video, and researchers found that those with high EI had higher levels of identifying the incorrect perpetrators. The researchers suggest that high EI had a paradoxical effect of impairing people's ability to detect deceit (Baker, 2012). The implications for this research are profound, because it provides another argument for the idea of emotional balance. If criminals and bad actors discovered a causal link between high EI and lack of deception detecting ability, those with high EI could become targets.

EQ Radio – A popular theory on brain wave activity is the idea that human brains are little Wi-Fi devices, that are constantly broadcasting subconscious emotions within our immediate proximity, and other brains near ours are downloading those emotional cues and processing them subconsciously. Essentially, this creates one larger social brain, which is comprised of everyone that is within immediate proximity of each other. That has always been an interesting, yet unproven theory, until now. Researchers at Massachusetts Institute of Technology have developed an "EQ Radio", which is a radio that can detect human emotions using wireless signals. The radio measures subtle changes in heart rhythm and breathing and associates those signals to emotional states. The radio broadcasts signals toward individuals and uses the reflections of those signals to measure heartbeat intervals, measuring differences in times of stress, arousal, happiness, or sadness (MIT, 2016). The researchers claim that the radio can sense emotions in others at 70% accuracy (humans can only identify their own emotions at a 36% success rate). This research is revolutionary, since it not only can identify emotions as they happen within individuals at twice the accuracy rate, but it can highlight to others what the emotional states of others currently are. Knowing what we know about emotions and decision making, having an ability to see the emotional states of others has infinite application.

Master the Future

Battles are unpredictable. That is why the ancient shinobi used hand-to-hand combat as last result. Not only did it bring the shinobi closest in proximity to the enemy, it also eliminated all advantage and surprise. Tai Jutsu was the art of mastering the unpredictable, understanding that humans were erratic and random, and ensuring that the shinobi would live to fight another day.

Organizations are no different, as they are simply a collection of people. Individual people, who make judgements that are supposedly rooted in logic and thought, but as you now know, this is not the case. Organizational directives are subjective decisions, made by people who are surrounded by irrationality, emotions they cannot process, and cognitive bias. To date, EI is the only predictor of workplace success that matches dynamic use of skill to desired business outcomes. IQ and personality, while important to be aware of in some aspects, generate only that; self-awareness. In order to keep the battle going, EI is the best skill set for the modern-day ninja to master. This ensures that the shinobi is engaged in the present, but also focused on the future.

– Shinobi Skill Acquired –

Tai Jutsu 体術

Epilogue

The Shinobi's Sunset

I have reflected in this book on all of the lessons I have learned from my great teachers, my fortunate experiences in coaching and consulting, and from my quest to discover psychological powers that created positive change. This book concentrates on my personal experience using emotional intelligence and the EQ-i 2.0 assessment to coach, consult, empower teams, improve lives, and develop leaders all over the world. I hope that after reading my experiences, you will agree with me that the psychology degree is as important, if not more important, than the management degree within modern business.

Understanding how teams work, how leaders make decisions, how emotions affect cognition, memory, and learning, are all important elements of emotional intelligence. Everything that I have learned came from two core principles that I try to employ every day: Be curious and fail fast.

The world is a vast and wonderful place, and I feel sadness for those who have no curiosity to explore it. Think of every new technology or invention that was ever created. Technically speaking, nothing "new" is ever developed. Essentially, the combination of already existing elements is identified, which creates a new product that humans can start to enjoy. Going back to the caveman days, the element of fire had always existed, it just took some creative dumb luck to realize that striking flint created a spark. Think of every discovery or new technology – it is simply a never-before known combination of material or a new way of looking at things that creates a new advancement. This is why I feel that nothing new is ever created, but merely found. This stems from being curious. Be curious about the world around you and you will enjoy all of the things this world has yet to reveal. Be curious about people, places, things, and the combinations of them, and you'll be amazed at what you discover. That's why I love emotional intelligence. The combinations are infinite, and there should be a curiosity to discover the emotional profile within each one of you, which is waiting to be unlocked so that you can each reach your full potential. Curiosity is the thirst for knowledge and the pursuit of it. Throughout history, there have been many views on the pursuit of knowledge. Plato believed that knowledge is innate and that learning and development are buried deep within the soul, while philosophers like Aristotle believed in tabula rasa, or blank slate, which posits that the soul is an empty template with no built-in content, and that knowledge is acquired through experience. Whichever epistemological idea that you subscribe to, a deep curiosity, focused inward on self-discovery or outward on the world around us, is the only way to truly learn. Being curious is a cornerstone of the human condition and higher cognition.

Curiosity isn't enough though. You have to try things, fail, and fail fast. Failing fast means that you go for it. Failing fast means that you never give up. It means that finished beats perfect, you have grit and persistence, and do not care what others think. It means that you constantly face rejection. Rejection is hard on everyone. It creates feelings of embarrassment, low self-worth and inner-doubt. It is completely understandable why people wish to avoid ever getting rejected, but getting rejected, every day, is actually a great thing. It is a great thing as long as the person possesses three key emotional intelligence skills: Self-Regard, Self-Actualization, and Emotional Self-Awareness.

People often frame their entire life plan and their daily actions around NOT getting rejected, which essentially translates into inaction. You don't ask the girl out, you don't ask for the sale, and you don't ask your boss for a raise, because of the paralyzing fear of rejection. In the end, you do nothing and you aren't rejected, but you didn't gain either. The result is no progression, no situational advancement, and frankly, a boring life. Those who get rejected every day, are some of the most successful people on the planet.

Most of the top consultants and best salesmen in the world subscribe to the theory of abundance, as opposed to the theory of scarcity (the idea that the pie is fixed, there are limited seats, and success is a distributive and zero-sum game) that modern society would have us believe. Abundance theory states that money and business opportunities, while technically not infinite, are plenty enough that we shouldn't live in fear of spending our money or worry about not putting together the perfect business deal, and that there is so much out there for each one of us that we should go after it every day, in every way. Success is integrative, meaning that the outcome is greater together than any of us can reach on our own.

As Mark Cuban once said, some of the most successful millionaires in the world have no fear of losing it all, because they know they can make it all again if they needed to (and some actually have, many times over). Those who fail to act, while waiting for the perfect plan and scenario to develop, never actually act. Successful people do not live in fear of rejection, but instead spend money at their leisure and cast a wide net when it comes to business opportunity.

It only takes one success to be considered successful. Think of the guy at the bar that asks 200 women for their number. He will most likely get rejected 199 times, but will most likely get one or two numbers, making his night a success. Think of the average job seeker, that sends out thousands of resumes. She will get hundreds of "thank you for applying but we have found someone who is better qualified" emails, but only needs to land one or two interviews.

There are hundreds of stories of people with high emotional intelligence, that persevere through difficult times, succeed once, and then go down in history as a success story. My favorite example is the story of Abraham Lincoln. From 1831 to 1858, he loses his job, is defeated for state legislature, fails in business, his sweetheart dies, has a nervous breakdown, is defeated for Illinois State Speaker, is defeated in run for Congress, defeated again in run for Congress, rejected as a land officer, defeated in run for U.S. Senate, defeated for Vice President nomination, and then defeated again in run for U.S. Senate. But then he was elected the President of the United States in 1860, and is widely considered one of the greatest Presidents of all time. Now I am speculating because I don't have his EQ-i 2.0 assessment results, but I would imagine that Honest Abe had very high emotional intelligence, specifically pertaining to the Self-Perception Composite.

Many of my coaching clients think that Self-Regard, Self-Actualization, and Emotional Self-Awareness are personality driven and only innate. As you now know, these are actually skills, that can be developed by anyone, with targeted coaching and consistent practice. Those with high Self-Perception skills possess an Internal Locus of Control (the belief that they control their own life) versus those with low Self-Perception skills that possess an External Locus of Control (the belief that their life is controlled by external factors outside of personal control).

If you are being rejected every day, that means you are asking for those sales, you are sending out resumes, you are talking to people you don't know, and you are constantly trying to become something better. When the eventual rejection comes, those with high emotional intelligence brush it off, realize it's part of the process, and don't let the external result impact internal feelings of self-worth or derail aspirations and goals.

I can't tell you how many times I have failed in business. I have failed more than I have succeeded, to be honest. I am constantly sending out proposals every day for my consulting business, and most of the time, I hear nothing back, or the response is a rejection. Here is the trick though, I technically haven't lost anything with each rejection that comes in! Maverick consultant Alan Weiss describes the scenario as such (I am paraphrasing): before you ask for the sale, you have nothing. Once you ask for the sale, and get rejected, you technically are right back where you started. So, you didn't really "lose" the sale. If anything, you should have gained knowledge on what to do better next time. So even in rejection, you come out ahead. The rejection should have no impact on your own self-view, your confidence, or your goals. It should be considered a learning opportunity and a symbol of your hard work.

This is the mindset of those with high emotional intelligence. The external actions and rejections of others do not and should not impact our inner confidence or the goals we set for ourselves, and the emotions that accompany the rejection should be sorted and categorized in our brains so that we don't attribute them as being created internally. If you aren't failing, you aren't trying. If you aren't getting rejected, you aren't successful.

Show me someone who fails every day, and that person is either currently a great success, or is about to be.

Daily rejection is a great thing, because it means you are abiding by abundance theory and you are going after it. You are trying to improve your life every day. However, daily rejection is only a great thing if you are equipped with the emotional intelligence skills and abilities to properly deal with it, and weaponize it into your greatest asset. We must consistently ask for what we want, go after what we want and visualize what we want, because the only way to truly predict our future is to create it.

- The IO Shinobi

References

Many thanks to the great researchers and gifted scientists that made this possible. I highly recommend reading each one of these individually; I have learned so much from every one of them.

Albuquerque, N., Guo, K., Wilkinson, A., Savalli, C., Otta, E., & Mills, D. (2016). Dogs recognize dog and human emotions. *Biology Letter.*

Allais, M. (1953). Le Comportement de l'Homme Rationnel devant le Risque: Critique des Postulats et Axiomes de l'Ecole Americaine. Econometrica. 21 (4): 503-546.

Anderson, J.R. (2010). Cognitive Psychology and Its Implications. New York, NY: Worth Publishers.

Ashkanasy, N.M. (2002). Studies of Cognition and Emotion in Organisations: Attribution, Affective Events, Emotional Intelligence and Perception of Emotion. Australian Journal of Management, 27,11-20.

Babiak, P., & Hare, R. (2006). When Psychopaths Go to Work.

Baker, A. (2012). Will get fooled again: Emotionally intelligent people are easily duped by high-stakes deceivers. *Legal and Criminological Psychology.*

Bar-On, R. (2013). http://www.reuvenbaron.org/wp/

Bar-On, R. (2004). The Bar-On Emotional Quotient Inventory (EQ-i): Rationale, description, and summary of psychometric properties. In Glenn Geher (Ed.), Measuring emotional intelligence: Common ground and controversy. Hauppauge, NY: Nova Science.

Bar-On, R. (2002). EQ-i Technical Manual. Toronto, Canada: Multi-Health Systems.

Bateman, A. W., Gunderson, J., & Mulder, R. (2015). Series: Treatment of personality disorder. The Lancet, 385735-743.

Baughman, H. M., Schwartz, S., Schermer, J. A., Veselka, L., Petrides, K. V., & Vernon, P. A. (2011). A behavioral-genetic study of alexithymia and its relationships with trait emotional intelligence. Twin Research and Human Genetics: The Official Journal of The International Society for Twin Studies, 14(6), 539-543.

Baumeister, R. F., & Bushman, B. (2014). Social Psychology and Human Nature, Comprehensive Edition. Belmont, CA: Wadsworth.

Baumeister, R. F., Vohs, K. D., & Tice, D. M. (2007). The strength model of self-control. *Current Directions in Psychological Science*, 16(6), 351-355.

Beasley, K. (1987). The Emotional Quotient. Mensa Research Journal.

Blank, I. (2008). Selecting Employees Based on Emotional Intelligence Competencies: Reap the Rewards and Minimize the Risk. *Employee Relations Law Journal*, *34*(3), 77-85.

Bonebright, D. A. (2010). 40 years of storming: a historical review of Tuckman's model of small group development. Human Resource Development International, 13(1), 111-120.

Borg, S. W., & Johnston, W. J. (2013). The IPS-EQ Model: Interpersonal Skills and Emotional Intelligence in a Sales Process. *Journal of Personal Selling & Sales Management*, *33*(1), 39-52.

Brooks, A., & Bitterly, B. (2017). Why It Pays Off to Be Funny at Work – Usually. *The Wall Street Journal.*

Briffa, M. (2013). The Influence of Personality on a Group-Level Process: Shy Hermit Crabs Make Longer Vacancy Chains. Ethology, 119(11), 1014-1023.

Carducci, B. (2009). The Psychology of Personality. John Wiley & Sons.

Chamorro-Premuzic, T. (2016). Strengths-Based Coaching Can Actually Weaken You. Harvard Business Review.

Cheng, D., & Wang, L. (2014). Examining the Energizing Effects of Humor: The Influence of Humor on Persistence Behavior. *Journal of Business and Psychology*, 1-14.

Corey, Gerald. (2012). *Theory and practice of counseling and psychotherapy,* 9th ed., Belmont, CA: Thomson Brooks/Cole.

Damasio, A. R. (1994). *Descartes' error: Emotion, reason, and the human brain.* New York: Quill.

Darwin, C. (1859). *On the origin of species by means of natural selection, or, the preservation of favoured races in the struggle for life.* London: J. Murray.

Dearborn, K. (2002). Studies in emotional intelligence redefine our approach to leadership development. Public Personnel Management, 37(4), 523-530.

DeVaney, S. A. (2015). Understanding the Millennial Generation. *Journal of Financial Service Professionals, 69*(6), 11-14.

Dietmeyer, Brian (2004). Strategic Negotiation: A Breakthrough Four-Step Process for Effective Business Negotiation. Kaplan Publishing. ISBN 978-0-7931-8304-3.

Dion, K., Berscheid, E., Walster, E., (1972). What is Beautiful is Good. Journal of Personality and Social Psychology, Vol. 24, No. 3, 285-290.

Easter, T. H., & Brooks, S. (2017). Our Leader Is Gone, Now What? Creating the Foundation for Stable Transitions. *People & Strategy, 40*(1), 28-32.

Eldesouky, L. (2016). Out of Sight, Out of Mind? Accuracy and Bias in Emotion Regulation Trait Judgments. *Journal of Personality.*

Ermer, E., Kahn, R. E., Salovey, P., & Kiehl, K. A. (2012). Emotional intelligence in incarcerated men with psychopathic traits. Journal of Personality and Social Psychology, 103(1), 194-204.

Ferres, N., & Connell J. (2014). Emotional intelligence in leaders: an antidote for cynicism towards change? Strategic Change, 13(2), 61-71.

Fiori, M., Antonietti, J., Mikolajczak, M., Luminet, O., Hansenne, M., & Rossier, J. (2014). What is the ability emotional intelligence test (MSCEIT) good for? An evaluation using item response theory. PLoS One, 9(6).

Garcia, S. M. (2002). POWER AND THE ILLUSION OF TRANSPARENCY IN NEGOTIATIONS. *Journal of Business & Psychology, 17*(1), 133-144.

Gardner, L., & Stough, C. (2002). Examining the relationship between leadership and emotional intelligence in senior level managers. Leadership & Organization Development Journal, 23(1/2), 68-78.

Ghiabi, B. & Besharat, M. Emotional Intelligence, Alexithymia, and Interpersonal Problems. Procedia – Social and Behavioral Sciences, Volume 30. P 98-102.

Goleman, D. (1995). Emotional Intelligence. New York, NY, England: Bantam Books, Inc.

Green, D. (2016). The Emotional Intelligence of Managers and the Effect on Virtual Workers. ProQuest.

Haas, B., Miller, J. (2013). Borderline Personality Traits and Brain Activity During Emotional Perspective Taking. *Personal Disorders.*

Haselton, M. G.; Nettle, D. & Andrews, P. W. (2005). *The evolution of cognitive bias.* In D. M. Buss (Ed.), The Handbook of Evolutionary Psychology: Hoboken, NJ, US: John Wiley & Sons Inc. pp. 724–746.

Harris, Nicole V., Jim Mirabella, and Richard Murphy. 2012. "IS EMOTIONAL INTELLIGENCE THE KEY TO MEDICAL SALES SUCCESS?: THE RELATIONSHIP BETWEEN EI AND SALES PERFORMANCE." *Review of Management Innovation & Creativity* 5, no. 16: 72-82.

Herjavec, R. (2016). Driven: How to Succeed in Business and Life. HarperCollins.

Herpertz, S., Nizielski, S., Hock, M., & Schütz, A. (2016). The Relevance of Emotional Intelligence in Personnel Selection for High Emotional Labor Jobs. *Plos ONE, 11*(4), 1.

Hogan & Hogan (2007). Hogan Personality Inventory. Tulsa, OK. Hogan Assessment Systems.

Jakobwitz, S.; Egan, V. (2006). "The 'dark triad' and normal personality traits". Personality and Individual Differences. 40 (2): 331 39.

Judd, T. (2015). Task Selection, Task Switching and Multitasking during Computer-Based Independent Study. *Australasian Journal of Educational Technology, 31*(2).

Kahneman, D. & Tversky, A. (1979). Prospect theory: An Analysis of Decision under Risk. Econometrica; 47: 263- 292.

Kamal, G., & Soheila Shakoori, Y. (2014). A study on relationship between emotional intelligence components of sales managers from Goleman's viewpoint and sales promotion activities in Iranian business enterprises. *Management Science Letters, Vol 4, Issue 7, Pp 1433-1440 (2014),* (7), 1433.

Kaplan, R. M. & Saccuzzo, O. P. (2010). Psychological testing: Principles, applications, and issues. Belmont, CA: Wadsworth.

Katz, N. H., & Sosa, A. (2015). The Emotional Advantage: The Added Value of the Emotionally Intelligent Negotiator. *Conflict Resolution Quarterly, 33*(1), 57-74.

Kelley, H.H. (1967). Attribution theory in social psychology. In D. Levine (Ed.) Nebraska Symposium on Motivation, Lincoln: University of Nebraska Press.

Kennedy, C. (2006). Guide to the management gurus: the best guide to business thinkers (5th ed.). London: Random House Business.

Kessler, SR; Bandeiii, AC; Spector, PE; Borman, WC; Nelson, CE; and Penney, LM (2010). Reexamining Machiavelli: A three-dimensional model of Machiavellianism in the workplace. Journal of Applied Social Psychology, 40, 1868–1896.

Kholoud S., A., Othman H., A., Elsayed M., A., & Neil, A. (2016). Relationships between emotional intelligence and sales performance in Kuwait. *Revista De Psicología Del Trabajo Y De Las Organizaciones, Vol 32, Issue 1, Pp 39-45 (2016),* (1), 39.

Koçaslan, G. (2014). Quantum Interpretation to Decision Making Under Risk: The Observer Effect in Allais Paradox. *Neuroquantology, 12*(3), 412-418.

Kotter, J. P. (2012). *Leading change.* Boston, Mass: Harvard Business School Press.

Kroger, J., Segovia, J., Sallee, L., & Lenard, C. (2015). Machiavellianism in Business Management and Corporations. Academy of Business Research Journal, 280-87.

Loewenstein, G. (2003). Hot-cold empathy gaps and medical decision making. Health Psychology 24(4) Suppl. S49-S56.

Mackay, C. (1841). *Extraordinary popular delusions and the madness of crowds.* New York: L.C. Page.

Malle, B. F. (2006). The actor-observer asymmetry in attribution: A (surprising) meta-analysis. *Psychological Bulletin, 132*(6), 895-919.

Massachusetts Institute of Technology (2016). Detecting emotions with wireless signals: Measuring your heartbeat and breath, device can tell if you're excited, happy, angry, or sad. *ScienceDaily.*

McAbee, S. T., & Connelly, B. S. (2016). A multi-rater framework for studying personality: The trait-reputation-identity model. Psychological Review, 123(5), 569-591.

McDaniel, M. A., DeLosh, E. L., Einstein, G. O., May, C. P., & Brady, P. (1995). The bizarreness effect: it's not surprising, it's complex. *Journal of Experimental Psychology: Learning, Memory and Cognition,* (2), 422.

McDaniel, M. A., & Einstein, G. O. (1986). Bizarre imagery as an effective memory aid: The importance of distinctiveness. *Journal of Experimental Psychology: Learning, Memory, And Cognition, 12*(1), 54-65.

McElroy, T.; Dowd, K. (2007). "Susceptibility to anchoring effects: How openness-to-experience influences responses to anchoring cues". *Judgment and Decision Making.* **2**: 48–53.

McRaney, D. (2010). "The Illusion of Transparency". *You Are Not So Smart.*

Milius, S. (2012). mixed results: Having the right blend of animal personalities can make or break a group. Science News, (8). 26.

MUNSHI, M. M., & HANJI, S. (2013). LINKING EMOTIONAL INTELLIGENCE, SALES PERFORMANCE AND SALES SUCCESS OF RETAIL SALESPEOPLE: A REVIEW APPROACH. *CLEAR International Journal of Research in Commerce & Management, 4*(12), 19-23.

Nahari, G., & Ben-Shakhar, G. (2013). Primacy Effect in Credibility Judgements: The Vulnerability of Verbal Cues to Biased Interpretations. *Applied Cognitive Psychology, 27* (2), 247-255.

Nicholas, C. A., & Cohen, A. L. (2016). The effect of interruption on the decision-making process. *Judgment & Decision Making, 11*(6), 611-626.

Nikolaou, I., & Tsaousis, I., (2002). Emotional intelligence in the workplace: Exploring its effects on occupational stress and organisational commitment. International Journal of Organizational Analysis, 10(4), 327-342.

Oginska-Bulik, N. (2005). Emotional intelligence in the workplace: exploring its effects on occupational stress and health outcomes in human service workers. International Journal Occupational Medicine and Environmental Health, 18(2), 167-75.

Ozguner, Z., & Ozguner, M. (2014). A managerial point of view on the relationship between of Maslow's hierarchy of needs and Herzberg's dual factor theory. International Journal of Business and Social Science, 5(7).

Palmer, B., Donaldson, G, & Stough, C. (2002). Emotional intelligence and life satisfaction. Personality and Individual Differences, 33,1091 -1100.

Palombo, D., Hayes, P., & Keane, M. (2016). Medial Temporal Lobe Contributions to Episodic Future Thinking: Scene Construction or Future Projection? *Cerebral Cortex Journal.*

Parker, J. D. A., Taylor, G. J., & Bagby, R. M. (2001). The relationship between emotional intelligence and alexithymia. Personality and Individual Differences, 30, 107–115.

Payne, W.L. (1985). A study of emotion: developing emotional intelligence; self-integration; relating to fear, pain and desire.

Pennington, D. (1982). Witness and Their Testimony: Effects of Ordering on Juror Verdicts. Journal of Applied Social Psychology.

Ruocco, A., Amirthavasagam, S., Choi-Kain, L., & McMain, S. (2013). Neural Correlates of Negative Emotionality in Borderline Personality Disorder: An Activation-Likelihood-Estimation Meta-Analysis. *Biological Psychiatry.*

Salles, A., Lin, D., Liebert, C., Esquivel, M., Lau, J. N., Greco, R. S., & Mueller, C. (2016). Grit as a predictor of risk of attrition in surgical residency. The American Journal of Surgery.

Savitsky, Kenneth; Gilovich, Thomas (2003). "The illusion of transparency and the alleviation of speech anxiety" (PDF). *Journal of Experimental Social Psychology.* **39** (6): 618–625.

Schiff, L. (2013). Business Brilliant: Surprising Lessons from the Greatest Self-Made Business Icons. Harper Business.

Schippers, M. C. (2014). Social Loafing Tendencies and Team Performance: The Compensating Effect of Agreeableness and Conscientiousness. *Academy Of Management Learning & Education, 13*(1), 62-81. doi:10.5465/amle.2012.0191

Singh, D. (2003). Emotional Intelligence at Work. New Delhi: Sage Publications.

Slaski, M., & Cartwright S. (2002). Health, performance and emotional intelligence: an exploratory study of retail managers. Stress and Health, 18, 63-68.

Slavin, R. (2010). Educational Psychology. Pearson Education Limited.

Snell, M. J. (2010). Solving the Problems of Groupthink in Health Care Facilities through the Application of Practical Originality. *Global Management Journal, 2*(2), 74-84.

Solomon, B. C., & Vazire, S. (2016). Knowledge of identity and reputation: Do people have knowledge of others' perceptions? Journal of Personality and Social Psychology, 111(3), 341-366.

Stein, S. (2011). The EQ Edge. Jossey-Bass, MHS.

Srikanth, S., & Sonawat, R. (2014). Emotional quotient (EQ): The essence of life. Indian Journal of Health and Wellbeing, 5(10), 1244-1248.

Surowiecki, J. (2004). *The wisdom of crowds.* New York: Anchor Books.

Suzuki, Y., Tamesue, D., Asahi, K., & Ishikawa, Y. (2015). Grit and Work Engagement: A Cross-Sectional Study. Plos One, 10(9), e0137501.

Swider, B. W., Barrick, M. R., & Harris, T. B. (2016). Initial impressions: What they are, what they are not, and how they influence structured interview outcomes. *Journal of Applied Psychology, 101*(5), 625-638.

Szycik, G. (2017). Lack of Evidence That Neural Empathic Responses Are Blunted in Excessive Users of Violent Video Games: An fMRI Study. *Front. Psychol.*

Thorndike, E. (1932). The Fundamentals of Learning. AMS Press Inc. ISBN 0-404-06429-9.

Turnbull, S. (2003), Ninja AD 1460–1650, Osprey Publishing.

University of Toronto, Rotman School of Management. "Higher emotional intelligence leads to better decision-making." ScienceDaily. ScienceDaily, 19 November 2013.

Vrij, A. (2008). *Detecting lies and deceit: Pitfalls and opportunities.* Chichester: John Wiley.

WALKER, W. R., & SKOWRONSKI, J. J. (2009). The Fading affect bias: But what the hell is it for? *Applied Cognitive Psychology, 23*(8), 1122-1136.

Weymes, E. (2003). Relationships not leadership sustain successful organisations. Journal of Change Management, 3(4), 319-331.

Wisker, Z. L., & Poulis, A. (2015). EMOTIONAL INTELLIGENCE AND SALES PERFORMANCE. A MYTH OR REALITY?. *International Journal of Business & Society, 16*(2), 185-200

Yip, J. & Cote, S. (2013). The Emotionally Intelligent Decision Maker. Sage Journals, Yale University.

Zhu, D. H. (2013). Group polarization on corporate boards: Theory and evidence on board decisions about acquisition premiums. Strategic Management Journal, 34(7), 800-822.

Index

3

360 assessment   2, 6, 22, 68, 70, 71, 72, 74, 75, 135, 181
    advanced interpretation   68
    coaching   73
    EQ360   7, 23, 24, 40, 41, 71, 74, 76, 112, 123, 141, 142, 143, 148, 162, 172, 173, 176, 181, 194, 220
    rater category   68, 72

A

adjourning   80
Aesop   171
Alexithymia   139, 140, 141, 143, 144, 151, 262
    configurations   140
    Toronto Alexithymia Scale-20   139
Allais, Maurice   179
Aristotle   255
Assertiveness   30, 31, 78, 87, 88, 108, 111, 112, 121, 151, 164, 166, 167, 170, 175, 193, 199

B

Bacon, Francis   168
Bar-On, Reuven   16, 20
Beasley, Keith   15
bias
    Actor-Observer Bias   182
    Allais Paradox   179, 180, 181, 264
    analysis paralysis   170, 171, 172
    Bandwagon Effect   166
    Bizarreness Effect   188
    Certainty Effect   179, 180, 181
    cognitive bias codex   161
    Confirmation Bias   168
    Conservatism Bias   170, 171
    Curse of Knowledge   173, 174
    Dutch Tulip mania   166
    Empathy Gap   174, 176
    extinct by instinct   172
    Fading Affect Bias   198
    False Consensus Effect   163
    Focalism   158, 164, 165, 170
    Framing Effect   176, 177, 178, 180
    Fundamental Attribution Error   182

Halo Effect 185
Humor Effect 191
IKEA Effect 178
Illusion of Asymmetric Insight 162
Illusion of Transparency 200, 264
Information Bias 170
Ostrich Effect 172
Primacy Effect 197, 265
Pseudocertainty Effect 179, 180, 181
Zeigarnik Effect 195
Book, Howard 11
Boyatzis, Richard 22
brain
amygdala 190
hippocampus 188, 190, 192, 247

C

Carnegie, Dale 47
Caruso, David 17
change leadership *See* change management
change management ii, 6, 18, 23, 125, 137, 152, 163, 188, 204, 267
adoption stage 210
decision stage 205
reasons for failure 210
resistance stage 205
The Valley of Despair 210
three distinct stages 204
Chapman, Gary 11
coaching
advanced balance 99
Alexithymia 140
defined 8
group report 91
Machiavellian 152
schizoid 146
within the five perspectives 64
Co-Active Coaching 11
Cognitive Behavior Modification 200
cognitive dissonance 74, 181
Columbus, Christopher 170
Cuban, Mark 256
curiosity xviii, 125, 204, 213, 255

D

Darwin, Charles 12, 16, 26, 29, 108, 124, 261
Deaton, Angus 57
Decision Making

Composite   34
Decision-Making   34, 118, 123, 195
disclaimers   63, 139, 140, 144, 150, 160
Drucker, Peter   216
Duckworth, Angela   50

E

Edward Thorndike   185
Emotional Expression   30, 107, 108, 111, 112, 140, 144, 151, 163, 164, 170, 197, 199
emotional intelligence   62, 262
    advanced balance   96
    advanced balanced defined   98
    as a clinical diagnostic tool   248
    balance   39
    Bar-On model   26
    Bar-On model, 15 factors of   27
    Bar-On model, development of   27
    bias   157
    Communicating with Animals Through Emotions   249
    defined   1
    Empathy and Violent Video Games   250
    EQ Radio   251
    heuristics   157
    Love is Blind   250
    one unequivocal fact   235
    overuse   96
    People Can't Spot Liars   251
    the core concept   20
    the future   241
    The Hippocampus and Future Thinking   247
    three major models   22
    underuse   96
Emotional Intelligence, Why It Can Matter More than IQ   17
emotional quotient   15
Emotional Self-Awareness28, 29, 99, 103, 104, 106, 121, 140, 141, 142, 154, 164, 165,
    168, 169, 170, 175, 176, 181, 183, 186, 187, 196, 197, 199, 201, 205, 255, 257
Empathy32, 33, 113, 114, 116, 121, 140, 146, 151, 163, 166, 167, 173, 174, 175, 176, 177,
    186, 187, 190, 193, 206, 207, 208, 221, 238, 248
EQ-i 2.0 xviii, 4, 5, 9, 16, 17, 20, 21, 22, 23, 25, 26, 27, 39, 42, 43, 45, 56, 59, 60, 62,
    64, 78, 83, 91, 96, 105, 115, 122, 128, 131, 135, 139, 140, 151, 153, 160, 206, 209,
    211, 213, 219, 220, 223, 226, 254, 257
    EQ-i xviii, 4, 5, 9, 16, 17, 20, 21, 22, 23, 25, 26, 27, 39, 42, 43, 45, 56, 59, 60, 62,
        64, 78, 83, 84, 91, 96, 105, 111, 115, 122, 128, 131, 135, 139, 140, 146, 148, 151,
        153, 160, 206, 207, 209, 211, 212, 213, 219, 220, 223, 226, 234, 254, 257, 260
    group report   23, 41, 78, 83, 87, 91, 92, 94, 135, 167, 174, 219
expert power   44
External Locus of Control   257

F

FAB
    Fading Affect Bias   198, 199
Flexibility   36, 124, 125, 145, 151, 164, 165, 166, 167, 168, 170, 171, 178, 196, 197, 211, 212, 213
forming   79
Frames of Mind   15
Freud, Sigmund   55, 68
    ego   14, 55
    id 55
    psychodynamic approach   55
    repressed memories   55
    superego   55

G

Gardner, Howard   15
Goleman, Daniel   xii, xiii, xv, 2, 13, 17, 18, 262, 263
grit   42, 47, 48, 49, 50, 51, 52, 198, 255, 265, 266
    discovery   50
    perseverance   36, 42, 43, 47, 50, 198
group polarization   90
groupthink   89

H

Happiness   38, 103, 130, 131
Herjavec, Robert   47, 263
heuristics   158, 159, 202, 205
    Affect   159, 198
    Anchoring   158, 164, 165, 170
    Availability   158
    Contagion   159
    Representative   158
    Scarcity   159
high use 89, 96, 99, 102, 103, 104, 106, 108, 109, 111, 113, 114, 116, 119, 120, 121, 123, 125, 126, 127, 129, 131, 163, 165, 167, 171, 173, 187, 207, 208, 209, 212, 213, 221, 226
Hitler, Adolf   189
Hogan, Robert   69
How to Win Friends and Influence People   47
humor
    theories of   192

I

Impulse Control   34, 35, 121, 163, 181
Independence   30, 31, 90, 109, 166, 167, 171, 172, 173, 177, 178, 181, 183, 190, 201,
    219, 220, 226
Internal Locus of Control   257
Interpersonal   15, 32, 89, 112, 113, 116, 140, 144, 148, 151, 173, 174, 190, 206, 207,
    208, 235, 236, 238, 261, 262
    Composite   32
Interpersonal Relationships   32, 206

K

Kahneman, Daniel   57, 158, 179, 180, 263
Kimsey-House, Henry and Karen   11
King, Martin Luther, Jr.   190

L

Level 1
    defined   4
    differences from Level 2   23
    review   25
Level 2
    defined   4
    differences from Level 1   23
Loewenstein, George   175, 264
low use 84, 89, 91, 96, 97, 98, 99, 100, 102, 103, 107, 108, 109, 111, 113, 114, 116, 119,
    120, 121, 125, 126, 130, 131, 142, 163, 169, 173, 174, 176, 177, 181, 187, 207, 212,
    221, 226

M

Machiavellian   149, 150, 151, 152, 153, 154, 189, 263, 264
    configuration   150
Magellan, Ferdinand   170
Marx, Karl   68
Maslow, Abraham   14
    hierarchy of needs   14
Mayer John   20
Mayer, John   17
Millennials   230, 231, 232
Million Dollar Consulting   11
MSCEIT
    ability test   17
    Mayer Salovey Caruso Emotional Intelligence Test   17, 22, 146, 262

N

negotiation 164, 165, 200
Newton, Isaac 170
ninjitsu skills 8
    Cho Ho 9, 230, 239, 240
    Henso-Jutsu 8, 68, 76, 77
    Inton-Jutsu 8, 54, 66, 67
    Kayaku-Jutsu 9, 138, 155, 156
    Naginata-Jutsu 9, 96, 133, 134
    Nyudaki No Jutsu 9, 216, 228, 229
    Nyukyo No Jutsu 9, 204, 214, 215
    Seishin Teki Kyoko 8, 52, 53
    Seishin Teki Kyoto 42
    Shinobi-Iri 9, 157, 202, 203, 204, 216
    Tai Jutsu 9, 241, 252, 253
    Ten-Mon 9, 78, 95
norming 79

O

onboarding
    70/20/10 model 233
Optimism 36, 37, 103, 124, 126, 127, 151, 172, 173, 193, 199, 211, 212, 213

P

Part 1 10
    defined 6
    wrap up 40
Part 2 41
    defined 6
    wrap up 135
Part 3 137
    defined 6
Payne, Wayne 15
performing 80
personality assessments
    strength-based 59
    strengths-based 59, 60, 62, 131
    trait-based 58, 62, 63, 64, 75, 182
    type-based 57, 58, 60, 61, 62
Peter Salovey 20
Plato 255
Presentation Zen 44
Problem Solving 34, 35, 99, 119, 123, 171, 172, 173, 177, 190, 196, 219
psychologists
    defined 8

within the five perspectives 64
psychology
  abundance theory 256
  assessment theory 60
  behavioral approach 56
  biological approach 57
  Borderline Personality Disorder 248
  classical conditioning 56
  cognitive approach 58
  configurations 6, 138, 139, 140, 141, 144, 145, 150, 151, 155, 159, 160, 181, 222
  Dark Triad 149, 150
  disorders 107, 138, 139, 143, 145, 154, 159, 160, 200, 248, 249
  dysfunction 7, 24, 56, 57, 60, 61, 65, 81, 82, 88, 89, 91, 132, 135, 140, 218
  dysfunctional 4, 57, 64, 65, 81, 89, 103, 200, 208
  emotional fit 216
  five major perspectives 54
  humanistic approach 59
  identity 40, 68, 69, 70, 71, 72, 73, 74, 75, 90, 102, 122, 123, 135, 143, 172, 226, 264, 266
  Levene's test for equality of variances 236
  my transition to it 157
  operant conditioning 56
  Paradox of Choice 172
  physical needs 57
  psychodynamic approach 55
  reputation 3, 40, 68, 70, 71, 72, 73, 74, 122, 135, 172, 176, 181
  scarcity theory 256
  stages of group development 79
  syndromes 138, 154, 155, 176
  two core principles 254
  workplace bully 149
Pythagoras 170

R

Reality Testing 34, 35, 120, 140, 144, 151, 162, 165, 170, 173, 174, 175, 177, 178, 183, 186, 190, 197, 201, 219, 221
Reynolds, Garr 44
Rohn, Jim 78

S

Salovey, Peter 1, 17
schizoid 143, 144, 145, 146, 147, 148, 149, 152, 177
  configuration 144
  psychopaths 143, 144, 146, 147, 149
  sociopaths 143
schizoids 143, 144
Schwartz, Barry 172, 260

selection 217
   EI assessments 218
   personality assessments 218
   three types of validation 217
Self-Actualization 28, 29, 90, 99, 102, 106, 178, 179, 201, 255, 257
self-awareness xi, 15, 22, 29, 39, 58, 62, 63, 65, 68, 69, 73, 75, 101, 128, 162, 165, 168, 174, 178, 180, 252
Self-Expression 30, 106, 107, 111, 121, 235, 236, 237, 238
   Composite 30
Self-Perception 28, 30, 99, 101, 106, 257
   Composite 28
Self-Regard 28, 29, 84, 101, 102, 106, 140, 144, 151, 162, 163, 173, 174, 193, 255, 257
selling 11, 42, 43, 45, 46, 47, 135, 164, 210
   combined with emotional intelligence 46
   finished beats perfect 45
   first lesson 47
   snowball recruit 46
   the profound principle 46
shinobi xv, 1, 3, 5, 8, 24, 42, 45, 52, 54, 68, 76, 78, 94, 96, 133, 138, 155, 157, 202, 204, 214, 230, 239, 241, 252
social intelligence 1, 2, 5, 7, 12, 13, 16, 17, 26, 29, 131, 185, 246
social loafing 88
Social Responsibility 32, 33, 114, 117, 144, 148, 151, 163, 164, 183, 206, 207, 209, 219, 220, 226, 227, 231
Stanley, Thomas 11
Stein, Steven 11
storming 79, 81
   groupthink 79, 89, 92, 119, 163, 166
   polarization 79, 90, 92, 267
   social loafing 79, 88, 92
Stress Management 36, 124, 211, 212
   Composite 36
Stress Tolerance 36, 37, 89, 125, 126, 127, 129, 151, 166, 196, 201, 211, 212, 213, 219
succession planning 221
   Diversity 222
   Identifying the high-potentials 222
   Internal versus external 222
   roadmap 223, 224

T

team dysfunction 81
The EQ Edge 4, 11, 20, 266
The Five Love Languages 11
The Millionaire Mind 11
Thorndike, Edward 2, 12
Tolstoy, Leo 168
Tuckman, Bruce 79, 80, 81, 261
Tversky, Amos 158, 180, 263

W

WAIS
    Wechsler Adult Intelligence Scale   13
Wechsler, David   13
Weiss, Alan   11, 258
Well Being Indicator   38
Wood, JB   210

Z

Zeigarnik, Bluma   195

42556604R00166

Made in the USA
Middletown, DE
15 April 2017